When Legends Rise Again

The Convergence of Capitalism and Christianity

by

William L. Roth, Jr.

Preface by Timothy Parsons-Heather

The Morning Star of Our Lord, Inc. is a nonprofit, tax-exempt, 501(c)(3), religious and charitable organization which is incorporated under the Laws of the State of Illinois. It has been established for the dissemination of various apologetic works in defense of the Truth of the Holy Gospel of Christianity. It is the intrinsic role of this Corporation to provide pastoral consolation to those lacking in faith, the infirm, homebound, incarcerated, deprived, dejected, and those who are otherwise suffering humanity for the sake of the Glory of the Kingdom of Jesus Christ. All proceeds from this book are being donated to other charitable causes to help feed, clothe, and house the poor, and for the reproduction of this spiritual manuscript for distribution on every continent of the world. If anyone would like to contribute to this worthy cause, you may do so through the following postal and website addresses.

The Morning Star of Our Lord, Inc.
Post Office Box 8584
Springfield, Illinois 62791-8584
www.ImmaculateMary.org

ISBN: 0-9671587-2-9

Printed in the United States of America

Cover Graphic provided by www.Comstock.com

When Legends Rise Again
The Convergence of Capitalism and Christianity

Table of Contents

Part One
These are the Facts as We Know Them

Part Two
The Ideal Capitalist State?

Part Three
The Universal Mandate of Christ

Part Four
The Convergence of Capitalism and Christianity

DEDICATION

to
Three Humble Bishops
The Diocese of Springfield in Illinois

Seated
His Excellency, Most Reverend George J. Lucas D.D.
Ordained Eighth Bishop on December 14, 1999

Retired
His Excellency, Most Reverend Daniel Leo Ryan, D.D.
Installed Seventh Bishop on January 18, 1984
Ordained Titular Bishop of Surista in Mauritania and
Auxiliary of Joliet, Illinois on September 30, 1981

His Excellency, Most Reverend Joseph A. McNicholas, D.D.
Installed Sixth Bishop on September 3, 1975
Called to Eternal Rest on April 17, 1983

How grateful our Heavenly Father must be for the quarter-century of service herein and ongoing that these three holy men have bestowed upon His Church through their lives of pastoral servitude, humility, and prayer. To thank them for elevating Jesus Christ who is so profoundly present in the Most Blessed Sacrament upon the Holy Altar of Sacrifice, I dedicate this book in remembrance of their humble guidance in leading their flock to Everlasting Salvation in the Blood of our Crucified Lord. I join with the Blessed Virgin Mary in beseeching Her Son to shower His great benediction upon these three noble souls who have upheld the honor and dignity of our Diocesan Cathedral of the Immaculate Conception. Thank you, Jesus, for the gift of their love in the lineage of your first Apostles!

-William L. Roth, Jr.

PREFACE
Intercontinental Malaise and Our Global Unease

It has been said in many places around the world, and quite eloquently so, that there is nothing even remotely metaphysical or transcendental about the prospects of acquiring more corporate or capital gain. Why, then, are we all working so hard to get ahead of everybody else in the race for the accumulation of imperishable goods and a much valued wealth? If any one of us ever owned a defensible response to such a question, there would be no reason for us to continue reading this book. The fact is, we are perpetually in the midst of gathering material resources to sustain ourselves in a very competitive world, especially in the technologically advanced Western Hemisphere. We have always known about the fragile nature of human life on Earth, and have become especially more aware of it as a result of the clandestine cells of global terrorism which have been slowly unraveling our system of free choices over the past decade or two. It seems to be a general area of agreement in the civilized community that there is no context in which the elimination of a government of democracy would make sense; and yet, we are slowly being forced to surrender the freedoms that most people take for granted nowadays because of the influence of evil forces that place our ordinary movements into great peril. We should always remember with distinction how our founding fathers sought a greater nation than the world had ever known when they first drafted the articles which became the United States Constitution, as effected and amended. But, each of them must have also stopped to ask themselves, as we do today, about what may truly be our jurisdiction over the lives of other men. Does our knowledge that we can affect their broader destiny, both publicly and privately, provide a third dimension to our national meaning and sense of community? We live in a world that asks far more questions than it ever tries to answer, that taxes more than it provides, that appeases to a greater degree than it holds itself accountable for our collective faults and failures, and which is usually satisfied with the status quo in the face of mediocrity when we should all be struggling to achieve a higher purpose for our being here at all.

If we are ever going to stop the forces which keep trying to diminish the freedoms that we enjoy so prolifically in the United States today, we must learn to retreat from our prejudices and preferences in deference to the dignity and well-being of all other peoples, most of whom we have never met in person. This does not mean that we should surrender our moral station in

i

knowing right from wrong, or to desist in admonishing others who are wittingly committing error to their own demise and at the expense of other souls. It simply refers to our reasoned abandonment of our partisan priors and being better listeners to those who do not yet understand our way of life, or our tantamount awareness of theirs. Much too often, we depend upon our public leaders to put a face on our national attitudes toward other customs and creeds, when most of those who represent us on the outside do not necessarily agree with our basic principles or human responsiveness. Indeed, there are countless public figures who have buffaloed and hoodwinked enough people in the general population to believe that they care sufficiently about humanity at large to get themselves elected, while trying to tell us that they are who they really *say* they are, rather than the selfish war-mongers and hypocrites that they are trying to conceal inside their truer selves. If only we could all agree on the spiritual nature of public service and private enterprise, alike, we would grow more proportionately toward the stately grace that will keep us from ever fighting with one another again. It is social order, freedom, and tolerance which has allowed our Christian faith to prosper and grow in America from the start; and this is a liberty that we must continue to protect at all costs. We are reminded of the "B.C." comic strip that appears in various Sunday newspapers around the country, so aptly composed by Johnny Hart. One of his paneled strips from September 2001 shows the proverbial alpha male who has chiseled a message on his stone tablet stating the following, *"Over here, we are systematically removing all mention of God from textbooks and public places, put there by our founding fathers,"* after which he deposits it into the ocean and waits another day for a reply to come floating back. The response that finally arrives at his shore is, *"Way to go, kid! Hell's gonna have a hoedown when you guys get there!"* Can we not see that the very noble Johnny Hart knows what is happening in the United States today? He realizes that the politics of agnosticism draws lines in order to box people in from expressing the liberating beauty of their own faithful beliefs, whereas the Holy Gospel removes the bridles that make our consciences as flat as Old Glory, herself, and sets us all free; the former is a definitive confinement of indifference, while the latter a means of mutual inspiration.

There is both candlepower and wattage in our opportunities to become the likeness of excellence in the eyes of God these days; but most of us run around the country trying to extinguish every semblance of higher motivation that happens to enlighten another heart inside our midst. We are a nation that espouses a world of capital over the reality of the omnipotent nature of our Divine Creator. What a scurrilous shame! What can we say about America when we espouse to capture an unlimited amount of material assets from the rest of the world when, by definition, this is supposed to be our mission? How do the other nations perceive us when they know that we can prosper only by assimilating what little resources they hold in their own hands for the paupers who inhabit their lands? There seems to be no threshold of materialism that we will not try to surpass because there is no self-imposed cap on the limits of personal wealth which Americans aspire to accumulate, amass, hoard, and retain. There is no *absolute deposit* or any such thing as too much surplus to us. We are in the process of profoundly seeing the awful effects of the 1980s unraveling before our very eyes; not only in our push for material gain, but also in the tragedies of losing our grasp on our behavioral consciences, too. We must have grown to become terrible parents to our children who were born back then, the little ones who were cultivated from amidst the unmitigated greed and lust which was transferred to the greater search for profit of the 1990s; the horrid culture of death that the United States has avowed, our loosened and abandoned morals that our fathers and grandfathers embraced so dearly after World War II, the desecration of our highest spiritual icons in the name of "modern art," our refusal to recognize the symptoms and effects of the mental derangement of our peers, our ineffective approach to crime of seeking punishment over treatment, our dissatisfaction with common decency, and the destruction of our faith-based institutions in every sovereign state. And, if this is not enough, our bias and discrimination has also led us into the parity of right-wing materialism versus left-wing immorality, the erosion of our physical environment, the depletion of our natural resources, international isolationism, global pollution, government scandals, the amassing of material waste, and a snowballing social apathy that continues to haunt us to this very day. Talk about a Halloween destruction of the greatest nation to ever rise on the seven continents between the seas!

Even after all of this evidence that we are heading in the wrong direction by working only for our own advancement before we turn our heads any other way, we continue to thumb our noses at our neighbors' plight and close our eyes when we see the shameful effects of our outright hatred and social unrest. Over the past twenty years, we have exchanged our bell-bottom denims and long side-burns for a more personal and private expedience; hailing the unholy trinity of "me, myself, and I." We have yet to recover from such a rogue, crass, and unnatural selfishness in favor of our disproportionate pursuit of even more private wealth, a haughty desire to succeed in aerospace technology while calling it the interest of national security; and we have spent ourselves both publicly and privately into unadulterated oblivion; racking-up a greater national debt in the decade of the 1980s than the sum of all quadrennial periods that preceded it combined. Hereafter, do we still have the audacity and gall to stand in front of the world stage and proclaim that we are the freest society on the face of the Earth? We are deluding ourselves about the facts of our domestic status, and following it by our misperception of primping our curls in front of the mirror everyday and lying to our own faces about whether the peril of our democracy is as horrible as it really seems. Who are we to believe that the community of nations must somehow revolve around our own personal needs and the mandates of our various bureaucratic departments? We call ourselves the only superpower left shining on the hilltop of the globe, declaring that Communism is dead and completely disappeared from sight; and yet, we continue to ignore the influence of the billions of people who still live in Red China, their extraordinary weapons and tactics, their pride in their atheistic approach to human persuasion, and their bulging arsenal of nuclear and conventional weapons. Is this the type of dictatorship that we want our country to become? It will, if we continue to expel the Spirit of God from the ranks of those who govern us. So many of our citizens have stated that a book about the relationship between the secular world and religious faith cannot be written, at least any that would effectively defend the reasons why we should focus our national sights back toward the Will of God. These are the ones who have sorely misjudged the power of the Holy Spirit to infiltrate the human heart in a beneficent way, to pulverize the progress of those who oppose the Almighty Father, and to flatten the enemies of righteousness as though God was scalping the face of the globe like a "buzz" haircut.

It is true that many common people and ordinary citizens often redress their grievances along our thoroughfares, in various media editorials, and on public signboards about the increased perversion of our American and global communities. However, when anyone who is properly informed stops to criticize the Western culture on a massive scale, these same people say with the pride of blind partisanship in their eyes, *"Don't you dare denigrate the United States of America,"* as though our observations are somehow unpatriotic in substance, nature, and intent. We have forgotten that our freedom to choose does not give us a license to choose wrongly or to decide a fate for our brothers and sisters that is lesser in dignity than that of our own. After all, we are every one in this life together. Once we have been conceived into our mother's temporal womb, our own mortality has already ushered us past the point of no return. Our birth is the hallmark of all goodness, and our death is God's accreditation of our resolute communion in Him. We are supposed to be protecting those who cannot fend for themselves, after all. These are not the times for anyone's new bravadoes or pretentious lifestyles anymore. What ever happened to the simple way of life that our forefathers sought from under their casualties of war and the intercontinental malaise of their earlier centuries? While most people in foreign nations are satisfied in settling for the scarce provisions of room and meal, we in America are not happy until we have acquired for ourselves the extravagances of ivory mansions and smorgasbords! Is our freedom in this great Republic truly defined by our measures of such profiteering? We disguise our selfish agendas inside the throes of politics, debate, compromise, consensus, acclamation, majority rule, and the like; all toward the purpose of saying, *"It must be alright if everyone else is doing it, too."* Our country is in great jeopardy and peril if we assume that God is going to allow us to get by with this type of delusion for very much longer. It seems that the virtues of our own self-governance often contradict what He wishes us to do; for our legislation occasionally contrasts with the aspirations we claim to be our inalienable civil liberties. We somehow dissect, decipher, define, and divulge the motivations of our fellow countrymen with the ulterior intention of discovering whom we, ourselves, have actually become. Is this not a more frightening process in attempting to discover the worth of our souls before God than making the totality of our being to coexist in communion with His only begotten Son?

It seems as though the United States has become both inspired and exasperated in the same coldly-calculating breath. We require great fidelity and obedience in the performance of our workplace laborers, but could not care less about the condition of their mortal souls before the eyes of Heaven or Hell. We often make qualitative judgements about the beliefs of our neighbors and friends before retrieving the facts about what they have suffered, how their childhood has shaped them today, and who has been brow-beating them for the past decades to finally do something wrong. At the risk of seeming too simply parabolic, it would suffice to say that East meets West at any point on the globe where we happen to be standing during any given moment in time. Hence, there is no need for us to utilize our political borders in defining an imaginary "us versus them" syndrome of choosing who we should adopt as our friends, and the rest we will regard as being our common enemies. Lest we forget that we might be among those whom God will place last in line in the procession of Saints someday, our bland projections and uncertain prophesies are only elementary guesses when it comes down to knowing whether Jesus Christ actually agrees with our

Western ways of life. By all means, we do not have to ever leave *terra firma* to see how this might be the case. Those who cry-out for a smaller national government, lower taxes, and less entitlement spending that might help the poor and elderly population in our midst are the same ones who pummel our doorsteps, blanket the airwaves, cram our personal mail boxes, and ring our telephones off the hook with their barrage of solicitous advertising, trying to get our private money transferred into the coffers of corporate America, whom most right-wing zealots say should be paying less taxes than the pauper living in an efficiency apartment above the local hardware store. It is this type of thinking that has moved the United States into creating a global network of economic unease. When our systems finally begin to fail, as they have on many occasions in the past, our people will again grip their wallets with the clasp of death; and those nations abroad who depend upon us for what little they can retrieve during the best of times will be left standing with nothing charitable from the greatest nation on Earth to feed their poor at all.

So, why has William Roth, Jr. written this book? Because he is among the many giants on the Earth who sees the fallacies in our thinking, and knows that we are not on a course which is ratified by the God of all Dominion. He realizes that we are suffering from a world-wide position vertigo because everything that is supposed to be stable about us seems to be spinning out of control. He is among the responsible citizens in America today who are asking how the world's most enterprising Republic has allowed its mutual assets and its very moral fiber to depreciate into such an unenviable state of compression and disease. People like William L. Roth, Jr. know that the molecules of the true liberty of humankind are found in the nature of our faith in a higher Being, and that they are the foodstuffs upon which all civil decency feeds. I have learned from William and from many thinkers like him that there is a definitive difference in having affection for someone just because we may happen to be related to them, or that we may have studied in the same classroom somewhere, or perhaps may have fought in the same wars together, and the Divine Love we must embrace for all of humankind, even those we will never meet face-to-face before we stoop to die. If we remember more about why we are here and where we are going, rather than refurbishing our grudges against those who might have offended us in the past, we will be on track to truly making this a better world in which to live. Some people claim that their childhood was so miserable that they wish to refer to their life's beginning as the age when they were first capable of taking it by control. But, if they decline to pack their God-given moral conscience with them inside that transition, or somehow never miraculously inherit it along the way, they have sadly not begun to live, even yet. We are on a constant search for the delicate balance between private continuity and public diversity; but our prejudices will always reveal the false nature of our intentions if we leave God out in the cold. This is the essence of our return to understanding the purposes and actions of the many American legends who have preceded us in creating this Nation, developed our interstate commerce and regulations, espoused the original doctrines of tolerance which have made us great alongside the other nations, and kept us from real harm in the face of so many world wars, religious conflicts, and radical racial tensions. *When Legends Rise Again* discusses our relationship with these foregone heroes, and is a mandatory discourse that will make our sprawling land a more decent home for many more generations to come. The moment we remember the quotations of their personal genius and the emphatic paraphrases that are found in this book, we will have taken a giant step toward becoming an elegant nation again.

Timothy Parsons-Heather
February 2002

Can a mother forget her infant,
or be without tenderness for the child of her womb?

Isaiah 49:15

INTRODUCTION
Technology Backfired, Progress Gone Awry

Humankind is given every opportunity in the world to do good on behalf of others, to seek the brightness in a future which seems always yet to be determined, and to flourish amidst the milestones of progress that our previous generations have set into place. Most of us wait to see what reaction the rest of humanity will have to our earliest potential, whether there is honesty beneath their critical thoughts and preponderance, or if our better ideas will ever take-hold in the public arena at large. Most people believe that there is nothing random in the Universe; for every bird that sings, every breeze that blows; any star that falls, and in every baby's cry; there is, and has always been, a natural progression of growth, change, and development to Creation in accordance with the Will of God since the Earth was first positioned in space. It would be safe to say that most of us know that there is an inevitable purpose in life, if not outright predestination. And, it will remain so unless we beseech the Almighty Father above to change it through the wielding of His power. There is some sort of understanding that seems to exist between God and the Earth; as the future belongs to the hunter who seeks, the prey who eludes, the connoisseurs who savor, the novelists who render, the jesters who laugh, and the children who play. Is not human life a part and parcel of this same imminent process of being shaped and advanced by the fusillade of Heaven over the lands below? What can be said of the nations who are not yet so united as to gather in a consortium of exchange from which only the barest of compromises seems to rise for the betterment of the world? Can any among us define the greater purpose of such moral reasoning if it is not to make us each and everyone a purer breed?

Our American nation has become sorely divided within itself, if not completely fractured by the lesions of hatred and isolationism which have sprouted from one neighborhood to the next. The people of the United States have made the way of their union a destiny that is almost assured to be rough sailing into the next few decades and beyond because we have defined Love down to its barest of meanings; to say that we know the hearts of other men, while looking completely away from everything that makes them ache from the core of their very being. Too many Americans have been left stranded and allowed to drift into the darkness over the rolling waves of misery, while millions of others are too proud to concede that they have stood along the shoreline and launched their brothers' plight upon the crest of their own indifferent arrogance. Can we be sure that this awful horror has not been wrought by our earlier refusal to value the essence of unborn human life from now three-decades past, and counting? We are unsightly because we have cast-away our pretty face by the guilt we have inherited and the shame that is ours to wear, wrought by the oceanic blood of the aborted unborn innocents who, in God, shall retrieve their justice at last. The world will finally reveal itself as a protector of the sanctity of life when people pass-away and the unborn children in their daughters' wombs are listed in the obituary columns as being among the survivors who are left to mourn. When America has finally accepted this Commandment of Heaven as our infinite source of Wisdom, no one else will ever be able to talk us out of it because we will have already mastered the art of persuasion and exercised complete control over the effectiveness of defending the Truth to our death.

The wasteful breath of those who have no faith has become a fashion which is now outdated and altogether obsolete. The effect and reflection of days gone-by may allow us to remember and record what our consciousness wills, but we shall thereafter extract only very little perspective from it if our course is not to make ourselves better known to God. Human perception is based upon our capacity to envision reality with the clarity of the Creator who made us in the flesh with a Spirit we cannot yet see. We can sculpt whatever world we choose to make inside the parameters of our minds, but our hearts will always be capable of telling us where the *real* one is. That is the one where people still lay in poverty and disease, where haughty crudeness is having a field day over the air waves and in public print, and where the deterioration of our conscience is growing wider by the day. If we take a good hard look at the United States electorate, do we exercise our franchise and suffrage only in accordance with how we are affected by the nation as a whole, or whether every segment of society gains the satisfaction of their needs and the redress of their personal grievances? The reflection of this prospect is what tests the mettle of our own democratic state, not to mention the genuineness of our faith. Every one of us should think about what our own legacy will be, once we have passed beyond the present age. It is not so much that a chord is struck which marks our new beginning, but that it echoes through the air and in our memories long after the orchestra has been dismissed. Will the reflection of our lives be among the fonder masterpieces through which our great-grandchildren will be consoled? Indeed, the diminishment of our better recollection is never quite like a pitfall into a canyon, but as though time has become an invisible auger that is somehow connected to our brain, slowly drawing-away the effects of the parading years and returning us to the innocence with which we first started learning as toddlers in the backyards of our friends.

We sometimes wonder why Jesus did not wait to be Crucified until such time when we had the availability of audio-visual equipment so we could simply play it out for every succeeding generation to see. God's answer to this premise is that there is no need for recording what is still ongoing upon the Altars of the Roman Catholic Church. Does it require our faith to see it well? There is no one alive who would maintain that it does not! But, *for* such faith, we are saved from the preeminent effect of certain death. We should wish not for replicas of the Passion of our Salvation, but for the suffering of Jesus, itself. This, too, is still proceeding in the lives of those paupers whom our American nation has refused to feed and those who live in squalor in distant parlours around the globe. Many are the times when citizens of our country have thrown their hands into the air and said, "We just cannot feed them all!" Sadly, however, these are the same individuals who have never really tried because they are much too concerned with fending for themselves. Is it more difficult to prepare for the running of a marathon than it is to discover that someone else has won? We have yet to take the tiniest steps in the direction of ameliorating society's ills, but have already surrendered it as being a long, lost cause. With this same lack of perspective, would the original founders of the first thirteen American Colonies ever expect that they would be the curators of the greatest superpower ever known to man? Did the framers of the United States Constitution discuss in a side-bar how much money their successors would require for sending a triad of men to the moon?

What would these legends have said to our modern-day democracy that they nurtured from the nests of their personal humility if someone had approached them from outside the stately halls where they were so solemnly sequestered and stated that they should allow their wives, fiances, and daughters the freedom to kill their Nation's progeny in their pregnant mothers' wombs? There is no doubt that these dead who penned the original charters of our American republic will return someday wearing the wings of God's Wrath on one shoulder and His Justice on the next, barnstorming through the gateways of the past and proclaiming at the top of their collective lungs, *"We have come back to retrieve the noble Nation to which we devoted our lives, for which our countrymen fought to their deaths, upon which our mothers' tears fell alongside the blood of their sons on the battlefields abreast, and over which you have no right to pervert and destroy the dignity we so properly instilled in the tenets of her Trust. Listen well, and lay low; for the time has come for your infectious immorality to greet its destined end! We have come this day bearing the swords which have been handed to us by Christ; and it is in His Holy Name that we shall remake this country again! You can run, but you can never hide; you marauders and thieves who have pilfered the honesty and Love in whose stead we are now marking steps; for God is right behind; and you had better shiver to the bone in wonderment what He will do with the pillaged acreage over which He is about to scatter your remains! Shed His Grace upon Thee, indeed! We will be more than jubilant to deliver your souls to Him in shreds for the evil you have allowed to perpetuate inside these sacred borders, and whose history we have come to rescue from the jowls of your error!"*

Imagine seeing George Washington glaring our peoples straight in the eye with the cold stare of Valley Forge upon his brow; Abraham Lincoln bearing the towering admonition of honesty to everything in his path; and Benjamin Franklin peering over the frames of his wiry spectacles as though awaiting an explanation for why we ever allowed time and fashion to steal our hearts from the decency by which they all long lived and prospered well. What about the Romantic lyricists who sang dirges and wrote so prophetically about how we would be the inheritors of a land of pleasured opportunity between the silvery seas, one that would never stoop for demagoguery or deceit, let alone the false witness that has plundered our neighbors' chance for making the most of the grandeur of the mountains and our kind civilities. There are countless poets-laureate and dignitaries, ambassadors and Senators, ex-officio parliamentarians, missionaries, and Generals who are about to break through the barriers of our wards of mortal reclusiveness and take us to the docks. Bygone popes, bishops, Martyrs, and parishioners will walk through the walls of our most endearing institutions and grab us by the throat until we cough-up a reasonable explanation as to why we have allowed this hallowed ground to shift so closely to the fiery inferno of Hell. Let us never believe that we will be vindicated before them without our own collective contrition, lest they decline to intercede on our behalf to the Christ who has Redeemed their steely souls for God.

By this same hope and revelation, we should henceforth make every effort to wrest the continent of America, the Western Hemisphere, and the entire globe away from the aftermath of our obstinance to do any better toward Salvation out of respect for the many statesmen who have left their own signature and seal on the modern-day world through the price of their sacrifices; personal, societal, interracial, and universal. We are the origin of the tawdry shambles which have befallen the twenty-first century for the rest of Creation to grieve. If our consciences are dead, then our souls should be amongst the first decedents to be also buried with them; for there is nary a man who ever lived who would not return to the Earth and guide us a better way. He knows what we know now; that this is our time to effect the reconciliation of the present and the impending future that will make human life a banner procession for the multitudes who are scorned. The bereavement of such Saints that are hailing above us now is about to be resolved in the face of our own judgement, as we are those who will have to muster an excuse for reneging in our mission to uphold their sound reasoning of the lessons they learned in such pain, agony, selflessness, and service. If legacies and legends are to serve only the living, then why do we keep burying our faces in the ground? Are we prepared to pronounce ourselves dead at the feet of our own denial; anticipating only the fateful sentence to which we have exposed our minds and hearts? We shall look upward and beyond the frail images that keep distracting us from the proper goals of life, because there is no other purpose to human dignity than to seek it from the first. We cannot discover Love if we wrap ourselves in hatred; and no goodness has ever sprung from under the spoils of disdain. Whatever happened to the primness and propriety that brought us to drive our motorcars down the road with our palms grasping the steering wheel at an imaginary ten-and-two, knowing that our little children were huddled safely in the back seat as we continued on?

The long-range methodologies we were bequeathed from our teachers, legislators, and friends have died in our hands because we have done everything we could possibly do to squeeze the lifeblood from them through the brash temperament of our sightlessness, our corruption, and our whims. We once rued ever being left alone as infants who looked for mentors to guide us into the yonder years and beyond; but now, we have dishonored them by living just for spite, by wasting what is needed to the point that millions of others now want for just a pittance and a share, by staking our entire legacy upon a flesh that is headed for the grave, and by our unmitigated lying, cheating, stealing, carousing; and telling the children of our day that these vices are quite an acceptable way to live. The essence of tomorrow cannot be found in anyone's libido or the fads of a secular world, but in what we do to escape them for the good of the spirituality which is the procurance of our sanctity and the finality of our grace. Then, when those lofty birds of a feather sing and our babies start to cry; we will know that only our reunion with the God of all Creation is the reason for our placement both hereto and hereon; that America must be beautiful from the inside-out, not by virtue of her rolling meadows or her pretzel cloverleafs, but in the simplest nobilities that we gain from espousing human Love. If Jesus finally decided to pull-the-plug on the passing of our tomorrows, would we know enough about Him to stop and wonder why? Is our awareness as scant as our willingness to discover what lies beyond the phases of the moon? Perhaps we should learn that America is, indeed, not only a melting-pot for the peoples of the world; but also the awesome cultured preservation of everything that has been best about man. We must protect and unite her as well as we know how; for God realizes that we are helpless without Him; with nothing but His deliverance to keep us safe and free.

There are more than a few grand possibilities in aspiring to not only realize this glistening essence of tomorrow, but to also become one with it inside the transfer of our consciousness toward our revolutionized new beginning. Whether we are painters whose concentration is focused upon automobiles, nature, figurines, or animals; we must all employ the same brush strokes that will allow us to compose a replicated assemblage of order, rather than some random tribute to our own psychic insomnia. If we search for the Truth this carefully, we will be drawn in conscience and action back to solving the problems of the physical world, because the shame we would bring upon ourselves if we declined would never let us speak to our spirits again. What do we really have to show for all of our advanced technologies and social progress over the past hundred years? Are we a better measure of people than those who lived almost explicitly off the land? Do we somehow believe that we are more worthy before God because of our sophisticated institutions of higher learning, our appellate courts and civic councils, and the unprecedented discoveries we have made in science and medicine? Is the restoration of our human decency in any way connected to our ability to conceive our children in laboratories, implanting artificial "hearts," reattaching severed limbs, or curing crippling diseases through the corrupt abuse of human stem cells? Does the cloning of certain species somehow vindicate us for the millions of little children whom we are killing in their mothers' wombs every year? There is no doubt that we will be responsible to somehow try to explain to God how we will give Him credit for our advanced intelligence at the end of time as we know it, while simultaneously continuing to utilize it for a means that is contrary to the Divine intentions of His Spirit of Holy Truth. We live in an era of soundbite journalism, shallow conversations, multi-millionaire sports dynasties, "canned" entertainers, artists, actors, and singers; and we have sought-out excuses not only to be quicker in solving our immediate problems, but also how to expeditiously capture the profit we believe should rightfully be ours for doing it before anybody else has a chance to act.

When we stop to ponder the cinema arts, motion picture productions, the abstract writings of modern authors, and lewd and illicit illustrations of physical infatuation; what are we actually saying about ourselves? Do we really believe that we hold the right to amend the time-honored social mores that so many people before us have fought tooth and toenail to keep from being infringed? Have we allowed our moral decency to go to wrack and ruin just because we want to somehow make a mark on the history of Creation for the legacy of our own generation; whether it be one of goodness or careless harm? If this is what we call progress, then we have totally missed the point; for progress is meant to infer that our most proficient approaches should be toward preserving the purity and integrity of our religious faith, the community of America as a land of sound judgement and critical thought, and a place where there are definitive limits as to how far we will allow our counterparts to go before we stop them from commandeering the reigns of our societal order and driving our civilization into the ground. There is little doubt that the hapless world is on its way to Hell in a handbasket; and we Americans have our collective palms placed tightly on its handles, carrying it like a coffin to an unknown grave somewhere.

Let us not deceive ourselves any longer; we have generated a culture of living in the United States that devalues the heralded virtues of the Holy Gospel, and which is not even slightly in alignment with the sacrificial nature of human life that God has asked us to embrace. Too much time has passed before us now to lay the blame on the faddish iconography of the Beatles phenomenon, or the tragedy of the Viet Nam War, or the crisis of President Nixon's Watergate scandal, the effects of the failed Equal Rights Amendment, or our voluntary exposition to the vast wasteland of the television screen. Everything that must be repaired and restored about our national fiber and fabric must be done from within us, by us, and in our present day. We have been told that there is nothing that can come from the outside which can violate us or render us impure; only those things which we choose to emanate from our spiritual core. We should not have to hold our consciences up to the dawn of light to see whether there is a watermark of authenticity to them; for every soul who is born in the flesh is given one to pursue and exercise from the moment they are conceived, to have and to hold, until the hour of our death. It has also been said that our balloons may sometimes lose their buoyancy and the grapes of our sweetness may turn into uncensored wrath; but this does not imply that our righteous "being" must also degenerate with them. If we allow it to do so, will God not stomp upon us, too, searching for wine; driving us farther into the pit of the Earth, knowing that the best nectar of our inner-selves has already evaporated into the thin air of our snobbish gloating? We must eventually learn that social progress and spiritual piety can walk hand-in-hand, just like that same George Washington and Abraham

Lincoln walked together in patriotic goodness, while mortal generations apart. They were common in their deeds because they both served the same God; therein making their souls timelessly united toward the cause of human freedom. We must hem our evocative curiosity about the future to their lessons of the past; to know that the civility of America can truly live again; and assure the rest of the world that we are in a stable state of acceptable grace before the Divine Creator who has given life to us all. If this sounds a bit too symbolic and poetic to be true, let us remember that our American eagles are still soaring through the air, whistling the tune of the Star Spangled Banner as they hover just overhead.

Our nation is hemorrhaging now more than it ever has before; from the violence on our streets, the crime behind closed doors, and from the dying goodness that we once espoused; now rolling like bloodshed into the cracks beneath our feet. It is the likeness of our greater men that is calling upon us now, seeking us to rise to the cohesion that will again make us one Republic, under God, and indivisible; although we have never really gotten the art of seeking liberty and justice for all quite right just yet. It is our great forefathers who are begging from beyond their graves for us to abandon our wanton disregard which we have garnered toward one another, praying from their lofty palaces inside the Mansions of Heaven that we who live below them might finally snap to our senses and somehow reel-in the years that we have blindly and haphazardly allowed to slowly slip away. They have no doubt that their successors of our age have permitted the advancements of our new technology to backfire on us, leaving our faces powdered and splattered with guilt and the stain of mortal sin; and that we have become *much* worse for the wear, diminished by the pilfering effects of time, effaced by our own collusion, and deceived by the ecological superiority that we claim to hold over the annals of history right now. Most everything that was supposed to make us a free society has heretofore bound us in chains; from the digital divide, to telephone modems, computer screens, microwave ovens, atom smashers, cellular phones, fax machines, global positioning systems, ATM electronic banking, and even casting our ballots for our public officials while seated behind the steering wheel of our fancy new automobiles. Whatever happened to our good old-fashioned personal interaction, the jokes we used to butt on the Main Street park bench downtown, and the loitering of amusement that kept us all laughing at the gas station along the State Route road? Most every place of business where we hold an account these days has a computer to conduct our affairs; and we call on the telephone to reach a digital voice that could not respond to a question if it meant another million-dollars' profit for the members of their Board. With the daily increase in the world's population, why are there less and less people to speak to when we seek someone to respond to our individual needs? Are corporate businesses too cheap to hire someone to answer the telephone anymore? Is this process of dehumanizing our affairs in any way on course with the community that our original founders had in mind? These are only among the epidermic changes that have taken the personal nature away from our common marketplaces and replaced them with a faceless sensation of a more anonymous air.

There is no doubt that the solvency of our entire social and collective conscience is at stake as we continue our march into the 21st century. We have gone from Romeo and Juliet, to Ken and Barbie; and now to any two individuals who think they can hoodwink God into believing that their illegitimate union has a useful purpose alongside His Sacred Kingdom. There have been not only presidents, but lyricists, lecturers, philosophers, and archeologists who have been sitting quietly in the wings, watching as our national integrity slowly emaciates toward certain extinction. While we used to be concerned about our enemies abroad who might strike us with terror or an invasion of troops, we should hope that this is only the slightest of what God might allow to occur. The corruption of our civilized union has little to do with violence, but with our willingness to climb into bed with unfettered evil, by the agnosticism of our ordinary citizens, the lackluster approach we take toward keeping the Sabbath holy anymore, and an appetite for materialistic greed that rivals none other in the history of man. These descriptions are not too exaggerated to be true, because the facts of our actions speak loudly for themselves. There will be no healing of the United States of America until we all stop what we are doing, take a deep breath of fresh air, and recant our demands of "I want, I need, I cannot, and I quit;" in favor of the more noble beatitudes of goodness, to which we must respond, "I will, I can, I hope, and I'll try." This should be not only the *Introduction* to any written manuscript about the convergence of capitalism and Christianity, but also a complement toward our better course of fusing the two without bringing greater shame upon the awful error that we have already embraced in the past. There is a new sense of anticipation which rests just beyond our initiation of this course. We can find it if we try; and only our individual sacrifices will allow us to succeed. This, in its most essential terms, is why the discussion about the truth of "In God We Trust," should continue without inhibition. We can change our minds about what we are doing, but it will not be enough to suffice for the wholesale alterations that must become a part of our entire new psyche and the amendment of our social behavior. Perhaps we will see now, after the wars of hatred have finally entered the borders in our greatest American cities, that we cannot approach the larger world with the same disdain that we have deployed against them in the past. It is time for victorious Love to overcome everything which ails us; a moment that is both precious in purpose and expiring as swiftly as we speak. Thereafter, if the angels still deny us our due recompense, it will be solely because we have already driven them away. It looks from here like the future may still be bright because it is yet quite dark in the places where we live. Let us hope for Earnest Hemingway's Sun to rise again very quickly so as to set our souls afire with the flames of the new beginning that he and millions of his own contemporaries were much too timid to face.

Part One
These are the Facts as We Know Them

Chapter One
The Crisis of Our Post-Modern Age

America is suffering from an internal identity crisis because we are continuing to bow to the temptation of trying to legitimize nearly every conduct of deviancy that happens to wander in our direction. "Can't we make an exception for just one more?" is what our so-called contemporary social progressives seem to require. Some people exit their front doors into the world every morning with an attitude of "...the clock is right and I'm ready," never disconcerting themselves with the consequences of their actions or the wayward paths down which they might be leading their apprentices and peers. This rolling snowball of immorality is not continuing its motion because the brakes of our consciences have failed, but because we are still refusing to apply pressure to the pedal when we are supposed to rise toward more redeemable courses of power and influence. Could this, perhaps, be accorded to the fact that the issues of our extreme personal nature that we formerly spoke about only to our pastors and psychiatrists are now being splattered all over our television screens these days on programs such as Oprah Winfrey, Sallie Jessie Raphael, Montel Williams, Maury Povich, and Jerry Springer; just to name a few? Such scandalizing "entertainment" would not succeed in being produced were it not for our own low collective self-esteem and our cowardly fear of actually becoming like those whose actions we deplore whenever they occasionally confront us head-on. Many other people are opportunists who lay claim to a public forum for the purpose of exposing the intricacies of broken hearts and twisted minds for their own financial gain. No one can argue that we do not live in a world composed of an infrastructure which thrives on the incipient indications of our social instabilities, the conveyance of our interpersonal pathologies, and an unfairly-acquired sense that we have the right to know everyone else's business whenever such fancies happen to take-hold. Those among us who wish they could travel forward through time are only fooling themselves because the precious ticks that they are trying to supercede are expiring by the droves in the process of their studying how to actually accomplish it in the first place. Is this not a reflection of how helpless we are to do anything more than rectify the problems we are facing today and to ensure that the impending years are better for our children to inherit than those that were left to us? This, just like advancing the causes of social justice and individual actualization, must be done from our present vantage point in history.

Indeed, the post-modern era in which we live is an oxymoron and contradiction in terms because we cannot truly live past our own heritage without the power it takes to transcend our errant culpability, our tendency to fail, and our motivational duplicities. There are too many pieces of information that we believe to be relevant to the advancement of our age, when they are actually no more than a collection of baseless opinions. Someone once asked me whether there might have ever been a year in the passing of all Creation that did not contain the birth date of anyone who was living in that particular generation. His question was a commentary about the sad condition of affairs regarding the relevancy of our curiosity and if we have yet come to our senses as to the true problems that need to be solved. Quite the contrary, it is important for us to concentrate our efforts upon formulating more than just delinquent hypotheses about the ongoing nature of our contemporary world; we should be tallying the number of people who have yet no place to lay their head and nothing to eat at the end of each day, and moving swiftly toward reducing that number to zero. It does not help much when the government of the United States has declared it to be against the law to teach the spiritual virtues of God in our public schools; which, in turn, is partly responsible for our adolescent children resorting to drugs and alcohol for an alternative escape. This same government, however, is the first to incarcerate our youth in prisons and detention centers for not complying with its definitions of right and wrong. To further complicate the issue, those who take to the airwaves and other media outlets to clamor for a smaller government with less social spending are the same ones who persist in asking the taxpayers to brunt the bill for all of this so-called alleviation of wrongdoing and "corrective rehabilitation." Moreover; surely we need the United States Congress and the 50 states' General Assemblies to take another look at tort reform by studying the effects of civil liability and material reparation settlements; while the real change has to occur in our desires as decent citizens to become more fair and honest from the outset; to be less greedy and more willing to dispose of such litigatious matters amicably between ourselves without the intercession of disinterested arbitrators and cloaked judges. The majority of American citizens proclaim that they act in most situations in accordance with the facts which are at their disposal, but only after they are filtered, strained, intercepted, and interpreted through the fine teeth of their own biases, misconceptions, prejudices, fallible judgements, and systems of belief.

It often seems as though our newborn children are entering a world that, in itself, appears to be just as infantile; and yet, acts sometimes as though it is quite brittle, old, and crippled to the point that it is on the brink of taking its last fragile steps before falling into shambles from its stately pose amongst the stars. Which of these globes do we really want our future generations to inherit? We will ultimately expose ourselves as being enemies of God if we do not befriend the sick and the dying, the grieving, all little children, and the poor and elderly who cannot fend for themselves. We are indictable as frauds if we expect Heaven to accept us as we *are* when we turn our backs upon those who have the least of every excellence that is available to all peoples of every race today. God either sustains or overrules our goals and objectives at His own discretion without supernatural prejudice, notwithstanding our own skewed versions of the facts as we know them. There is no doubt that He keeps a constantly keen eye on the course of mortal events in America as we wile away the hours through our seductive tenors and material conscriptions. He knows who is truly capable of leading our nation to greatness; but, do we always heed the admonitions of His Will? Most of our revered leaders have entered public service and thereafter "discovered" themselves, rather than suddenly becoming the likeness of true giants and later searching for a venue through which to channel it. The vast majority of good people dream about true selflessness before ever aspiring to pursue it, not knowing if they will ever persuade their peers to acknowledge their hopes for a better world or the electorate to ever give them a chance to prove it by the casting of their ballots on their behalf. Most of us would consider it a great accomplishment to be mentioned in the same sentence or breath with those whom countless citizens already admire. The question revolves around our individual capacity to be prepared to lead a society of people before we ever first don the honorable crest of becoming a "public official" or civil servant. Without the honest integrity of the Spirit of God as our mentor, we will ultimately fail the course of taking any government to its destined purpose of reclaiming freedom and justice for all. We have seen the throes, perils, and tragedies of many faithless tyrants in the past and to this very day that have made a mockery of innocuous benevolence and led their countries into evil ways and ultimate ruins.

Doctors, lawyers, and counselors must be soundly prepared and qualified to enter their chosen professions; and they must carry the proper license and certifications to prove it. But, what of those who occupy the offices within the public sector in the jurisdiction of the several American states? As long as enough people support a given candidate, that is who is chosen to take the oath of office and the reigns in their hands and engage the breadth of their tenure. So long as the majority of those who vote choose them over someone else, with the exception of the presidential Electoral College rule, applied most recently in November 2000, they are the legally cited "elect" who will become incumbent to the extent of the prescription of their constitutional duties and political responsibilities. To be clear, this so-called "majority" might be taken from only a quarter or half of the registered voting bloc of citizens who bother to go to the polls which, in itself, is a pooled subset of the entire census of people in a given district; many of whom do not even register to vote in the first place. This speaks to the continuing crisis of our post-modern age because the lackadaisical and callous view we have toward democracy these days is a perilous sign that there are really only a few among us who are choosing the parameters of the republic in which we live and the extent of the liberties that actually exist anymore. Our public leaders will respond only to those who are hollering loud enough, those who say they will either vote for them or someone else when another term of office nears an end. When the rock-group The Eagles sang their lyrics stating that every refuge has its price in the song, *Lying Eyes*, they might just as well have been inadvertently implying that we can find no support or encouragement from our government unless we take the time to listen to what our candidates are saying and whether they are catering to those who want change for the sake of change, or attempting to acquire an elitist administration bent on turning the agenda of our democracy toward a more limited scope; not the least of which is one that may lead us farther away from God. Our founders and predecessors have left us, intact, a system of spiritual values and a means through which we can freely express our religious liberties; and we should be vigilant against anyone, whatever their motivations, enticements, or walk of life; who may try to suppress them or expunge them altogether.

We own only a bland, impotent, and irrelevant consciousness if we do not connect and suture it to the virtues of higher reasoning, responsible conduct, and moral refinement. This, too, is one of the more viable aspects of a post-modern age that will keep our focus on the righteous purposes of God. We need to begin trusting one another again, without requiring bond and blood to prove it. What can we say of a world that mandates so many licenses, leases, contracts, warrantees, sureties, oaths, promises, agreements, and writs? Is there no sound bartering anymore that can leave our sense of trust in one piece, at least for the course of the passage of a single night? Do we need to execute a promissory note for every dime that is lent to a pauper who is only trying to get back on his feet again? A nation that genuflects to the invisible influences of the almighty dollar is in a pretty sad state of affairs, especially when we hire hit-men to collect our bad debts and bring foreclosure upon the collateral property of anyone who happens to allow a due date for a payment to slip-by a couple of times during his moments of leans profits or uncontrollable strife. The crisis of our post-modern age begins in these things; and it will also be abated and absolved by our collective revisiting of the way we share the necessities of life and the fruits of the land which should belong to everyone. There are millions of reams of paperwork which behold the truth that we do not really trust one another anymore; in bank vaults, lockboxes, the files at our county's Recorder of Deeds, and even in our back-pocket wallets, sometimes. The state of our capitalistic condition is such that we continually transfer wealth to one another to get the commodities we need to survive; and our lust for money should be no greater than this. Why, then, is there a list in Forbes Magazine and other such periodicals that hail Who's Who amongst the world's current billionaires?

There is little risk of sounding too judgmental should the rest of the people in the world look down upon such an elitist group as those who are hoarding millions of dollars in assets as being a figurative death row of those who will someday be the last to be blessed by the Eternal Hand of God at the end of the mortal world because the Truth in the Holy Gospel speaks quite loudly enough for itself. Do the words, "...sell what you have, and give it to the poor," sound familiar to anyone? The basic input-output system which is inherent in the conscience of every man says that there is something awfully inequitable in the extravagant means through which some of us live. A case in point exists with reference to the discovery of our need for a broad-based election campaign reform. We have learned from the past that capitalism does not always infer that the proper virtues of democracy will always be enforced. After all, the actions of people are oftentimes "bought" through the influence of financial bribery; policies can be sold to the highest bidder; responsibility can be delegated to less-qualified personnel; prejudices can be pork-barreled; and certain assets can be forcibly detained or even held hostage until someone concedes to the demands of the controlling interests. The reverse can also be true. Do we remember how many ordinary citizens obtained a drivers license in the State of Illinois in the 1990s by paying cash under the table to the public officials who were entrusted to dispense them only to those who were legally examined and otherwise qualified? It is irrefutable that our national integrity can be weighed beside the substance of our actions; but sometimes what we accomplish in its name sits in direct contravention to the mandates of the law; many of which are almost too ridiculous to be upheld. This springs from the fact that most states have made it possible for small villages and rural areas to receive grants for local use if they will press their constituents into compliance with the mandates of the state. This, in itself, has led to a backlash against our American democracy because private citizens in remote places are now having many of their rights stripped away. When Grandpa leaves the local pub after drinking a couple of beers and drives two blocks to his home on Jackson Street at 15 miles-per-hour, chances are high that an overzealous policeman with a blank DUI citation on his clipboard will fall-in behind him and pull him over if his car swerves even an inch past the center line.

Does anybody recognize that local chapters of village law enforcement agencies collect the larger portion of their proceeds from new regulations that are meant to protect people in mostly urban areas where the threat of perilous danger is quite increased? Such a system of legalized profiteering for the local public coffers is often at the expense of the least harmful among us. Now, we are being told that little towns across the country are making it illegal for residents to burn their trash in the backyard alleyway where their ancestors have been discarding it for the past 200 years because the smoke is in violation of the regulations of the Environmental Protection Agency. It is furthermore an infraction for a rural homeowner to drain the oil from his automobile's engine crankcase onto the ground; but the government can come alongside this same person's property and spread millions of gallons of crude oil over the road so that everyone will have a place to drive; and nobody ever blinks an eye. Some municipalities have even passed ordinances making it a violation to ride a bicycle on the sidewalk; often in villages so small that a pedestrian might be seen passing-by once every twenty or thirty minutes, at most. The fact is, we have all gone overboard in determining what should comprise the most conservative definitions of right and wrong; and have lost our sense of common decency in the mix. We own the relics of tremendous civil victories from our highlighted historical past, but we refuse to claim them for our newer generations now, saying that they are too archaic to be applicable anymore. What we are really stating is that too many blind hypocrites are taking over who claim to be cracking-down on crime, while at the same time collecting tens-of-thousands of dollars to pad their municipal budget. What makes this so deceptive is that these same officials later beat their breasts with pride that they have not raised taxes at anytime during the tenure of their office. To counter this inconsistency, we should employ every conceivable action and travel any available avenue to retain the distinction that has made us the role-model for civil and human rights around the globe. We do not have to wait for any foreign legions to overtake our government because we are already slowly destroying our democracy from the inside out. If we continue our present-day course, our freedom will eventually become as inanimate as the statues and monuments of the American heroes alongside our thoroughfares who framed it from the first.

To add insult to injury in this ongoing crisis of our post-modern age, we shamelessly refuse to communicate with one another anymore. We speak too often in slogans, retorts, and cliches; and electronic mailing has taken the place of our impassioned speeches both in person and on the podium in front of City Hall. More emphasis needs to be reinstated in the value of the distinctions that make each of us individual amongst the crowd of many faces. Marketers and chain-stores do not know their customers when we come in; they only hope that we are carrying a certain amount of cold, hard cash or plastic fun-money that they can get their greedy clutches on. Credit card companies are enticing impressionable people into accumulating a fortune in overextended purchases; the same companies who are lobbying our members of Congress to make it almost impossible to file an effective petition in federal court for debt-relief or bankruptcy protection. The mammoth task at hand is for us to convince the masses that true wealth resides inside the human heart; not in what vehicle we choose to drive, where we eat our meals, or how many financiers it takes to fill the inside of our New York penthouse for drinks and caviare. We have quite another adjustment to make on our own domestic front as we try to protect ourselves from the racist factions who are trying to destroy us just because they do not agree with who we are and what religion we choose to practice. But, hereto, they seem to be more offended by how we spread our capitalist philosophy around the globe under the guise of international commerce than how we kneel to pray. The greatest tribute we can leave to the memory of our lost loved ones in the face of the new-world terrorists attacks is to try to make peace with their killers; so that no misunderstanding, confusion, or vile hatred can ever lead to such horrible destruction again. We bruise one another both physically and psychologically quite often these days; and it is time for this, too, to come to an end. We are waging a war against more than a global or sovereign enemy who espouses clandestine terror; we are also battling against the inner-forces that make us a lesser country, too; and God is allowing the casualties to mount upon our own mainland so we can see the dire effects of our previous prosecutions in other regions right here at home. There were about 281.4 million Americans counted in the 2000 census; and we often tend to believe that this number is the extent to which any tallying of souls around the world should go. Yes; we have actually adopted such an isolationist approach.

We tend to forget that squirrels, rabbits, and birds know when they are seeing another in their species out in the wild; and this is how we should also learn to recognize our fellow man from amidst the camouflage of everything about us that is lifeless and inhumane. We already own a prolific penchant for protecting what is ours; so let us not forget to apply it to our honest faith in embracing every single creature of our Almighty Father when we collect our thoughts for the day. After all, there is little difference between ourselves and the constitution of most any other man or woman alive. It has been said that we are 99.9% identical in our biological composition, no matter to what race we belong. President Bill Clinton mentioned this in one of his State of the Union addresses to a joint session of Congress just before he left office, after which he also hurriedly said, "This may make some of you feel uncomfortable," to which the muffled sound of guffawing could be heard. Most of us, however, thought his point was quite well taken, and a matter for intense contemplation about who we think our real enemies have become. We can say the same thing about our perception of how Heaven engulfs us along every boundary of our territorial mortality. Whatever select or pious images which individual people or prayerful groups wish to harbor about the Orders of the Angels or the Mansions of Paradise are surely alright with God; as they are our way of enhancing our personal aspirations for getting there someday. There is a great deal to be said about how we perceive our souls in relation to the entire body of Creation around us. The spiritual bibliography of our sacred references should span the course of human history, all the way back to the Descent of the Holy Spirit of the Son of God from His judgement seat in Heaven. He knows what hopes and dreams we nurture inside our hearts. While we are in the mood for dictating the terms of how we think the world should end, perhaps we ought to reconsider whether true "living" has ever really begun in America and in every other hemisphere. Have we acquired a disposition which illuminates with courtesy the proper codes of conduct that can expel every demonic force within our midst? Do we profess the Creed of the First Apostles with the same aura of absolute belief inside our epoch of time? Heaven help us if we ever approach the Throne of God when we die in the same way that some among us casually stroll past His Altar of Sacrifice in our greatest Cathedrals these days; offering only a snide parting glance to whereupon our Eternal Salvation has been wrought.

Perhaps we should reserve the after-dinner hours or take a pause before we retire to our beds for the night for a more thoughtful meditation about the Kingdom of God oftener than we do; and for Our Savior and Nation, for the unity of races, for the inclusion of every transgressor inside the Divine Mercy of Jesus Christ, and for the intentions that were placed alongside our timid spirits from whence we were only giddy little children. The better pages of our storybook lives surely have yet to be written, with calmer days and happy endings, when our country and its citizens can really become everything good that we were meant to be, before our ancestors placed their mass-exodus from the continent of Europe into motion. There will always be more work to do to make our democracy complete and a place of true dominion for those who are weak and without a home; even if it is accomplished by our beneficiaries long after we have gone to the grave. Our task is to the solace of every shattered soul we meet; and to somehow broker a peaceful accord for those who are still warring half-a-world away. How great a benison it would be if we could discover the blessings of our homeland as easily as we scratch-off an instant lottery ticket at the convenience-store counter down the block when we rush-in to pay for our gasoline. Unfortunately for us, however, we have to wait longer, until the time is ripe and God reveals our fateful draw beyond the destinies which are meant for each and everyone. There is no denying, here again, that our informal modernism depends upon the constructs of His Will; and this is why so many people grow quite impatient during the interim; leading lives of profanity and conducting their affairs with a futile thirst for the pungent and sensational. Does the measure of a decent man or a collective society rest upon our stature as a nation on the world stage amassed? Do we need to stand at the summit of materialism to be able to see the Truth better than any other people alive on the planet today? Is the pinnacle of greatness a reflection of the effects of a superior military-industrial complex or our advancements in self-defense? If we hold the most massive arsenals in the history of civilization, why must we be so afraid? What is the true source of our unfounded paranoia? As the ancient Chinese proverb so properly states in relation to this, "That the birds of worry and care fly about your head, this you cannot change; but that they build nests in your hair, this you can prevent." Perhaps this, in itself, is sufficient for us to be wary of those who would destroy our systems of freedom, as rough and poorly administered as they may be; while we are doing the best we know how to protect them despite the human weaknesses which still haunt us to this day.

    We ought to be wondering about the time to come when Jesus Christ finally returns as He has promised and sets the world aflame; that we will surely not have time to reach for our fire extinguishers, sound the disaster alarms, and head for the emergency exits of the material world, as though they would ever make any difference in its outcome. Indeed, there will be no need for such panic, evacuation, and expulsion in accompaniment with our final day because we will all see the same charismatic climax to human existence at once. We shall know at the last that there was never anything factual about the new-age philosophy that some "maternal" Earth would protect us from the Divine Justice of the Almighty Father. The question continues to remain as to whether we will ever become shocked enough by our own vile deportment for it to matter in the end. *I am not referring to the hometown, decent, honest, sincere citizens who make-up so many of our civil societies and vast landscapes everywhere.* I am speaking about those who race to the cities to be a part of the action, who pierce their brows with lances and smear facial makeup across their cheeks under the marquee lights, who lay in adulterous beds while their spouses are out working at night, who spend money like it is growing on trees, who crouch in the shadows while waiting for an innocent victim to come along, and who wear a necktie by daybreak and fangs after-hours. It seems like some of us are going like gangbusters to get ahead of everyone else, and are ultimately forced to liquidate our assets to pay our medical bills from years of smoking, drinking, and carousing; or even to foot the cost of our own funeral; while our hungry widows and heirs whom we never bothered to assist in getting a proper education or a gainful beginning in life are left alone to fend for themselves. Have we not all seen the harrowing madness on the floor of the New York Stock Exchange at ten o'clock in the morning most days? There are too many unexplained situations, documented miracles, and paranormal events going-on around us nowadays to warrant this type of perverse hysteria anymore. Most all of us have seen the inexplicable phenomenon of the pet dogs whose owners suffer from clinical epilepsy. Some of these animals can actually predict when their human companions are going to suffer a seizure, well in advance of its occurrence; and in time for the patient to take the proper course of action so as to endure it safely, as a precaution so no injury will be sustained. Do these benevolent canines care more about the plight of the afflicted than we do?

Human existence should not consist of excursions into exotic places, life-threatening heights, or in harboring vengeful nightmares. We should be pondering in advance how peaceful it will be to see the Face of God someday, and making the Earth the likeness of that image as much as we may rightfully instill. If there are vexatious elements to our ordinary days, we should take the necessary steps to eliminate them, at least from within the lives of other people, if we can. Some social circles celebrate the "angels among us," in their window displays and dinner theaters; but what about all the saints-to-be who have already accepted their share of the Holy Cross so that God's hunger for justice can be appeased in the face of the millions of others who ignore Him everyday; those whom He would probably just as soon strike dead in their tracks than preside over their arrogance?   There is, indeed, a day of reconciliation coming to the perils of life; and it surely is not too far in the offing.   Could it be true that autumn arrives because God is sending the sun closer to the southern horizon to make way for the real Light to appear someday; reflected from the blazing Saber of Jesus Christ? Is this a prediction of another Fall of man as we wake to see that the daylight of Dawn has diminished the harvest moon? We know that our individual disciplines and collective chastisements are reckoned to be only a portion of this new beginning for America and the entire world; for all the globe to become one subsistence with the universe again. Beyond these things, there will be no night or darkness; all anguish will be transformed into high jubilation; thunderstorms by dusk will become dewdrops at our feet at the rising of the day; illiterate souls will be able to survey *War and Peace* in the matter of an instant; the blind will read the articles of the Final Judgement of God aloud with their hands waving through the air, the lame will be the majorettes in His Victory Parade, the deaf will respond to our interrogatories before we ever pose them, and the indigent will finally capture the keys to the storehouse of plenty within the Sacred Heart of Christ. These mystical prophesies are not a figment of someone's imagination or their illusions of grandeur; they are the cumulative Truth of the finishing of our faith and the repatriation of every soul who loves God with fidelity into the infinity of His Kingdom beyond the highest Firmament!

There are a lot of people who have asked why Pontius Pilate did not simply erect three vertical poles close to one another and connect them all together with a single horizontal beam to construct the Cross of Jesus Christ and the other pair of crosses which would bear the two criminals who were condemned along with Him on Good Friday. There are reasons aplenty for it; and all of them belong to God. He desired that no corrupt blood of sinful man would ever tarnish the Cross of His Sacrificed Son so that the world would forever know that the guilt of fallen souls could not hang with the innocence of perfect Love across the Arbor of human Redemption. Thereafter, the good would always be separated from the bad, the sheep from the goats, and the wheat from the chaff; and the Most Holy Trinity would never include the failed legacy of humankind; and that the Father and the Holy Spirit would remain invisible until the Son of Man shall return in Glory and recoup His Kingdom again. Moreover, what is the Almighty Creator telling us now? That we should initiate our will to move closer of our own accord to the grieving, the impoverished, the dying, those who have already surrendered loved-ones to death; and those who are lost or missing without explanation, or perhaps enchained by the shackles of illicit substances and hallucinatory contraband. We seem to be living in a generation where millions of people around the globe are almost dead-asleep in atheism; and their souls are parched for an awakening-sip of spirituality; one that their pride and obstinance will not allow them to savor quite yet. Whether we call it the accidental stature of the status quo, an effect of social *laissez faire*, or just business as usual; this squalid decadence of our mortal souls has got to change for the better very soon. It may take the architects of our new economy by surprise to discover that their progress has been of little benefit to all the anonymous Bettys and Alices across America who are still working restaurant tables for $3.25 an hour plus tips; or the little Joes who are standing on the production lines at the local candy factories. There is no doubt that God has allowed us to literally construct our own physical parables about the instruments of His Holy Word throughout the course of history, especially in the early 20th century with respect to the many luxury ocean-liners that have already been flushed into the churning depths of the seas. While the first-class passengers on these vessels were sipping from fine gold-laced China teacups on the clemency of the forward decks, countless sweating laborers were shoveling coal into the boilers in the engine rooms just below the water line to keep their steamers rolling along; while cool breezes were fanning the tanny faces of the polished social aristocrats sitting under their umbrellas, and basking in the sun. Why is this scene of contrast such an appropriate premonition of God's Kingdom to come? Because those among us who are still sweltering are about to be delivered from a dark world of peril and strife; while the unwitting elite will be allowed to sink deeply into the abyss of their own self-condemnation.

It is true that poverty-stricken people cannot hypnotize or cast a spell on the affluent who ignore them to get them to share the provisions of their wealth. But, believe it or not; Our Divine Lord will hear them as though they are waiving a pocket-watch before His eyes and listening to their words, *"...you are getting very sleepy now."* This is the powerful effect that our prayers have on Him when we recite them from the heart to the advancement of everything that is good in His sacred vision for the family of man. How happy He would be to know that He could close His eyes and rest, realizing that all the mortals below Him on the Earth have finally captured their portion of the "plentiful" which He has allotted for everyone. Is this a dream which is too good to be true? You can probably tell by now that the author of this book is no millionaire, either; for one who might be standing in my place would surely not be calling for a newer sense of justice that would cause them to relinquish a material fortune in the name of a Savior whose precious Face only a few who are living have ever seen or Sacred Voice heard by the power of the Holy Spirit and miraculous apparition. We should acknowledge all together what every man should know; that we must be more proud of our God than we are of ourselves; that no Mercy will be afforded to us by Him unless we offer it in-kind to those who have offended us; that there is no greater community of mortals under the stars than those who huddle like puppies at midnight near the Sacred Breast of the Divine Love of Paradise; and that the future will hold only what we forge for it; either to the good of everyone, or to the lessening of the sanctity that will make us all true legends again. Why does it always seem as though those who believe in God with the greatest faith are the same people who have suffered the most? The reason is quite obvious by now; the Holy Cross of Jesus Christ is our only venue to achieving a clear and concise understanding of the Creator, the Savior, and the Blessed Martyr who has given us the breath of life.

Therefore, what else can be appropriately said to summarize a discussion about our ongoing crisis of this post-modern age that will not seem too maudlin or schmaltzy to the more critical observer? We must assuredly assert that, if we want the legacy of the United States of America to always whisper stately in the breeze like the ceremonial bunting at a World Series Title game, we had better make sure that we play fairly and effectively enough to get there; with our caps on straight and fresh air in our lungs. Is it possible for us to sound too much like holy-rollers who swoon from the rafters in our efforts to emphasize the need to grow closer to God again? If we look upon bettering ourselves in the flood of His Grace and making reparation for our erratic nature, too; will we never-mind the ridicule and totally accept what our detractors have to say in the same way that our greatest inventors withstood the gall which was heaped upon them? *"Ride in a carriage that is not drawn by a horse? How naive do you think we are?"* This is the taunting tone which greeted the likes of Henry Ford as he passed such dubious naysayers on the street. Could they have ever guessed that Thomas Edison's light bulbs would be strapped to an automobile, too; or that the radio would play songs across the airwaves from a studio phonograph; all to the demise of those who said it could never be done? Let's face it; America is the nation of people who invented nearly every conceivable advancement of the industrial age; from the microchip to untold developments in technological design; we brought the world out of the dark ages in human growth and independence, professional sports and social civility; we have created ingenious ways to communicate world-wide in a matter of seconds, perfected nearly every contemporary cutting-edge and exploratory medical procedure, promoted the preservation of the environment that would not stifle our national progress, set-aside a vast number of acres as national wildlife refuges, brought social entitlement programs to the fore which have become a safety net for millions of our disadvantaged, saved the world from tyranny by leading the charge against Fascism, Marxism, and Communism; we set foot on the surface of the moon before any other country; we were the first to implement a massive immunization program against deadly and crippling diseases; we established a United Nations organization on our eastern shores to strengthen the bonds of civility between the sovereign republics on all seven continents; we have explored deeply into our domestic caves and oceans, discovered innovative new ways to deliver international aid to poorer regions, championed reciprocal free-trade and global enterprise in nearly every quarter of the world; we have exported military intelligence, weapons, and personnel so as to bring stability and peace to battling neighbors, protected the entire planet from nuclear annihilation, and have sent discovery satellites so deep into outer space that we shall never see their like again. In the wake of all this human excellence, why can we not also make the decision to say "yes" to God in everything else He has given us to do; to forego our outlandish imperialism, stop looking at the bottom line of our balance sheets everyday, and finally stand upright for Christian conviction, holiness, honesty, purity, prayerfulness, and faith?

Are we yet too precocious, apprehensive, and petulant to accept the reasoning that a higher "being" has been the source of our every good fortune and historical progress? Although it has become a ritual of habit for us to wake from our beds and change our shirt and socks from the ones we wore yesterday; we somehow still persist in clinging to the same old faithless indifference when it comes our turn to making the entire globe as free and enriched as we are here in the United States. We have already shown ourselves to be at the top of the class in personal achievement and social modernization; but too many Americans are continuing to search for as much as a simple remnant of the nation of decency we used to be; knowing all along that our body politick is badly aching, bruised, fractured, and nearly broken in half. We live under a peculiar Bill of Rights which allows those who despise our government to express it quite freely within the established parameters of the First Amendment. Unfortunately, however, this same liberty may be bleeding-over into making our disdain for our fellow Americans a new doctrine for public debate. We falsely believe that Our Divine Creator will be as permissive and indifferent toward our interpersonal discord as our founding fathers were about allowing our earliest citizens to say nearly anything they wanted. We are notorious for missing the mark in realizing what is ailing our disheveled brothers and sisters, both psychologically and physically; often mistaking their inner-suffering for a self-imposed reticence or a shy disposition. Let us vow to defeat this crisis of identity which has overcome our nation by opening our hearts ever more widely, reaching deeply inside them, and extracting the virtues from within our own goodness that will allow righteous Love to saturate the commonwealth of everyone alive.

Our hearts have been shaped by the untimely sequence of human events, emboldened by simple achievements, embittered by tragic losses; and molded, fabricated, and designed to survive; if not prevail, over all which diminishes the seemingly invincible human spirit. Every cause and each purpose of life made available to us by God we have either squandered, disregarded, or destroyed—the fertile opportunities for peace and good will, the chance that we can make real progress toward becoming the least of what He expects us to be. The hopeless and helpless of men always cry "when will it all end," while the courageous and hopeful inquire, "when will it all begin?" The Almighty Father will bring us the morning; indeed, it is already before our eyes should we invoke the fortitude to open them. We fear that we will be afraid to let go when the time arrives for us to no longer hang on. We worry that our rise might also be our malefaction, refusing to exchange our pride for valorous faith. Indeed, we resist God's overtures and dismiss His Grace as mere coincidence. We look to Him for change, but do not submit to the cultivation that will grow us fruitfully or give us a new beginning. We must trust that God will ratify our good intentions and complete our unfinished works if we embark upon them in Him; for He is the Author and Finisher of our faith. His Love is our pen to the page and His Will is an affection bequeathed to an errant world that is bold enough to admit its transgressions and willing to make amends to the advancement of world peace and personal purity. Nowhere but in our hearts can our lives come to fruition. Our hopes tucked neatly inside them can grow skyward if we offer them to the daylight sun. This is where the last days of our part in Creation will be protracted. What began in the Heart of God an Eternity ago must be finished by us in our time, here and now. By giving ourselves to Jesus Christ,

His Father will reclaim us, just as He sent us away. There is no alternative to God than Christ. He is, and there is no other. So, when children cry and people suffer, we know that we are helplessly not God. When hatred poisons our lives, we are simultaneously not Love. And, in this, we are lost, wandering through the darkness of our own ignorance and indifference, searching for a reason why God will not change us. All of this, while we have forthrightly been changed! Our transformation is incurred at our Baptism. If we pull the bottom of the shade to the window of our future just a pinch, we will be startled by how fast it flies upward before us, revealing all that God wishes us to know and to become. It is Light outside. It is forever; and it is God. It is day once again; and it is Love. Is the most beautiful sun always the one which sets? We think so now; but let us go with it, over the horizon to a new world that we do not recognize from here. At least, let us dispatch our hopes and wait in faith while Jesus opens our gift of Love for Him inside His Land of Love. This Omnipotent and charitable Champion will reciprocate with all His good might and thanksgiving. His is the benediction we seek, for the night is our wait for the Paradise He sends.

Chapter Two
Renouncing Secular Materialism

————————————

There are some people living on the Earth who would give their lives, limbs, properties, and fortunes for simple peace of mind. Do we find it in what we own, who we are or wish to be, what we wear on our mortal frames, the words we utter everyday, or the record of our past and the hopes we harbor for the future? Perhaps the art of being a biological person should be fashioned by our acknowledgment that we have been created from the distinct Love of Almighty God in communion with Nature and our outermost limits; so that we fully understand our dominion over the Earth as those who have been called to live in alignment with the purpose of returning to the Heaven from which we were cast. Is true refinement and happiness the substance of our daydreams, our reaction to other men, our ability to parse wit and Wisdom, or to bewail our perception and reciprocity? Perhaps our physical environment can lend a better understanding about our inner-selves, but is this all we must really desire to know? My intention in this book is not to sneer at the progress of the Americas or to say that we are not a worthy people before the presence of God and His Court. Quite the contrary, I am recognizing how blessed we are as a human species; that we have come farther than any other peoples of the world during any other era in history toward understanding the tangible aspects of our mortal existence in relation to the spiritual hierarchy of the afterlife. There is no doubt, however, that our fixation with material things and the artifacts we have produced through our own productivity and ingenuity have kept us from devoting as much time to our relationship with God than we would otherwise have given Him in their absence. Is there something novel, honorable, therapeutic, or even slightly noble in contemplating the touchable ambience of our surroundings or the "things" that we utilize as tethers to the source of our creative aspirations? It seems as though the more we learn about spirituality as the years expire, our souls are asking us ever more loudly to listen for a sound that is not unlike that which is made by a hacksaw as it cuts through a hollow tube. The nearer the severance of the tube into half, the lower the tone of the tenor we hear. Is this a parable to the way we light upon the surface of reality once we are old enough to know the difference between Heaven and Earth, somewhat like descending a stairway from having our heads in the clouds to finally ascertaining what is worth pursuing on a practical plane?

It is quite an ominous sign that we continue to hold-out against Our Lord in indignation when we continue the struggle for material possessions;

for it is only when our consciousness is "sown to the Spirit" that we can finally comprehend the meaning of life; or so Saint Paul has stated in his prophetic Epistles. I have come to the conclusion that there is no such circumstance as being disproportionately too spiritual or deciding too much for the sublime "metaphysical" in our encounter with the material world or in our relationships in social circles and secular affairs. In fact, we are told in definitive terms by the Roman Catholic Catechism that the Truth of the universe resides mainly in the Spirit of God as He is situated on His Throne in Heaven with Jesus Christ at His Right Hand, and through the Holy Spirit on the Earth, which is the substance of the Sacraments that are the original graces for our Baptism, conversion, faith, and transformation into the righteous-filled people we are supposed to become. It is surely true that the future which we must usher into our present day is like a decanter that should be filled with our proof to the Almighty Father that we have recognized the error of our ways, made a firm purpose of amendment for our future conduct, and plan to live only in accordance with the New Testament Gospel which has been revealed by the Holy Paraclete to us through His biblical authors. The fact that Jesus Christ is present in the Eucharistic Sacrament of the Roman Catholic Church proves again that our greatest possessions in life shall be rendered from the hands of those who are ordained to be His priests; for the Eucharist is the Body, Blood, Soul, and Divinity of the One and the same Savior Jesus Christ who hung on the Cross for three hours to expiate our sins from Creation; and is our peace, our life, and our everlasting Redemption. Hereafter, can there truly be anything less than the Sacrament of His Sacrifice or an authentic relic of His Martyrs and Saints that is truly worth pursuing with the determination of our souls? There is no doubt that whatever has been blessed in His Holy Name at the hands of His priests is also included in this sacred deposit of sanctified gifts. Why, then, do we continue to pursue the likes of modern-day automobiles, luxurious appointments for our homes, elegant robes for our backs, and a surplus of funds and wares that we can only perceive and selfishly claim as our own?

It seems to me that the purpose for the eloquence of the Holy Scriptures is to cool our tempers and stop the ongoing fighting for material gain which will only return to the dust to which our bodies will be bequeathed. Planes, trains, and automobiles are no more than three "nouns" which compose several modes of commutation; all of which will become obsolete in time because their motion is manufactured by a body of men whose days are both absolute and numbered. Henceforth, we have discovered that we cannot run from the Truth because it stands in perpetuity wherever we choose to go. Seven of the most important words in the Mosaic Psalms are these; *Cast me not out from your presence*, (Ps 51). This penitential supplication of the Psalmist is a plea for God to understand that we realize His power in rendering us helpless before the Divinity of His sight. Indeed, if we pursue only what we believe as having a sense of value in the physical world, are we not already casting ourselves away from Him before He has completed His opportunity to draw us all in? What do we do, instead? We continue to seek Him in every other aspect of Creation; the animals, Nature, the birds of the air, and the swirling cosmos over our heads. Each of these should be protected from ever being corrupted by our transgressions; but they, too, are only the effects of His Love as we know it to be. Our purpose is to motivate our consciences to seek *Him*; not just the aspects of His universe that we can see and otherwise sense, record, and explore. Johann Wolfgang von Goethe once wrote that, *"...Nature is the living, visible garment of God."* His vision was not completely comprehensive because it falls short of being the inevitable Truth of everything that composes the strands and cross-hairs of our basic fabric of faith. God has not put-on Nature; but has made it out of nothing with His own Hands. He harbored no specified elements that could have existed prior to Him from which to work because He forthrightly created them, too. Goethe's quotation, while kindly poetic in stance, is somewhat reversed because it implies that Nature existed somewhere in time before God poised Himself to "put it on." This reflects the same skewed vision that we have of Heaven today. We are the products of the Love who has given us life and, therefore, should seek to be restored to the centerpiece of God's Feast Table from which our souls have fallen like crumbs to the Angels who are still melodiously crooning underneath. No better understanding could be obtained than for us to know that our factual life is not constricted inside the visible existence in which we work, walk, and have our being; but rather in the systematic faith that is our Light of the ages, both now and forevermore; and this is the reason we should surrender our grip on the objects for which we work our entire lives to obtain. This is the essential thesis of why we mourn over those who continue to shun God during substantial periods in their lives, or perhaps disregard Him altogether until the moment they finally die.

If we wish to make a name for ourselves in the secular world, would it not be better if we were to be remembered for our efforts in diminishing its distracting effects on our brothers' and sisters' lives? Is not secularism the reason why there are so many people who have cast their Eternal Salvation aside for the exchange of pursuing greater notoriety and personal acclaim? Is the defense of a system of democracy seen as a great virtue in the eyes of God if that democratic system is to the exclusion of Jesus Christ in the end? Where is true freedom when we are bound inside the revolving circle of waging and spending for the entire of our days; leaving what assets we own to our heirs by which they will fall to the exact same error? This seems to be somewhat of a contradiction to seeking the Kingdom of God that we are asked to pursue from the moment we are born from the womb. Perhaps the German motto of the Prince of Wales, *ich dien*, meaning, *I serve*, is a suitable preference for the purpose of human life because everything we have and own is to the provision of happiness, peace, and security of all other men. This is the great oath of honor that we owe both humankind and God, alike; and this is what will make us heroes inside the Judgement of His Son. It is important that such service is not solely toward the preservation of secular independence, but for the advancement of the all-important spiritual presence of our more faithful side, as well. Do we suppose that R. J. Gatling (1818-1903) would rather now be renowned for how he might have brought peace through Christian conviction in reflection of his years from the other side of life than through the inventing of a gun which can fire successive rounds in a matter of seconds? This might give us pause to think about what type of defenses we are employing and teaching against the enemies of Love in the world today. We have transformed the old-fashioned catapult into the modern-day howitzer not so we could end the waging of war, but so that engaging in it would be to the greater detriment of our enemies and the increased number of casualties of our foes. Here again, does this concur with the tenets of the faith of peoples such as those in the United States of America who profess to lead lives in the likeness of Christ? There is no evidence that He ever held a weapon in His Holy Hands, threw a stone at one of His enemies, cast lots for the property of the damned, or construed a battle plan that would rout those who opposed Him by brute or physical force. All He asked us to do was to Love!

Another reason why so many of us sound the gongs to the advancement of the secular world is because there seems to be no stated parameter anywhere on record as to how much we are supposed to pray. After all, are we each and everyone meant to become secluded in cloistered homes where those who recite their holy hours almost perpetually rarely see the light of day? Who would become the doctors to heal our sick, those who tend to the young, or the scholars and scientists who develop our social progress and teach the methods of research? Who would prepare our food for supper and bear the children who are the fruitful multiplication of God's people around the globe? Herein, we can detect the active Will and intention of the Holy Spirit inside those who are given their various vocations, whether they are to the purpose of living as the ordered and ordained, or that of a parent or laborer; each is meant to be at the beck and call of the spiritual nature of Divine intervention. The sun still rises in the morning and our hearts are not yet withering like the leaves of fall into the husbandry of winter. Our better days are most assuredly standing ahead of us now because the interfacing of Christianity and secularism is still being modified; wherein the secular world will ultimately succumb to the values and principles of the Love of God; the raw power that the rest of the world who rejects Him is still lacking. Jesus Christ is the Savior of all sinners on the Earth; but He has not done so by establishing, sustaining, ratifying, or even faintly agreeing with the properties of human life which have nothing to do with the Cross. If He is being either ignored or impugned at any physical location on the globe today, it is a place which is bound for certain destruction and extinction because such will never be a parcel in the Kingdom of the Redeemed. The term "secular" describes an event which occurs only one time in an age or a given century. Jesus Christ is the King all ages and the Ruler of every single millennium. He is the perpetual Man of God in Creation; and von Goethe is to posthumously know that Jesus is the visible Garment of the Almighty Father in the physical world in which we, too, are to clothe our own souls. We have been called to "...put on Christ;" and this means to wear Him from the inside-out, where the Holy Spirit flows from within, like flowers budding from under the soil, and the bays of human goodness becoming engulfed by the streams of Truth and Love which we own in our bounty of faith. Thereafter, our sectile bodies may be plucked from amidst our spirits, but we will forever be in God's possession throughout all eternity.

What, then, does this mean regarding the residual places in our hearts where we admire the work of our hands; such as our carpentry and artful renditions, our crafts and furniture, and our other more simplistic and sentimental replicas? Would it not be proper to assume that these cherished archives have been also blessed into sanctity by the Great High Priest, Jesus, the Son of God, Himself? Whereupon they have been construed and constructed in memory of His goodness and likeness, and are a reflection of our filial Love for our brethren in Him, then these are assuredly among the quite tenable articles of our faith. They are not the redundant conveniences, extravagances, and superfluous pieces that we should cast-aside, but are the manifest evidence of the memoirs which uphold our good temperament to remain steadfast in the charge for a better world to come. Our more sincere intellect tells us, too, that our elegant church buildings and Cathedrals are not extraordinary properties that should be whittled from our presence like our multi-million dollar homes. Our religious statues, rosaries, pendants, and crucifixes are not to be considered as casual possessions because they are a portion of our environment that keeps us connected to our faith in God and humanity, alike. Even our stereos and televisions can be considered to be sanctified machines, especially when they are broadcasting programs such as the crusades of the Reverend Billy Graham, the 700 Club, Fr. John Corapi, Mother Angelica's EWTN network in Alabama, or a Papal Mass from a far-off country across the world. However, when these great venues are utilized for disseminating the violence and impurity that is scandalizing our youth today, they are considered a liability against the Christian conversion of our nation. Even our ribbons, trophies, and plaques of recognition are commendable relics when they reflect the excellence of human achievement; but not to the demise of an opponent who is equally deserving in the discernment of God. We should be filling our trophy cases with hardware that celebrates our victories over poverty and disease, over war and famine, and over hatred and bigotry; not whether we can put more points on an athletic scoreboard or run faster afoot than someone else.

Oh, we can just hear the howls of protest now! There are people screaming all over the country while maintaining the premise that we should wield supremacy over our personal effects! A mother may be complaining that her son's saxophone is no violation against the Testament of Our Lord! The answer is that she is correct only when such musical instruments are sounded to console us in the presence of the Holy Spirit, or to place the Sacred Scriptures into song, or to conduct the liturgical processions before the greater throngs of men. Any melody that sings from a musical instrument, or a vision which flows from the canvass of a portraiture, or a scene that streams from the most inspiring architecture to move our spirits closer to understanding the Kingdom of God as Jesus Christ has lent it to be is surely alright by Him! And, what about the stately presence of our national monuments and the solemnity of our war memorials? Indeed, what does God think of our sprawling expansion bridges and burrowing subways, or our granite-hewn cenotaphs for our predecessors, prophets, and kings? Here again, should any of these be of the peaceful accord of human decency, reminding us how great were the people who first introduced our generation to having respect for God, they are as natural to the lay of the land as the islands and streams that He forged with His own Hands. There must surely be a linear engagement which exists somewhere or a prima facie buffer that allows us to take a humble raft or a sailboat out to sea at times to reflect and be closer to God, and to ponder reconciling with our brothers again; but never once a smug yacht or a haughty cruise ship to betray the expanse of His exemplary simplicity before the rest of the world and our peers. Whatever composes this mortal precipice must surely determine whether our intentions are toward the amelioration of our personal discord with our families, friends, and enemies; or takes us, instead, to some other evasive self-fulfillment where we are only thinking of ourselves. Whatever the pose, it is inside this "zone" of enlightenment that we are allowed to capture the world for the purpose of becoming closer to God by escaping the commotion of those who are trying to persuade us to leave Him behind. And, what about our armaments, race-cars, space-ships, and family jewels? Unless we can discover a greater and more benevolent purpose for their being here, we had probably better sell them to somebody who will melt them down and make dinner plates for those who have nothing to eat, and thereafter transfer the proceeds to the poor.

Might it be essentially true that, if our possessions sustain life, preserve human health, and foster a higher dignity for man, then they are surely not inherently wrong? The perspective of passing time shall be our determiner as to whether we have made any headway toward legitimizing our physical inventories, just in case we get caught holding them like bags in our arms when Jesus Christ returns and asks us to take Him by the Hand. He knows, however, that if we are touching the face of a marble rendition of His Holy Family somewhere, this is quite another concern; one which is substantially defensible within the breadth of His Plan. There is no doubt that there are plenty of people in America who are getting pretty tired of hearing Protestants clamoring to the Catholics that we are not supposed to have any graven images in our possession while professing our allegiance to Christ. The fact remains that the Roman Catechism does not prohibit the placement of suitable statues of the many Saints, Jesus, Mary, and Joseph in our midst when we pray for this hedonist world. It seems awfully hypocritical that these same Protestants will travel thousands of miles to bow at the feet of the statues of their favorite movie stars and sports heroes, and look-up in awesome wonder at the faces on Mt. Rushmore and the dignified Statue of Liberty. Do they suppose that these stony likenesses must be alright because they are entirely secular in form? I have been waiting for 40 years for a Protestant leader to come forward and tell me why it is alright to honor a graven image of a sinner and not a canonized Saint or the Son of their Almighty God! They must come to understand that the measure of human history cannot judge the worthiness of our spoils because Jesus Christ has already transcended our own passage and the theories of their blind possessionists, too. If we were ever going to render a descriptive narrative about the United States today, would we not also include the faith which our ancestors promised to extol? No historian ever stops at just scouring the countryside in his mind, and thereafter pens his meandering thoughts, because he first travels the outline of our living heritage to serve as his guiding points. And, if such a chronology is to be completely accurate, it would be forced to include our conformity with founding our nation under the advice and consent of the power of God.

We need to somehow extinguish the menacing habit of looking backward and pondering only the moments in history where our democratic institutions took a turn, or whether their hinges swung to or fro, and examine once and for all the spiritual characteristics of our leaders which allowed them to see the Truth in their day. Our national pride must become vulcanized by our greater, more comprehensive purpose of preserving freedom because it is a virtue of the Fruits of Love, not because we think we are supposed to be more at liberty to shape the future before any other region or race. This does not mean that we should lower ourselves to the level that many other nations have fallen, of course. Were it not for our ambidextrous capacity to survive in a world which is filled with so many dying socialists republics and anti-Christian extremists, we would have surrendered our willingness to capitalize on the Truth of human Love long before modern terrorism ever attempted to bind our raised hand behind our backs, like little children sitting in class. The fact is, we live in a country which espouses the human community at no expense to our rights to further our private individualism, profess ingenuity in our daily chores, and voluntarily participate at our own discretion. Moreover, most of us give back to America far more than we extract from her surplus; while we continue to share our common modes of transportation, by-ways, and intersections; trusting one another even to the point of drinking from a tap which runs with water that is purified by people we do not even know. This means that we are completely aware of the intrinsic decency and close public security which has "become" America. If only we could broaden this same sense of well-being to the inclusion of a total belief in the Gospel of Jesus Christ as the record of our Eternal Salvation, we would be near the summit of completely understanding the reason why our mentors placed their pens and seals to the Preamble of our Federal Constitution. Let us not delude ourselves anymore; we continue to face an onslaught of opposition to our social freedom as those dignitaries originally proposed it. We live in a perilous time, upon an ever-more volatile globe. This is especially why our choices should be toward the evangelization of the God upon whom the likes of James Madison and Thomas Jefferson ultimately relied. They stood empty handed and proclaimed themselves to be free! Does this not teach us that we should let go of the material world and return to their same stability; acknowledging that we have turned too far away from their particular brand of noble democracy as it was initially intended to be?

I am not promoting the reversal of the itemized Amendments to the Constitution which have garnered even more rights for those whose lives were still held in bondage in the days when our nation was born. The subjective precursor of our century which was altogether lacking in theirs is that their form of free-enterprise had yet to corrupt their definitive moral creed. They were certainly listed as being among those whom we would describe today as being "sinners;" but must we broaden the scope of their error just because we hold the ordinances to do it? Our forefathers were much more interested in being free than they were in becoming rich. Now, however, we subscribe to the inalienable right to pursue both of these and, therein, have become severed from the high value they placed upon life and the dignified presence of man. In their own simplistic way, these thoughtful people who articulated the Truth with wooden pallets in their mouths, while wielding feathered pens, knew that true liberty was to be found in their promise to lay their lives on the line when speaking of the unlikely event that they would ever be able to succeed without the solicited intercession of God. In more concise language, they realized that they would have to pray for guidance and strength if the United States of America was to become everything they had perceived in their dreams. This same requirement is no-less true for us today; but it has somehow become a violation of other people's civil liberties to ask them to beseech the invocation of Heaven to come to our aid nowadays. If this is not an erosion of the freedoms that we were promised when John Hancock first took to the podium and spoke so passionately before the council of our founders, then we have no business defending our shores anymore. His desire was to instill a new courage in those who were afraid to recite the words *e pluribus unum*, one out of many, so that we would all be united in faith, morality, strength, and allegiance. He would have defied anyone alive in his age to imagine that we would ever live in a nation where so much capital is concentrated in so few hands. Let us remember this with intensity when we go waiving our tri-colored flags around the world these days! Are we saying that we are a sovereign nation because we have captured the greatest wealth, to the tune of trillions of American dollars? The small nation of Afghanistan that we bombed in October of 2001 has one-fiftieth of the wealth that our stock markets plummeted during the single week following the terrorist attacks which felled the World Trade Center towers, ignited the Pentagon, and downed the commercial airliner which was filled with our heroes in rural Pennsylvania.

None of this ease of wealthy acquisition even existed when the United States was first chartered by our great founders because they were a prescient people who vested in our generation, as unwitting as their actions might have been, the capacity to deal with the 21st century complications that would arise from the more perfect union to which they were increasingly devoted. Let the record show that we have not perfected it yet! We continue to be strapped to the gurneys of our own self-indulgence, profiteering, gambling, substance abuse, and isolationism. And, if this is what we call human liberty, then we have got ourselves an old-fashioned addiction to the very corruption that Jesus Christ has asked us to shed. Our vision has become deluded by our progress; and our blindness is leading us toward relinquishing control of ourselves and our nation to the ills of, "...defining deviancy down," as the eloquent former New York Senator Daniel Patrick Moynihan has so appropriately described. We are indicted both by our present misdemeanor and our remorseless intentions to carry it into the future without addressing the awful effects that our behavior is having on our children at home. We fill our living spaces with toys for Christmas, birthday presents, and anniversary gifts; not knowing that they are all distractions from the true reunion that we need to engage at the center of our hearts. We have finally lost sight of the coalescent nature of interpersonal Love; replacing it with the same kind of skewed vision that brought Wolfgang von Goethe to proclaim that the Almighty Father has put on a Nature that He, Himself, has given to us upon an Earth which is no larger than a footstool under His heels. If we are to ever return to the plateau of Sir Thomas More's Utopia in America today, we must stop being distracted by the provisions at our hands and train our attention toward the Christian Doctrine of the Messiah on the Cross; not to materialism, never to atheism, and certainly not to the secular agenda which has made such a travesty of the hopes and dreams of the legends who first put our democracy in place. This is the process of our true renouncing of the secular materialism which has become the origin of the emaciation of our decency and the erosion of the freedoms that were meant to be ours all along.

As strange as it may sound, the Son of God has a very romantic Heart, and is still deeply in Love with humankind to this day. His presence cleaves to those who embrace true freedom; especially when His Salvation is hailed as the supreme reason for its resourcefulness. He fields our questions about His holiness with great honor and dispatch, sending His pious Angels to sit at our sides when we ponder how to make His humanity more free. He knew every one of these great democratic dreamers from the moment they were born, as well as He recognizes us today. His wholesome genius prevails over our every invention, except those which are a detriment to His Kingdom. Beyond any doubt, we can inviolately hold to our faithful accords and retire to our cordoned parlours where we kneel to pray in much greater peace now, as a result. The Holy Paraclete is our motherboard of metaphoric balms and storehouse of memories which keeps our hearts ticking along, never feigning affection for our best interests; and always anticipating which one of us will suffix our days by loving Him in holiness before we are called to die. It is surely enough to say that leaving our possessions behind is paramount amidst this solemn recession. Surely the Heavenly Father is pleased by our charter buses which deliver His flock to the occasional Eucharistic Congress, and the civilian aerotransports that fly us to His Mother's miraculous Marian shrines. Would He not, however, reprove us for our pride in our B-52s, our nuclear submarines, and our spy satellites which hover so sheepishly overhead? We must concede that the argent world is filled to the brim with our proteges, partners in crime, and secular voids which will eventually drive us all to recline upon our psychiatrist's couch and ask what is ailing us from within. Thereto, unless he owns the foresight of God, Himself, he will conclude that he really does not know; and then proclaim that it was nice to see us, while uttering those inevitable words, *"...that will be fifty dollars, in advance."* It does not take a Philadelphia lawyer to understand that there are scores of shapes, sizes, periscopes, and panoramas that must wait for another day to be deployed; for we are on a mission to discover who we really are in the perception of Jesus Christ; and damn anything that can be procured with a bargaining chip which might try to hinder our path.

　　We shall never stoop for centenarian trials or ascend to beveled-decks before we have seen our way clear to knowing God as perfectly as we can; for this is a charge that only our faith in His Son can acquire. Togetherness is our strength and device, for there is no more time for our cowardly hermitages anymore. We oftentimes sit alone in our upstairs rooms and scribble notes in our unfinished diaries, listening to the sound of our pen scrawling our heart's consolation on the hollow surface of our wooden-top desk; sounding like mice gnawing on the baseboard beneath our kitchen sink. We wonder, too, whether God will ever make an anthology of them all for the Saints to read, so they will know what we were thinking when we felt so lost and forsaken on our own. We ponder the politics of the day on a massive scale, daydreaming about what it might be like to become a part of something else; not quite so damaging to the mortal fabric with which we keep trying to cover our heads to get away from it all. When we see our fellow patriots asleep alongside their legacies, will any of us be the honorable ones who can see their Heaven so clearly that we will leave well-enough alone? Will we ever see ourselves as the bumblebee who was never so callous to be forced to sting, the spider who knitted a winter coat for the flies that were caught in his traps, or the bear who took no time to hibernate for fear of missing the reveille of God? We are the Americans who hold custody of a nation of many companions; and we have inherited the goal of taking her closer to the spires of true Dominion than she has ever been before. The titanic objectives of all the ages are now in our hands, like that proverbial torch in the darkness; while other worlds see us flailing about so swiftly in the blandness of our neutral indifference that we risk fanning it out. Imagine having this gruesome asterisk next to our name in the annals of time, "...the age which allowed America to die." The fact remains that the United States is bleeding gravely from our own error; and we need sanctified acres, rolling plains, and western flats to lay our battle-scarred, wounded, and dead upon. All of these are found inside the storied Fruits of the Holy Spirit which are already growing within our hope and certitude like apples on a tree. We need not run to the orchard of the outer-world to get them, for they are planted, nurtured, and harvested at the center of our hearts.

Let our nation and our countrymen never stray from the charity which is so defined by the Roman Catechism, "*The whole concern of doctrine and its teaching must be directed to the Love that never ends. Whether something is proposed for belief, for hope, or for action; the Love of Our Lord must always be made accessible, so that anyone can see that all the works of perfect Christian virtue spring from Love, and have no other objective than to arrive at Love.*" (Preface, 10, cf. 1 Corinthians 13:8) In this blessed assurance, we finally know that our American nation has been founded not only upon human freedom, but also firmly within our intrinsic supernatural connection to the souls who established it; they who blessed us with the Fruits of the Holy Spirit which guided them in Love, joy, peace, patience, kindness, goodness, faithfulness, gentleness, and self-control. How could any republic ever fall from grace if she is so destined to share these holy virtues with the rest of the world? It is inside this perfection of our Almighty God that the Paraclete animates Creation, awakens our faith, enables our communication with Jesus Christ, gives us the words to say in the solitude of our prayers, restores our

Divine likeness with Heaven, reveals the Most Blessed Trinity, brings about the unity of the Church, and confirms the charismatic healing of our citizens in accordance with our public communion with the Truth. This is the real direction that America should be going; not suspending ourselves in mid-air above a boiling cauldron of polytheism or, worse, the agnostic practices of the pragmatic elite. Every ship on the open seas which is not sailing under the masthead of Christ's Redemptive Cross is definitely headed for a date with a coral reef somewhere, or even a dry-dock that will render it fit for inhabitation only by the rat-race of infidels who have nowhere else to go. Is this the fate we want to see for the Good Ship America? Is our main hatchway getting ready to collapse from the rush of our citizens trying to acquire a taste of history while seeking what made those gold-rushers of '49 so headstrong, worrisome, and blind?

The glowing embers we see before our eyes are what remains of the world of propriety that the earlier ages left behind; and it is our generation who will either smother it under our molten selfishness for material goods, or inflame it once again with hope by allowing the entire of humanity plentiful room to breath in light of our spiritual charity. With all her shambles, shattered dreams, and broken hearts; America is still a land of high promise because we own the civility that allows us to foster a greater hope for the future, and beyond. We are a mature, poised, polished, and experienced lot of publicans who ought to be confident enough on the world stage to reveal our innermost desire to ensure a global peace. But, we often display a certain pathos toward our own successes and a weakness in the knees which leaves us trembling in fear that someone from abroad is about to arrive on our shores and steal our progress like thieves in the night. The awful prospect of which I speak is not of other mortal men, but the ripe judgement of God who will say that we have had our chance; but we somehow left His most endearing creatures shivering in the cold. It is true; we have a certain lack of inner-security which brings us to hide behind our possessions and wealth; and only by losing them will we ever be able to take the pacifier of corporate gain from inside our mouths and speak with utter integrity that we do not need it anymore. We know that rain, sleet, snow, or darkness of night will never stop the delivery of our mail; but we decline to stick our heads out our front doors on the most beautiful days of the year when the Holy Spirit makes the call for us to collect all peoples under the Cross in the Name of the God of all nations. Our suspicion seems too great that we might lose our leveled mansions outside MacArthur Park, or somehow not be able to walk past an ongoing Mass without being forced to stop inside and pray. The courage and vision which led our founding fathers to mold our nation from the first is not yet dead in time; for we are their likeness when we call upon the same Holy Spirit who served as their guide and Lord. If we are to move forward in victory and shun the perils of defeat, we must imitate their faith and good works, crossing more than just the Atlantic, the Potomac, and the Delaware to seek our freedom again, while reaching all the way to Paradise for the infinite Wisdom through which God will proclaim once more, *"... I have shed My Grace on Thee."*

It is not a signal that we will relinquish our modesty if we continue to reach-out to one another, both domestically and across the globe, to share our technologies, medical advances, discoveries in communication, transportation, and defense; so why are we so afraid to take our faith in God to other lands where there is so much civil strife and hatred that it makes even the most hardened of conscience cringe in pain? What a miracle it would be if a natural earthquake were to strike the heart of our nation, causing the oceans to crest over our mainland beaches, and rendering the entire continent of North America to be reshaped into the form of the Cross. Would we finally believe thereafter that we are meant to evangelize Christianity with every resource, fiber, and resolution within our strength and means? God already knows that we are guilty of spreading our error in a broader sense which gives us a twisted view of the Truth. While Caucasian Americans are so worried that their race will be a minority in time, they have still allowed the systematic extermination of millions of their own children in the wombs of their impregnated mothers; all to the excuse that any more little ones would inhibit their ability to seek greater prosperity and more comfortable lives. Only time will tell what price we shall pay for mortal transgressions as great as these!

In the final analysis, we are being constringed inside a vice of our own rendering; pressuring ourselves to gather what we can effectively claim in order to practice the deceptive artifice of material possessionism, while continuing to anticipate how to pare our resources to the bare minimum so as to satisfy the veiled inquisitiveness which most of us espouse in pursuing the presence and identity of God. Humanity must become able to contrast the differences between our provisions of necessity and our casual accessories; although this task is made quite formidable in a capitalist country because our prospect of succeeding always relies upon the mutual exchange of our privatized funds. The idea that we might somehow sacrifice our patriotic liberties should we decide to return to the simpler means through which our earliest countrymen lived is quite an untenable premise. If not for the proliferation and stockpiling of our own wares under the guise of human freedom, there would probably be no need for social welfare anymore because everyone would own a share of the whole. No one is suggesting that we should mutate our federal government into some type of communist enterprise, but we will eventually be splintered into two large pieces in the near future; the rich and the poor, if we do not take action to redress the grievance of such a large gap between them in America very soon. Indeed, the chasm separating those who "own" and their subordinates who "labor" has never been wider in U.S. history. Who would have guessed that there would be such parity in a nation in which hundreds-of-thousands died in the Civil War to ensure the integrity of our states' cohesion when we are allowing it to manifest nonetheless by the inequitable distribution of our commodities and wealth? In our hearts, with our thoughts, and through our actions, we are gradually becoming a nation-divided because of the secular materialism which is slowly bringing us down; and not a musket-shell or cannon ball has yet been launched against our neighbors and friends. The subtly of this phenomenon makes most of us assume that it is neither a matter for immediate concern nor a prophecy worthy of hypothetical conjecture. However, will we address it sufficiently in advance to preclude the physical violence by which nearly every other aspect of our social infrastructure has been previously evolved? Can we anticipate what our fellow citizens will do if we continue to leave them out of the process of supply and demand? If we should decline to include them now, would it be improper for us to assume that our national burglar alarm is about to start sounding its loudest in America's most recent memory?

A Trilogy of Verse

279   *Tie the Strings to my Life, My Lord,*
Then, I am ready to go!
Just a look at the Horses—
Rapid! That will do!
Put me in on the firmest side—
So I shall never fall—
For we must ride to the Judgement—
And it's partly, down Hill—
But, never I mind the steepest—
And never I mind the Sea—
Held fast in Everlasting Race—
By my own Choice, and Thee—
Goodbye to the Life I used to live—
And the World I used to know—
And kiss the Hills for me, just once—
Then—I am ready to go!

441   *This is my letter to the World*
That never wrote to Me—
The simple News that Nature told—
With tender Majesty
Her message is committed
To Hands I cannot see—
For love of Her—sweet countrymen—
Judge tenderly—of Me

849   *The good Will of a Flower*
The Man who would possess
Must first present a
Certificate
Of minted Holiness!

Miss Emily Elizabeth Dickinson (1830-1886)
Amherst, Massachusetts

Chapter Three
Let Go the Captives All!

———————————————————

It seems to be increasingly obvious that we do not lock people inside jail cells or confine them in prisons solely because they are unfit to live in our society anymore, but because we do not really know what else to do with them. We do not sentence them to "hard time" because we wish to reverse or expunge the nature of their offenses because there is truly no way of turning back the clock once their crimes have been committed. So, we must be operating upon spiteful vengeance when we put our convicted citizens away so that we will always know where they are, that they will not be the ones who might repeat additional infractions against a more decent society. This whole idea of "corrective rehabilitation" through physical detention is almost too absurd to be true. If we think we can bring someone closer to love and kindness by placing them behind bars, then we are less capable of sound judgement than those poor souls whom we remand to the custody of the Department of Corrections. The entire prospect of restricting someone's physical mobility or confining them inside a predetermined parameter reeks of the Medieval Ages, back when those who were considered to be unfit to live among the rest of society were placed in stocks and chains, and taken to a dark, moldy dungeon beneath the lower bowels of the downtown square. What exacerbates this errant philosophy is the fact that we have placed almost one in 250 people in America today in some type of penitential system; while the crimes for which they have been sentenced are oftentimes quite paltry when compared to the corruption that is allowed to manifest elsewhere with almost everyone around it turning their backs in disinterest. It is high-time that we took another serious look at the aspects of crime and punishment to see whether we can determine the true cause of various human actions which are not in accord with our basic broad-based statutes and regulations. Have we ever considered that most crimes are not the result of someone's premeditated hatred for their neighbors and adversaries, but rather spontaneous actions by which they are venting a frustration for another undisclosed pathology? In other words, their reprehensible conduct is just a cover for a more serious psychological problem. Except for most white-collar conspiracies, calculated murder, and crimes against humanity, most of those who violate the law are quite normal people who have simply arrived at their breaking point.

It is worth noting that, in America at least, no one can be sentenced to imprisonment unless he is convicted by a circuit judge or a jury of his peers.   However, this must be preceded by his indictment by a district attorney; having been placed into custody by a law enforcement agency, a police officer under oath, or a federal marshal in their particular jurisdiction. Even these individuals have no legal power to detain someone unless it is granted them by the public laws through which they are operating; passed either by a given state's legislature or an act of the United States Congress. We must glean from these circumstances that every criminal who has been incarcerated or otherwise punished by the state or federal government has allegedly infringed upon the "will" of the public officials who have been appointed by their electors to promulgate the definition of unacceptable conduct and should, therefore, be held in contempt before the general population. However, in light of the fact that less than one-half of the eligible voters in most districts actually select these representatives; are not the other half of their fellow citizens allowing such men and women to be imprisoned by proxy? This speaks directly to the importance of our need to vote in every public election and to understand the position that those who are seeking office are taking toward civil justice during any given point in history. During the 1980s, for example, when the voters of the State of Illinois aligned with the national government in electing extremely conservative officials, we saw a rash of new prisons being built and a massive set of new laws that were meant to remove so-called "less desirable" people from society altogether by confining them to penitentiaries and detention centers. Was this not a type of "ethnic" cleansing that the world thought to be so offensive during most of the 20th century? Their purpose was not so much to discover the cause of crime in the first place as it was to segregate those who did not accede to the opinions of the majority population or who were offensive in nature from the rest of society; thus unwittingly creating a sub-culture that was composed of those who were unable to influence or limit the scope of the laws by which they were being punished. Indeed, this is further aggravated by the fact that most convicted felons have been stripped of their rights to cast their ballots or to bear firearms. Are we saying that we fear that so many parolees are making-up the electorate these days that they might all show-up at the polls on election day and exercise their franchise for candidates who could overturn the very criminal statutes which made them offenders in the first place? Moreover, are we saying that we will deny them the right to bear arms so they will not commit another crime, or because we do not want them to gather en masse and reclaim their dignified citizenship by force?

The obvious question to all of this is whether we are guiding the world by the substance of our hearts; or are we, instead, castigating those among us who just do not yet understand human life because they are afraid of us? Or, do we harbor contempt for those who are too frustrated to matriculate into a society of callous adults, not to mention the thousands who live under the influence of the forces of their acquired habits which make them unable to peacefully coexist with the rest of humanity? Maybe too many of the rest of us grew-up watching the likes of Matt Dillon, John Wayne, Ben Cartwright, Clint Eastwood, and Nash Bridges blowing the life out of their enemies with shotguns, rifles, and pistols on television that it seems all too natural for us to find a group of people who occasionally make a mistake to be our scapegoats for the sentimental reprisals of our early-childhood heroes. Let me be very clear; *I am not advocating the release of those inmates from closed institutions and treatment centers who are likely to bring harm to someone else or a particular segment of society should they be set free because, if we did, we would be partially responsible before God for facilitating their mortal sins and offenses.* On the other hand, however, there are still scores of American citizens who would cry foul if a Roman Catholic Mass were ever to be offered inside a public school gymnasium or on the House or Senate floor of the U.S. Congress; while these same secular activists often ask our Christian clergy to travel to our prisons to extend pastoral counseling to the inmates there; long after it is too late to teach them any form of spirituality before they first fell prey to our penal institutions. Indeed, we allow motion picture producers to spread explicitly lewd conduct all over the silver screens and, thereafter, we prosecute our children and more impressionable adults for imitating it; locking some of them so deeply into the black holes of solitary confinement and mental despair that they will never make their way back out again. And, as if this is not enough, we make the ones whom we have labeled as "sex offenders" register their addresses with the State Police, allowing their neighbors to taunt and harass them for the rest of their lives. Anyone can print a photograph of a convicted person off the Internet and send it wherever they please with the full blessing of the United States government, the Federal Bureau of Investigation, the Department of Justice, and the United States Postal Service. What we fail to recognize is that mind-altering substances are the reason why most people lose their best judgement and concede to the temptations which hit them in the face everyday. At the same time, we live in a society where anyone who is considered to be mentally unfit to answer the charges against them is allowed to be placed into a psychiatric ward until they are considered cured; whereupon they are allowed to go free again. Is our system of justice saying that someone whose judgement has been impaired by their addiction and ingestion of an intoxicating substance, controlled or otherwise, must be held more accountable than those who simply suffer from some sort of a pathological mental disorder? If not, then over three-quarters of the prison population in the United States of America has been incarcerated for the wrong reason.

The moral basis for understanding how inhumane it is to lock people behind brick, mortar, and iron is found in actually acknowledging the crass nature of the prison environment and the debasing effects it brings to the dignity of *all* humankind. The most sensitive nature of this entire discussion is revealed once a convicted defendant is sentenced and has been forced to be corporally removed from the rest of society and confined inside a jail cell. The co-author and publisher of my first two books, Timothy Parsons-Heather, has visited the Illinois prison system on a number of occasions to lend consolation to some of the inmates there; and he has told me about the rude and impersonal treatment that is given to them at times. We have both received quite heartbreaking mail from some of the prisoners who have had plenty of time to think about their lives from a more broad perspective now; and all of them can find a fulcrum in their years when someone who was supposed to be beside them to offer guidance and support had either deserted them or did not care enough about them to offer it from the start. They realize that they are unable to commune with nature anymore once they have been incarcerated; for they cannot feel the midnight wind against their faces or see the twinkling stars and moonbeams breaking across their brows. They need not concern themselves that the swirling breezes would ever extinguish their flickering candles of hope because most of them do not even know what one is. Even those who have served at length "to pay their debt to society" and are released back into freedom again tell us that they can hardly remember the judges who sentenced them or the first prison guard who ever locked them behind a steel door. But, they will always remember the faces of those who finally set them free. There are so many psychological changes which occur to these people during their service inside a prison that it is almost impossible to recount on a page. How do they view America after having been exposed to its brash prescription for justice? Indeed, how do they perceive their own worth after having suffered the experience of being holed-up for so long? Most of them surrender their own self-dignity while thinking that their souls must be worth no more than that of a dog or cat, since they have been bound inside a cage like a wild animal would be detained.

Most all of those who have been released from time spent in detention centers envision the world differently with regard to how the poor are treated in comparison to those who are more wealthy. We do not have to look very far to see that rich people who deal in illicit contraband are approached as though they are mental patients; that they are addicts who have a disease and are placed into a drug rehabilitation program. However, middle-class and poor people who are caught with such substances in their possession are handled like common criminals, railroaded through the justice system, and prosecuted to the full extent of the law. To much the same hypocrisy, well-to-do citizens who shoplift from a convenience store are pitied as being kleptomaniacs and are escorted to their personal psychiatrist for counseling. But, their poorer counterparts are labeled as being thieves, and are rushed-off to jail in the back seat of a siren-screaming police cruiser. It is this kind of inequity that makes certain people bitter and more apt to become repeat offenders. Many of them see themselves as being in the segment of society who must be pushed through the "system" so as to justify the employment of those who have entered careers as judges, law enforcement personnel, and Department of Corrections officers. They begin to wonder whether they are among the "forced atrocities" who are taken to the cleaners so the client-base of these particular professions can remain at an accredited level. For many of them, life was once a glimmering city of aspiration which has suddenly deteriorated into an absolute mortal darkness because of one fateful mistake that will haunt them for the rest of their days. Their pride in their native homeland is suddenly transformed from being a symbolic flag waving proudly through the air into one hanging completely furled and limp from atop a steel pole. The regression of the psyche of someone who has been inside a jail or penitentiary is almost too catastrophic to relate. They know that many of the laws which are promulgated in our legislative houses might be sustainable to the sinners who originally passed them, but are absolutely over the line in the eyesight of God. And, conversely, there are many codes of conduct that are deemed to be acceptable in civil society which are outright mortal sins according to the Holy Gospel of Christ. To what extremes am I forthrightly speaking? It has become against the law in many states for poor people to panhandle in public, but it is not illegal for their daughters to walk into a Planned Parenthood clinic and kill their unborn children by getting an abortion.

We ought to be placing greater emphasis on making society more fair for everyone and, thereafter, rendering the basis for crime less attractive to those who are living without whatever they need to survive. The more resources we direct toward such prevention will allow us to focus less upon the urgency for retaliatory punishment. Our misguided approach in looking for the reason why people break the law is like cracking-open a chestnut, tossing-out the core, and consuming the shell. We ignore the central basis of the issue by refusing to acknowledge that we have failed as a nation and society to screen everyone *into* the process of gaining a fruitful life; leaving too many out in the cold by the pompous nature of our individual greed. The United States is simply missing the point about how to truly change the hearts of those who seem not to be able to live within the means of our acceptable social constraints. Their minds, actions, and ultimately, their fate rests upon whether we can do better to make the lives of every one of our citizens more successful and dignified. Most of us are too quick to point the finger of guilt toward someone else, refusing to accept our share of the blame, and systematically unwilling to absolve those who have trespassed against our way of life. Does this bear any semblance to a republic of mercy, pardon, forgiveness, and brotherhood? Even when one of our fifty governors grants executive clemency to an offender, the sentence may be commuted, but the record of their guilt remains unexpunged long after they have gone to their grave. Is this what these poor souls write about in their personal memoirs during the middle of the night? In response to having read my first book about the Immaculate Mother of God, *Morning Star Over America*, a thankful prison inmate wrote back, *"...I'm very blessed to have such a caring and kind-hearted friend such as you. I'm not one to show my feelings, or even try to 'feel' in general; and I know it shouldn't be that way. Though, when I read the book you gave me, I read the entry of October 3, 1992 and I felt as if someone put a blanket on my shoulders because my shoulders started to tingle before my own eyes shed tears on the truth I had just read. I'm not Catholic, but I know Jesus had sat down next to me at that moment in time, and let me know '...I feel what you're feeling,' like I could almost hear him say this."* The particular part of the book that he was reading was about the perpetual help of the Blessed Virgin Mary, and how She comforts all Her little children under the protection of Her Mantle. That was the "blanket" that this humble inmate was referring to at the time.

An apocalyptic question remains unanswered by all humankind. Do we love one another in the image and likeness of this same Jesus Christ and His Mother, Mary? In a subsequent letter to our offices, we read about a man's feelings for his father, *"...I would die for him. Yet, he has never looked me in the eyes and told me that he loved me; ever. What is...love? What does love on Earth feel like? How does a heart survive on emptiness, yet live another day in search of it?"* This same sorrowing inmate wrote of the horrible retaliation that a number of his peers had endured, including his own solitary confinement inside an unlighted cell that was barely six-feet square because of his refusal to reveal the identity of his fellow prisoners who had allegedly committed a misdemeanor which was quite insignificant in nature. These despondent souls frequently write reams of poetry, musical lyrics, and tragic essays about their inner-feelings and emotions; and oftentimes paint extremely beautiful portraits and create mosaic images of the impressions in their hearts; so much the likeness of Jesus and His angels that it would bring tears to your eyes. And yet, there they remain; forsaken, discarded, scorned, and abandoned. In the words of yet another inmate whose letter we received, *"...I would really like to learn more about God. I went to church when I was a little boy, but I really don't remember much. I know God sent his son Jesus down from Heaven and was born from Mary. I believe in the Holy Spirit. I have faith that God is working in my life. I have no one who writes to me...my Dad died. He was never around anyway. I know if I knew God better, I wouldn't be here. I was wondering if you can write to me and teach me more about God. I really want to change my life. Can you help me, please? If you're too busy, I will understand."* Needless to say, we contacted this person immediately and directed him to a Roman Catholic priest at the Office of Chaplaincy inside the prison where he was being held. But, in a much larger sense, what are these downcast human beings trying to divulge to us? Is it not an accurate assumption to believe that they would never have been subjected to the temptations which caused them to breach the law and to be placed in the custody of the State if we had taken their spirits more closely to the perfection of God long before they ever matured into adults? I am convinced that if most of the people who are being held behind concrete walls and barbed-wire fences today were given the offering of love and spiritual guidance upon their early release, they would never violate the statutes and ordinances of our American society again.

Regrettably, however, we do not very often give our offenders such second chances while effecting our own recourse for dealing with their more egregious transgressions. The most faulty and grotesque aspect of our response to crime these days is the calculated vengeance which is meted-out through capital punishment; known truthfully to be no more than State-sponsored homicide. To me and many other Christians of like mind, taking the life of a person who has been convicted of a crime is the epitome of the proclamation by the Son of God that whosoever is without sin should be allowed to cast the first stone. Christ bears a warning for those who take human life, whether the victim is an innocent soul or someone who has been declared guilty of a capital offense. If we commit an act that is contradictory to the culture of life which He espouses, teaches, and commands; we will be subjected to the same measure from Him that we are protracting against those we detest. The United States Council of Catholic Bishops put it quite accurately in their "Statement on Capital Punishment" in 1980 and again in 1995, *"...crime is both a manifestation of the great mysteries of evil and human freedom, and an aspect of the very complex reality that is contemporary society. We should not expect simple or easy solutions to what is a profound evil, and even less should we rely on capital punishment to provide a solution."* The essential nature of this tenet is the same as when Jesus spoke; we are all prey to the same temptations of evil, regardless on what side of the law we find ourselves. Even Pope John Paul II stated that we *"...ought not go to the extreme of executing the offender except in cases of absolute necessity,...when it would not be possible to otherwise defend society. Today, however, as a result of the steady improvements in the organization of the penal system, such cases are very rare, if not practically non-existent."* In concise terms, the Vicar of Jesus Christ is asking why it is necessary to take the lives of condemned criminals to protect society when we have already spent billions of dollars on prison beds; acting as though we have no place to house them and are, therefore, forced to extract them from humanity altogether. The U.S. Supreme Court can whitewash it to any hue they desire, attempt to explain it away through haughty legalese, and even send the matter back to the individual states; but the fact remains that capital punishment is no more than killing someone else because it makes us feel better; that the American society has somehow compensated the family of a victim for their loss; and that we can continue our lives thereafter without having the thought of such criminals ever entering our minds again.

When we strap someone into an electric chair or onto a table-top and hit them with a fatal surge of electricity or a lethal dose of drugs, we are admitting that we as a people, a Nation, and a State, are ruthless cowards; that we are no more civilized than the man we have condemned, and are unwilling to follow the same virtues of love and forgiveness which we require as dignified individuals from everyone else. In addition, it costs more to send the arguments through the courts to appeal each capital punishment case than it does to leave the condemned inmates in their cells for the rest of their lives. Therefore, the premise that the taxpayers are tired of financing room and board for those they have sentenced to die is a hollow pretense which can be refuted by the facts. Any family member of a victim whose killer has been put to death who says that they "feel relieved" or that their lost loved-one can now rest in peace has absolutely no respect for the Holy Gospel of Jesus Christ and is doing everything conceivable to isolate themselves from the Truth. Indeed, their argument that other people who have never lost a family member to murder or other reckless manslaughter should not oppose capital punishment rings just as false. They know, and the perceiving population understands, that what they are really saying about a soul who has been executed by the State is that, *"...he finally got what he deserved."* This is not social justice, it is outright premeditated murder. Unfortunately for all of us, we should fear that this is what God will tell us, too, when we see Him after we die and try to explain our defiant response to, "...Thou Shalt Not Kill."

To the victor, who keeps to My
ways until the end,
I will give authority over the nations.
He will rule them with an iron rod.
Like clay vessels will they be smashed,
just as I received authority
from My Father.
And, to him, I will give the Morning Star.

Rev. 2:26-28

Chapter Four
The Cost of Doing Business

Does America possess the wherewithal to see the mission through that will permanently extinguish the broad chasm between the elite few who hold the most material assets and the residual of society, composed of the majority of middle-class citizens who must depend on them as the source of their next meal? The artifice that the wealthy actually do intend to help the poor is only a mirage to those who are still hoping for their fair share of the spoils of a successful democracy. What good is philanthropy in the United States if its effect is to create another generation of capitalists who look directly overhead as they ascend their corporate ladders toward their own eccentricity? Just because a college professor may award a "Grade A, Superior" to a student in a given subject does not imply that either of them has mastered the theoretics of their chosen field. It is obvious that America owns some of the greatest institutions of higher education in the history of growing the intellect; but are we teaching one another for the purpose of learning a pragmatic approach to secular reasoning; or are we properly transcending our material academics in order to broaden our view of the unexplained nature of the invincible power in the human heart? When one of our patriarchal citizens has been recognized as having succeeded in private business or being the most effective in creating solutions toward enhancing our world-wide industrial base, does this infer that personal greatness lies in our capacity to compound free enterprise for the sake of itself? Is there not something of more priority and essence to achieving our stated objectives than this? There is no question that philanthropy cannot be equated with charity if we continue to hold the bulk of our cache for ourselves. If we say that we might give someone a fish and they will eat for a day; but, if we *teach* them to fish, they can eat for a lifetime; how does this play-out when we consider our own generosity? Should we not, thereafter, offer a daily bequest to the poor and needy for the purpose of giving them our entire lives, instead? Would this not make us the best of all teachers?

For most Americans, capitalism means taking care of ourselves and our dependents at the cost of acquiring someone else's wealth before they have an opportunity to secure it. After all, this is what competition in the marketplace is all about; but it is also how particular segments of society are forced into an indentured state. Those who have been offered no means to secure a greater education, the mentally and physically challenged, minority races, and people who have not quite understood the meaning of secular profiteering are at a stark disadvantage in America today. It has always been "...every man for himself," when it comes to vying for the available dollars that are sifted from the United States treasury. As we learned from the previous chapter, it is the lack of any means to acquire such wealth that leads many poor people into lives of crime. So, what must happen in order to keep them and their children from becoming the "chronic" poor who remain on the street to struggle the best they know how? The U.S. government has been quite charitable throughout the decades to recognize their plight; but it has only limited resources, and is constrained by a bloc of conservative activists who fear that America has become a growing "welfare state." This was the thrust for the movement which was initiated by the likes of former U.S. House Speaker Newt Gingrich and brought such caustic voices as Rush Limbaugh and Ann Coulter into the limelight on radio and television airwaves. The essence of their argument is that there are too many Americans who are drawing public aid funds, and are not working to earn it. There is no doubt that some of them are; but certainly not enough to bring an end to the welfare system as it has been known for the past 40 years. Great strides have been made to enlist public aid recipients in various work programs, and to place a cap on the number of years they can receive benefits. Replacing printed food stamps with a debit card has also reduced fraudulent claims by a vast measure these days.

However, those who oppose public aid altogether are forgetting that no one ever sends in his tax return on April 15th with an extra donation, payable to "...those who cannot afford to live without it." In other words, America has set-aside a huge amount of taxpayer money to feed the poor because it is quite apparent that the private sector is keeping most of their profits for themselves. They beat their competitors to the bank with the bottom-line of their businesses, retrieve a deposit ticket, and never look over their shoulders to see if there is anyone there who might be too old, too ill, or too broken-down to be able to open such an account for themselves. We enter the drive-through while piloting our new sedans, knock the ashes from our cigars out our electric windows, look at the paupers leaning against the facade of the building across the street, and carry-on as though we are somehow living in another space and time continuum from them. *I am not suggesting that we are wilfully stingy or crass to those we do not recognize; but it is just a habit we have learned from our predecessors and the nature of the capitalist country in which we live.* If there were no taxes collected in the United States at all, would there be a single ounce of help for those who have no way of life? Do we inadvertently refuse to acknowledge the mandates of the Holy Gospel because we have learned to allow the government to tend to them, instead; the same government from which we have evicted the Divine Spirit of God? Even *He* knows that there is great disparity in how the wealth in America is dispersed. What would He say about a nation which allows its oil companies to charge so much for home heating oil that the government, itself, must subsidize its purchase for those who cannot afford it? How is this different from the U.S. Congress simply deciding to return the tax money that these companies have paid for any other anonymous reason? In effect, these fuel suppliers have said that they are paying too much into the public coffers for the use of common facilities, so they have chosen to increase prices to a level that will allow them to reap humongous profits from the consumers who can afford it, and thereafter be repaid by the government for those who cannot. This may not be an outright corporate monopoly, but it is certainly a covert abuse of our free-market system.

There has never been a justifiable reason why the cost of commodities must increase when demand is higher because it is during these peaks when private industries are making the most profit. When they say that production expenses are higher during these periods, are they trying to hoodwink the American people into believing that their cost-per-unit is inflated by some unknown supernatural force which cannot be seen with the human eye? Their mysterious cravings for increased earnings cannot be concealed behind some inflationary index or threshold of debt. Were it not for the Federal Trade Commission and the individual States' Attorneys General, there is no telling what we would be paying for a gallon of gasoline or a KWH of electric power. To most of us who cannot afford to finance their huge corporate skyscrapers and windfall budgets, life is not about a bulging surplus, our passbook savings, or the average of the Dow for today, but whether we have fed and clothed our children by the time they close their eyes to go to sleep at night. Our efforts are leaned toward paying our insurance premiums and getting to the County Treasure's Office when our real-estate taxes come due. Indeed, our life should be more concerned with such simplicity, responsibility, and spiritual amplitude; not whether the fine-print in the market section of this morning's newspaper reflects that our investments posted a gain yesterday. We somehow deceive our little children into accepting that their growth must also include a simultaneous birth into the advancement of market economies, stock futures, portfolios, retrievable coefficients, and mutual bonds. Not only that, we vacillate between determining whether all our assets should be inherently public in nature and trying to capture the most for ourselves. If we are ever going to diminish the infamous "welfare state" which causes Newt Gingrich's inner-conscience to cringe, we are eventually going to be forced to answer the question as to whether every American citizen has been given easement to an equal playing field and an opportunity to succeed.

It is true that the bulk of the U.S. Federal Budget is expended for paying the interest on the national debt, feeding the 45 million Americans on Social Security, financing the Medicare program, and maintaining the Department of Defense; not to mention "... a few other smaller administrative line-items." Some critics have accurately labeled the latter of these as being "pork-barrel" projects that individual senators and representatives send back home to bribe their constituents into voting for them again when their term of office comes to an end. The real problem resides in our battle with the triple-headed beast of materialism, wasteful spending, and our isolationist approach to public policy. Moreover, by the time we add everyone else's lust for political power and public influence into the mix, we have quite a liability on our hands. Is it no wonder that we are having difficulty funding our operations and maintenance accounts, paying off our reserve notes, and the litany of other social and environmental initiatives which are the pets of many extremist from one coast to the other. This, in itself, stands contrary to the ideals of public service in the way they were first defined by the framers of our republic. It is part of our genre for creating a monster of a government, instead of an established system of bureaucratic efficiency which does only what we allow. We have taken the "person" out of our public agencies and replaced it by an unsavory "us versus them" syndrome to conducting our social affairs. There is no spirit in our mood because there is very little of it in our hearts. And, if this is the cost of doing business in America today, then we are well on our way to petitioning the world bankruptcy court without any means to begin again. If we are the wealthiest nation on the Earth, and there is no doubt that we are; then the entire globe is on the brink of economic collapse.

Let us take another, more serious, look at those who have applied for public assistance through the Social Security Administration as an example. First of all, those who are old enough to retire are applying for their due benefits in great numbers these days; and this segment of citizens will explode in the next two decades when our baby-boomers begin to retire. It is all well and good to ensure the proper payments to these individuals because they are the ones whose payroll taxes are financing the benefits to our recipients today. However, when the United States Congress chose to alter the definition of "eligible recipient" to include those who are not yet old enough to retire, there was a massive exodus from the labor-force door to the waiting lines at the Social Security offices by those who could have earned a self-sufficient living if only they would have disciplined themselves to do so. This is not to say that the poor and disabled who are not yet of sufficient age to retire ought not to receive any benefits. I am speaking about the people who are drawing so-called SSI, or "Social Security Disability," who have been judged by their personal physicians to be unable to work because they are addicted to drugs and alcohol, or who have some other malady which keeps them from finding gainful employment in the manual workforce. Of course, these are determined on a case-by-case basis; but there is no doubt that some in their ranks have manipulated the system to their own advantage. Scores of them are receiving taxpayers' money because they have been diagnosed as being mentally unstable due to their ongoing addictions to hard liquor or contraband. But, there are countless others who receive a check from the government every month, cash it at the local package store, and take the proceeds with them to the downtown tavern and proceed to get stone-cold drunk while sitting beside the average, everyday workers who just left their factory production lines. It would not be so bad if they were somewhat discreet about it, but many of them pound their fists on the sidebars and boast about how they are bilking the United States government for every dollar they can.

How must this sound to the common hardworking man who might be sitting in a chair at a table right behind those who are abusing their fellow taxpayers to such an extent? What does he have to say when he hears these same freeloaders gloating that they just inherited several thousand dollars from a deceased relative, with which they just purchased a new car, but they have to conceal their new inheritance from their case-workers for fear of losing their monthly benefits? It is no wonder that many Americans have become so callous about helping the poor in our nation when there are people like that around. But, is the number of people who lie and cheat worth eliminating the entire system and risking denying benefits to the bonafide poor? Is such tawdry conduct *also* a category in the cost of doing business in America today? When the country music industry first released its song about a "Welfare Cadillac" several years ago, were they able to shed any light on this subject or force a change in how we identify those who are not really in need? If the "Republican Contract with America" of 1994 eliminated the majority of those who were cheating from the public assistance roles by putting them back into the labor force, then perhaps its fruit was not completely bitter to the taste of the American Pie. The more prudent question which remains to be answered, however, is whether there were any paupers who were actually in need who have since been denied assistance because the regulations have changed or they are incapable of sufficiently stating their case on their own.

As well-intentioned as it is, our capitalist democracy leaves a large number of people with nothing on their dinner plates these days because there is so much disparity in how we reap our profits. And, if we are ever going to share a genuine admiration for the Truth, we must begin to choose how we approach our national marketing by lending more charitably, defending one another more passionately, and finally coming to grips more concisely with our common faults. It is not mean-spirited to ask someone to work for the goods and services they receive, but it is wholly wrong to demand it from those who have no resources when they unavoidably fall physically or psychologically ill. What good is a nation of sound means if it is not empowered toward the greater advancement of every single individual? Must we become a society of the "select" in order to show our best side to the rest of the world? Are our foodstuffs, entertainments, and fashions so attractive that we should ignore the rest of humanity who have no palpable way to procure them? I co-authored an essay entitled *A Brief Polemic on American Entitlement Programs* in February 1999 that was presented to the Department of Public Administration at the University of Illinois which made the case for actually reducing the federal role in delivering our public aid programs for the poor and disadvantaged. Why? Simply because we will be able to leave that same drive-through bank facility and know that we can make a difference here at home; that our less-fortunate friends are being aided by their own peers. It seems like a pro-Christian proposition to put a recognizable face behind the hands which are nourishing those who are in need, so they will not feel so much like animals being fed from a trough. While I am neither a conservative nor anti-federalist, I believe that there should be a certain degree of "defederalization" within the various public assistance programs in the United States; while exploring the possibility that the local states might be a more fiscally responsible and effective venue for administering assisted housing and other anti-poverty programs to the indigent than those which have previously been completely under national control. It lends a certain comfort to those who must turn to the taxpayers when they are enduring a period of personal crisis. After all, there are millions who are still being hurt by the fiscal inequalities in our country; and a few bad apples must not bring us to turn our backs on them.

Americans will condone a measured amount of inefficiency, duplication, and ambiguity in the funding of entitlement programs because they believe that such systems are intrinsically flawed, i.e., that they are *another* part of the cost of doing business in the United States today. Indeed, most of us expect to write-off a given amount of our tax-dollars as simply going to waste. We assume that those who qualify for public assistance will be honest, and that some of them will probably always need some type of external safety-net in place. Before 1996, it seemed as though any attempt to juxtapose a substantial rehabilitation of the national entitlement system while carrying-out the day-to-day operations of our public agencies was like trying to work on an automobile while it was still traveling down the road. There have been many errant assumptions made by the general public, the United States Congress, and the state legislatures that should be clarified for the record. Very few underprivileged Americans will bow to the loss of their pride to capture what little dignity they gain by remaining on a welfare roll. No amount of benevolence by an otherwise indifferent electorate has ever brought a public official to do better by the poor until he or she has truly felt that it was warranted. There is also the proposition that many less-fortunate people would not even consider applying for public aid if they thought there was none to be had. What would they do then? Would they continue to beg, try to live off the land, or eventually perish amidst a self-imposed poverty? Does our nation of opportunity provide for their own self-actualization at the same time that we force them to compete in our ferocious free-market economy? Perhaps we are not asking such tough questions in the public fora because we are still too busy fending for ourselves. We live in a republic that exists by virtue of a common treasury, but we do everything possible to pay the least amount we legally can. Why should we sustain the salutary characteristics of the New Frontier and The Great Society in a nation which is still calling-out for the death of the sixty-year-old New Deal that continues to be in dire need of such structural reformation?

Politics aside, we are recycling generation-for-generation our public welfare rolls, rather than creating wholesale opportunities for substantive change. Contrary to popular belief, our entitlement programs will not atrophy like a leg in a cast should we take the time to continue to mend what is broken in them. After all, there are still able-bodied souls sitting at the bar inside a corner pub who are receiving welfare benefits because they are too lazy to go to work. It is no wonder, then, that the tax base in the impoverished inner-cities and rural areas is insufficient to allow for a guttural abandonment of federal subsidy to meet the needs of the chronic and working poor. And yet, these same dollars breed the addiction to welfare that keeps those metropolitan slums sweltering in crime, substance abuse, and infrastructure deterioration; quite the paradox for our advanced western civilization that is living its 225th year and has just entered the 21st century some $5 trillion in-the-hole. We have a hard-enough sell on our hands while trying to convince state legislators to promulgate laws and set-aside enough funds in their coffers to help the poor they see on the sidewalks outside their chambers. And yet, a Nebraska farmer is paying for dried milk and cigarettes for an unwed mother in Chicago whose face he will never see. Even through the prism of these facts, our Christian faith tells us that our duties are greater than to simply feed and house only the poor we know. National poverty can be heard calling for relief across the states' boundaries and into the courthouses of every city. As contradictory as it may sound; our burrows, counties, parishes, and commonwealths will never be united as long as we allow isolationists to succeed in attacking continental problems with regional solutions. We have proved in recent decades that poverty is not indigenous to any given geography, but can transiently shift to other areas of "opportunity" for the materialization of higher social relief. The past rulings of the U.S. Supreme Court have confirmed that the Constitution calls for assisting the impoverished according to wherever they may roam; summarily overthrowing the call to deny AFDC benefits to families residing in a given state for less than 364 days.

These are only a few of the propositions that liberals and conservatives have been arguing for years, whether the topic of discussion includes the guarantee of substantive socioeconomic freedom or our collective progress toward spiritual maturation. We will never close the gap between rich and poor if we stand-out in opposition to the strategic salve that will ameliorate the personal deficits which cause poverty in the first place, e.g. the need for class equity, a more level plane of educational opportunity, and shared religious and moral values. We are often offended when anyone tells us what to believe until it arrives in a package that is wrapped in subsidized vouchers and cash incentives. This is why there will never be a strict dichotomy between the national and state governments on the issue of social advancement. No one will ever be able to deny that a given state is one-fiftieth of our nation, which can neither succeed without benefitting the other forty-nine, nor be allowed to fall into disrepair without desecrating the entire union. The issue is certainly not closed regarding how much responsibility, vis-a-vis liability, that the several states should share while carrying the burden of funding entitlement programs for the poor and elderly. One thing is for sure, we will have to do it at a level that can be trusted not to fail, should the national economy continue to decline in the next two-to-ten years. The main aspect which makes this such an important issue is the rendezvous of the retirement of those who were born just after World War II through the early 1960s with the highest price for personal and medical care we have known in the history of this great nation, projected to capitalize between 2015 and 2030. The questions are already forthcoming, "Who will pay, and how much?" What agencies do we see, if any, that will still be in existence by then to deliver these programs? The national train of thought has run quite amok lately about this awful prospect. We may be returning to the "glitzy" self-ingratiation of the 1980s if we never look any farther toward eliminating the poverty of others than what we can keep inside our own wallets. We are a greater people than this, and we will succeed through that nobility.

Retired couples of the next twenty years will not wish to spend their hard-earned nest eggs by feeding someone else's delinquent children, whether they are on the street or locked inside a prison cell. Working families will be just as adamantly opposed to financing a nation which is burdened with the practicalities of their elders' geriatrics. This supports a strong argument toward a nationalist approach for ending social deprivation, at the same time that these retirees will be forever reluctant to pay any higher local property and sales taxes, and user fees. In this same breath, however, they are also stating that they do not want Uncle Sam telling them how to spend their hard-earned savings. Therefore, we are not at a crossroad in American history based solely on the arrival of a new millennium. Our last crossroad struck us broadside in 1865, when we chose to continue to be one nation through the bloodshed of hundreds of thousands of our own civilian warriors. We have since been wandering the countryside looking for an outlet to true freedom from fear, from unwelcome change, and from our foreign neighbors with deadly weapons. Our moral duty is not whether, or why, we should modernize our entitlement programs, but how and when. The war on poverty of the 1960s may have brought us all to exhaustion for the fight, but a lot of innocent children received food in their mouths and a place to lay their heads in the process. We must not forsake their modern-day successors as we bring the management of such assistance to the states' level. And, we have to do this together, with the spirit of humane decency in our sights and hearts. The lesson of the Great Depression of the 1930s left all boats sitting in dry-dock because we fell as a republic of divided people. That is why we have been subconsciously afraid to rise as one nation ever since.

While there is no such phenomenon as a negative absolute, we are just scraping-by with the barest essentials in a democracy that is flat-busted, but cannot be forced into insolvency because of its patriotic, historical, and moral responsibilities to survive. In all of the discussion about who is going to come to the aid of those who have no means of living, the time has arrived for us to accept that it is everyone's problem; not just the national government, the separate states, or the local townships. We are a country of *one* people who must aspire to see the experience of our democracy succeed in our time. This cannot be done without our factual admission that we have not loved one another as we ought; that our mirrors are lying to us if we peer into them and feel comfortable that we are seeing the faces of united Americans who have done all they could possibly achieve to extricate our neighbors from the valleys of poverty and despair. No matter how we dissect it, there is no question that the changes we require are a product of our inner-beings; not the power of a federal government; not the mandates and restrictions which seep from under our state capital domes; and certainly not by simply turning our backs to the problem in the hope that it will all go away. This is a matter for the properties and beatitudes of Christian goodness; one that causes our very consciousness to tweak; and one in which we can recognize that, if not for fate, we would be one another. If we are waiting for a national crisis to occur to awaken us to the fragile nature of human life, then let our world wars, our international melees, and our domestic terrorism sound our alarms.

The purpose of placing this chapter in my book has not been to profile an expose' about the failures of our political systems or how our democratic experience has developed, matured, and unfolded; but to raise the issue that it is our own individual consciences and actions which define who we are as a social family in comparison to the rest of the world. We own no government of anarchy or royalty to guide our every whim because we are much too independent a people to ever live that way. Our purposes are to survive in a freer society that is as old as any democracy in the history of Creation; to try to elicit our own idealism as best as we can within the constraints of our shared imperfections; to be able to carry our heads higher in reflection of the many heroes who have given their life's breath making our generation better than theirs; and to plead for civility with those whom we have the capacity to communicate in forging a world of lasting peace. Our fragile economy is only a minute part of the problems that humanity at large is facing in our particular age. The resolution to the discovery of moral justice cannot be found in politics because, by its very nature, it must be composed of partisan issues and nearly every shade of interpretation. We do not live in freedom because of our political peculiarities, but because we have chosen to overcome them through the unique stature of our desire to defend our liberties. When I speak of the cost of doing business in America these days, it is not to lay claim to any higher ground than any of our ancestors might have attained, but to see past our own blindness into the future, where there will no longer be a need for mandated social programs; a time for the expansion of the community spirit which led our original colonists to pray together for a new nation under God. Many great patriots have told us that they have defended a republic which would never be completely finished before they grew old and died. Their prophetic sentiments still ring true for us today, for we have yet to fulfill every dream that was lifted to the Heavens in Philadelphia so many generations ago.

What you are about to read in the next chapters is a celebration of the mobility of our people, our Articles of Incorporation, and our unique civil courage. We have already conquered the land, unfortunately taking some of it by aggression from its rightful owners; but we have also conquered our enemies and the elements, our own self-doubts, and disease and discomfort. We have waged an all-out war against the adversaries of freedom; those who, by their own posthumous admission, could not see their way clear to hope intensely enough that a world superpower could be constructed from a back room of young-spirited men wearing white wigs and buckled slippers. Our national tenacity has been challenged from every corner of the globe; from the air, across the seas, from the worst that Nature has to offer, to our own bickering and divisions from within. I would not, therefore, agree with those who say that America is the "greatest" nation because there are certainly mixed emotions in defining what that means. Forty million aborted unborn children will be nothing to brag about when we see the Sacred Heart of Jesus Christ, and neither will our insufficient excuses as to why we allowed thirty million people to log-on to the World Wide Web to look at pornographic depictions everyday. If our best hours have yet to come, let us rush the clock in advance by being different ourselves; by skipping the parts which are too ugly for our fractured souls to see, and by allowing untamed human decency to devour us once and for all. These are the hopes which I carry in my heart when I speak of the cost of doing business.

Our own mothers and fathers, whether we knew them or not, have always wanted the best for their children; although they may have occasionally lost sight of how to accomplish it at times. Some of us were abandoned at birth, perhaps deposited on a doorstep to the chiming of a bell; left for dead in hope that we would never be found; or even dropped-off in a mineshaft in the middle of the night. Even so, the Messiah of all dominion still loves us; He encourages our faith; He strengthens our desires to be free; and He savors the moment when we will finally erect our nation in the image and likeness of His Cross. For fear of being unintentionally ambiguous; there is no substitute for the Truth in governing our democracy, in the compassionate enforcement of our laws, and in the sharing of our wealth. The best benefit that we can claim as a sovereign people is to do these things well because we are the reflection of His Love on a continent which has never once said "no" to devoting our best. Indeed, nary has an age in America required it more intensely than we do right now.

Part Two
The Ideal Capitalist State?

Chapter Five
Our Geographical Expansion

I used to believe that the solutions to our more moderate problems were only one arithmetic equation away and that the concepts of the affirmative and the negative were as boldly clear as black and white. But, now that I have grown to be much older, I realize that progress on any front is more likely to be a mixture of confrontation and compromise; especially with reference to the growth, development, and management of our American United States. Permissiveness is almost an understood quality in the minds of our youth these days because very few of their parents have the backbone to stand up to admonish them or chasten their friends. When we ponder what transpired back in Europe before our founding fathers came across the Atlantic Ocean, would it be too great a stretch of the imagination to assume that they, too, were like our unpredictable youth of today; searching to create something that they could not quickly define; aching to actualize a life which could stand on its own without the authority of a crown prince or a pontiff to hound them from aside? There is no doubt that they must have penned their thoughts before they left; and we have yet to know what most of them probably scribbled only to themselves. When they appointed a time for this cataclysmic event, with permission from their Royalty, of course, they sailed toward the west inside their vessels on an uncertain ocean which was probably just as shocked as they were to find itself supporting their dreams, following the path of the retreating sun; leaving their homeland acres behind and untold fathoms beneath their keels. If the poetry of their age was any indication, they must have braved the whitecaps with pride, cursed the torrid monsoons; while risking the contracts of nausea, scurvy, and starvation, itself; and oftentimes unable to recognize their own jaundiced apprehension. The unwitting western hemisphere in which we live today had no way of knowing what was about to befall its placid fields and rolling plains in the span of the next twenty decades. There would be a new nation formed and fettered across its plats; and its earthquakes would become her labor pains and the Falls of Niagra her broken water which would portend the origin of the berth for new freedom in which many-a-patriots would retire. However, could it not also have seen the divisions in which it would be severed, the slaves it would detain, the wrenching battles it would endure; or the bloodbaths with the British, the strangers from their bottom, and the klondike of the North?

Hear! Hear! Would this new republic ever have been able to foresee the fracture which would impale her across the middle, the bluebeards from the gray, that opened-wide to split her unity entirely in two? Are these the extraneous forces which would shape her elder statesmen, her heroes and matriarchs, and her peacemakers, too? Or, did the God of their fathers create them of His own accord and dispatch them to the Earth at this most apropos juncture in mortal time? History would not peer kindly upon this baker's dozen of sovereign commonwealths as the map of their boundaries would look not unlike a jigsaw puzzle that had somehow gone awry. The intrepid men and women who claimed this country as their own were the collective Jonahs who were on an irreversible westward mission and, as ironic as it sounds, would swallow a whale of a continent themselves and cough-up a fortune in gold, minerals, preambles, proclamations, and stake-outs for their familial plots. Indeed, our predecessors embarked upon a new world like avenging angels who would try their best to play-out their New Yankee rendition of "...climb every mountain; ford every stream." They could not have known back then that linear time would be endlessly divided by the vision of their quest, as nearly everything to have and hold would be instilled by the lessons they would teach. It seemed almost as though the most momentous points in human history would be thereafter charted; that all progress, unity, and advancement would become the hallmark of their age. There would be a scripted public Constitution which would bellow from the page; one which is still no more than a trite contraption to keep our consciences at bay and our deportment more civil to the ear. The advantage of hindsight has already enlightened us that America of 200 years ago was grossly unprepared for the apathy which would devour its own beloved citizens. Their fellow pragmatists came preaching a promise of inalienable civil liberties, and a ten-spot to spare for a Bill of Rights; but they did very little to promote the inherent equality of every race of man.

They would trade-away their parliaments for newly elected presidents; exchange their House of Lords for lend-leases; and would restrain themselves from being venomous until it came to the rights of the states over the comprehensive configuration of the colored Union Jack. But, all change and fairness would prevail for awhile, and "...oh what a day that would bring!" Nothing of commodity was adjusted for inflation because personal greed had not quite yet set in. Their protocol was to levy taxes, but never too high, and only when they were necessary; but they were reticent to proffer the privilege of voting to women and those who held no title to any tracts of land. And, by all means, there was nothing that could be captured in the imagination of Normal Rockwell which was missing from the beauty of this national treasure that lay nestled between the oceanic shores. Its citizens brought together a coalition of wisdom, compassion, intelligence, prophecy, and quite explicit care to shape a country that would eventually, if only by the boldness of the ensuing generations, provide for the freedom of each and all; from natural-born to immigrant; disregarding color and origin, notwithstanding their creeds professed, and particularly inviolate of personal religious faith. Unfortunately, however, they had yet in the beginning to lay a glove on the fatalistic despair which would taunt the oppressed, the infirm, and the poor. The latent question also exists as to whether this new republic would live to serve itself, or would she be the poster-child for all the world, especially the land from which they fled? In the midst of their Senate Floor filibusters, would their publicans and orators need a little dose of smelling salts from Her Majesty's vinaigrette to keep them all from falling asleep?

Centered within all this presaged augury, the future portended the truth that all of these high hopes would be contingent upon the people's capacity to deal with the intricate details that were all but inevitable by then. Would we be able to embrace the brotherhood it would require to transform the parenthetic colonies of America into a completely United States? The answer lies in our casual observation of our country as it is now. Do we remember Lot, the nephew of Abraham, whose wife was turned into a pillar of salt when she looked back during their flight from Sodom; as recorded in the Old Testament Scriptures? (Genesis 19:26) Is this why we are so afraid to reveal to ourselves that we have erred in the past and are unwilling to amend our future as well? When are we going to stop deceiving ourselves about how much we really care about comforting the afflictions of our fellow citizens in America today? We wave the flag over our heads and pantomime the words to our favorite patriotic songs, but we never really live-up to the meaning of their lyrics or take their melodies to heart. Of course, we fall in line like elegant swans whenever natural disasters occur, or perhaps when we are attacked by foreign legions. We are told that patronizing sinners do as much. But, when will we engage this same genuine interest in the perpetual crises that keep our elderly and infirm laying flat on their backs everyday? As I have indicated before, we are never forced to relinquish our individual tenor when we stand up for them. We all like to emit the fragrance of our personal identity to everyone we meet; and this is alright by the chorus of Saints who are watching our every move. We never mix all the colognes on our dresser into one crock and splash it onto our face. Quite the contrary, our English Leather, Brut, Tommy Hilfiger, Wild Country, and Stetson can stand alone as their own aroma; but they are still *ours* in one concentric location in the corner of our bedroom. We embrace them, we are proud of them, and we like to exude them wherever we may go. Is this not also how we should personally enrapture the community of all peoples inside the ivory of our hearts?

Did our founding fathers prepare any of their succeeding generations for the unmitigated greed that would soon become an attribute of our American capitalistic culture? The mechanics who work on our automobiles charge a whopping dollar-a-minute for their labors; food manufacturers are putting less ingredients into their packages and collecting the same amount for the product; million-dollar athletes go on strike for higher wages; we often get hooked on chain letters and pyramid schemes; gas stations are charging fifty-cents for us to put self-service air into our own tires; women are collecting alimony and child-support payments from three and four different ex-husbands; our cars and vans cost five times as much as they did thirty years ago, but are made almost completely out of velcro and plastic; predatory lenders send us blank checks in the mail to use as we please, then charge 20% interest to pay it back; our land-line telephones cost $25 a month whether we ever make a single call on them; or did Alexander Graham Bell forget to tell us about certain line charges, federal access fees, day rates, night rates, local government charges, 911 costs, fees for municipal and state infrastructure maintenance, number portability surcharges, federal universal connectivity fees, sales taxes, and even an extra $1.50 for the pleasure of having the telephone company sending us their statement? Let us not forget that our kids' tennis shoes are now $75.00 a pair; breakfast cereal is $5.00 a box; we are allowed to join a fit-club for $40.00 per month, but only if we promise by written contract to pay them for at least two years hence whether we enter their premises or not. Our merchants boast of their sales of concrete religious statues for *only* $200 each, and our Sunday newspaper in which they list them costs triple the amount of the weekday editions because they are jammed-full of their subscribers' local business solicitous advertisements. Might we say that the capitalist machine is running quite robustly in the United States today? The idea that a dollar does not have the purchasing power that it did in decades past is more than a play on words or our linguistic diversion from the truth. We have inadvertently decreased the value of our currency because we have gratuitously required more of it in our modern-day pocketbooks than our more fiscally responsible predecessors did. Not only that; what about our unsavory social conduct? We have suddenly invented a new travel policy called "road rage;" our daily conversations and television programs are filled with profane expletives; we cut each other off in the supermarket checkout lane; we argue over who gets the parking spaces closest to the door; we curse at our neighbors across the fence; and we take the lives of our innocent brothers by driving hell-bent for election after having just guzzled two six-packs of beer at the neighborhood bowling alley bar. We see all of this happening on a more than occasional basis, but we still declare what a decent people we are and that we would fight to the death to protect such a sacred peace.

　　　　We must remember that these things will be a remnant for the record of our nation once we are gone. We know that American history is a function of the human memory, and is not something we can either touch or see. But, our grandchildren can fully experience from whence it first originated. Such will be the vestige of our conduct today; and we are the ones to blame. And, yet, we also know that America is the most studied of all the democracies on the Earth for Civics buffs and demographics professors in most every developed foreign land. Why? Is it in the way that we are so dedicated to our rustic legacies, dauntless adventurism, and national pride? It seems as though our highly esteemed mobility has become somewhat of a global phenomenon these days. We would like to believe that this is a response to the growth in the diversity of our population and that it was our economic prosperity which rolled the spur against the hide of our republic to expand its way westward in the last two centuries; not our collective greed or the global imperialism which kept us so divided from the Soviet Union for the entire second half of the 20th century. And yet, how can we ever convince the rest of the world that we have espoused democratic freedom when we have already conscripted Alaska, Hawaii, American Samoa, and the U.S. Virgin Islands under the ranks of our jurisdiction? Does our economic prosperity and the selection of our wealthy popularly-elected leaders look anything less than imperialistic to an inquisitive young eighth-grader sitting in the front row of a classroom in rural China somewhere? Moreover, do we call ourselves "free" simply because we can afford to? After all, the only time when we have even slightly appeared to be socialist in nature was after the markets plunged on Black Tuesday, October 29, 1929 at the New York Stock Exchange, which brought with it the Great Depression and the election of Franklin Delano Roosevelt as President of the United States. It was not that he had no democratic syntax to his vernacular; but we were all forced by common poverty into enlisting his proposals for federalizing so many economic, social, and labor programs. The Work

Progress Administration, the Civilian Conservation Corps, and Social Security were all the offspring of his compassionate leadership. If not for the vision and wisdom of this great man, how would their children have eaten; and, moreover, where would we be today? We once complained about Russia's global expansion by military aggression, but did we not end our own national bankruptcy by entering World War II? It may certainly take painstaking planning to establish a solvent nation; but it requires a lingering liberty and devoted love to finally set one free; not just artillery shells and emissaries' diplomacy. In the hindsight of history, the fall of Communism in the U.S.S.R. was the result of the proactive prayers of Christians all over the world and the powerful recitation of the Most Holy Rosary of the Blessed Virgin Mary that finally brought it down. Such pious invocations were the cumulative and active voice of the free world that hit atheism right between the eyes with the steel bullet of Christian Truth; and we are waiting to see whether the *lack* of such prayer for the conversion of the United States will be the exit wound which will ultimately portend our own demise. If we are going to take a global view of the geographical expansion of the values of our system of American ethics, we must come to the conclusion that it was not the great Western democracy that felled the Soviet Republic or anything that U.S. President Ronald Reagan ever dreamed of doing. It was the faith and courage of one humble Polish shipyard worker named Lech Walesa, who was awarded the 1983 Nobel Peace Prize, and the Supreme Pontiff of his chosen Church, who was also Polish, Pope John Paul II; both of whom were under the omnipotent guidance and intercession of Mary, the Mother of God. Walesa was the "Rosa Parks" of the Solidarity movement; the Vicar of Christ was his spiritual director; and the Messianic Gospel according to the Saints was his beatific mandate. The point to be made quite clear is that, if such Divine power can transform an entire continent from tyranny into freedom and from atheism to religious belief, then why can we not call upon this same Pope, his Roman Catholic Church, and the Immaculate Mother of our Creator to change our hearts into accepting the deifying Love of God in order to eradicate every form of sin from within our midst in America today? When we speak about our geographical expansion, we would be remiss if we declined to enlist the charge that we were given by our founding fathers to enhance the integrity of our spiritual lives, too.

The American Dream, therefore, is not about carriage bolts and tensile strength because it is a product of the pursuit of our modern drama and civic romance. It is about people who are daring enough to dream again, to live at the exact center of our relationship between two separate worlds; the one that exists surreally before our eyes, and the true commission of duty and respect that we are all called to achieve as decent human beings between one another. It is a product of our hope, faith, and opportunity; the same virtues which took Lech Walesa to the summit of legendary greatness; and our seizing of every opportunity for taking the last sip of Christian perfection which blooms from the core of the human heart. This is the defined resilience of true liberty; not whether we have succeeded in the marketplace, consecrated the superior banns of our democratic oath, or boasted of the valuable liquidity of our personal assets. True freedom is about waking in the morning and discarding the obsolete illusion that we cannot make a difference anymore. It means belonging to one another *not* for convenience or temporal dependence, but because our shared charismatic anticipation of an absolute world of peace will not allow us to be distracted by any form of whim. Perfect liberation is the satisfying of our desire to achieve the most profoundly beautiful spiritual sanctity that the world has ever known. Then, once we have finally seen that these things are within our grasp, we will be able to look anew at Christmas and Easter in America and say with confidence, "...God is here." Once we have recognized that human love is sovereign to any nation and that each of us must take our derivation from within it, then we will have begun the daunting task of making the expansion of our American spirit the model civilization, not only for the present, but for the full deposit of the future as well. Our tenure as American citizens must be based upon how we respond to one another domestically and throughout the rest of the world. One of the greatest aspects about living in the United States is that anyone can aspire to ascend into the governing class. The problem which still remains, however, is that such power is almost exclusively commensurate with our ability to acquire an empire of wealth. This social inequity is the very essence of what is prohibiting us from becoming a nation of truly noble people.

The uncertain torrents of unabridged freedom often make us appear to be a lesser society than our own potential would have us believe. If we are, in fact, to become the fashioned example of a properly governed and populous "...city on a hill..." before the rest of the globe, are we capable of ascertaining how they perceive us from distances so far and wide? Has our geographical expansion made us look unnecessarily selfish to those who have had no modernized means to cross the seas? There was a unique case-study that was completed in the mid-1990s which was taken from the World Development Forum and the Encyclopedia Britannica Book of the Year that posed the question, "...what if the entire population of the Earth was only a village of a thousand people?" How would the outlay of our fiscal condition and religious preferences stack up to one another? The focus of the study was an accounting of the composition of nearly six billion people whose attributes and beliefs precisely reflected a sample of one-thousand. They discovered that 564 of them would be Asian, 210 European, 86 African, 80 South American, and only 60 of them would be North American. A total of 329 people would be Christian, 174 Muslim, 131 Hindu, 61 Buddhist, 52 animists, three Jewish, 34 would be members of other smaller religions, and an unbelievable 216 of the thousand would claim to bear no faith in any religion at all. And, now, for the worst news. An extreme minority of only 60 people of 1,000 would hold half of the income of the entire world! Five-hundred of them would be hungry, 600 of them would live in shanty towns, and 700 of them would be completely illiterate and otherwise never formally educated. Just to make sure that the reference is clear; sixty of the total one-thousand would live in North America; and sixty of them would also hold over half of the profitable income. Could it be possible that these same two small segments of the world's population might have some direct tangible correlation? If we took a cursory look at the other continents and evaluated their standard of living, the prevailing condition of their general health, and their broader sense of self-esteem, might we assume that they are *not* the ones who are hoarding the greatest wealth? Are we able to also infer that the United States is the only nation which has a majority of Christians in it, but we also hold more than our percentage of the total assets? Do we remember what we learned in our high school algebra class that, *if A is equal to B, and B is equal to C, then A is equal to C?* We do not have to be blindfolded and play "pin the tail on the donkey" to realize that it is our lifestyles which are denying even the most basic of needs to those 500 hungry people half-way around the globe, and the 600 who are living in grass huts just outside a jungle or on the side of a canyon somewhere. As the great American television journalist, writer, and elder statesman, David Brinkley, might wish to say, *"...think about it."*

We can reminisce for years about what a great country we are; celebrate our patriotism all we want to; decorate it in red, white, and blue streamers; shoot fireworks into the skies on the Fourth of July; parade our university majorettes down the boulevards of our largest cities; fly our mighty F18 military warplanes overhead at every public event; listen to the Marine Corps Band playing the National Anthem in front of the Washington Monument; and have our media outlets run heart-stopping footage on TV of how beautiful is our countryside and what great devotion we should proffer our nation and its people. But, the fact remains true that the rest of the world is starving to death, while we are getting more obese by the hour, sitting on a cushion of over $10 trillion in gross national trade. If (the late) Mother Teresa of Calcutta was still alive to speak on behalf of the poorest of the poor today; would she not continue to admonish the entire Western Hemisphere about the rendering of demographics from that same World Development Forum report? If half the world's population is going without food, sixty percent are living in shacks, and 70% cannot read or write, then what purpose do we think we own before the Face of God for the existence of our own national modesty? What strikes the rest of the world so strangely is that America is *proud* to be so aloof. We suffer from a great delusion if we believe that most other regions envy the way we live over here. We are slaves to almost everything we pursue; our homes, our places of employment, our powerful influence over the public debate, and the fact that there are few among us who could miss a month's salary and not lose everything we own to the finance and mortgage companies. There are actually certain sects in third-world nations who hear news about the United States and look with pity upon us because we are so blinded against any allegiance to a higher God through our wilful addiction to materialism, self-righteousness, and outright corporal lust. Even in this poor light, we continue to laud our every move as though it springs from the center of the moral universe. We fall to our knees before popular basketball players, professional golfers, and race-car drivers; but rarely look in the direction of the thousands of humble missionaries who are serving God's "...least of these" in foreign impoverished and undeveloped places.

There is a term derived from Latin, *gravid*; which means "...burdened or loaded." The reason that it is so applicable in describing the United States is because we have heaped more upon the land within our continental borders than any earthen soil should be required to withstand; physically, socially, and emotionally. Our geographical expansion has taken us from the Eastern seaboard to the Ohio River valley, to the Great Lakes and the slums of Chicago and Detroit, and under the Rocky Mountain foothills where we find the glitz, glamor, and immorality of the city of Las Vegas, with its legalized prostitution, gambling, carousing, and inexplicable drug abuse. We have built our homes in the suburbs, in elite penthouses, at the summit of hills beside the streams, and even beneath the crabgrass. Our factories are steaming with toxic gases from sea to shining sea; nuclear power plants are just pining to finally melt-down; the northern "rust belt" is about to go bust, the midwestern "corn belt" would rather turn their grain into fuel than give it to the hungry poor; our military bases are being abandoned by the scores, and strip-mining has left a shambles of an otherwise beautiful landscape. Was Joni Mitchell right all along? Have we actually paved paradise and put-up a parking lot? Was this part of her reflections about President Eisenhower's decision to lay-out our interstate highway systems during the 1950s for transporting nuclear warheads around the countryside to their selective underground sites? What an unexpected boon they have become for the ease of civilian travel for millions of Americans who like to visit great distances from home! Indeed, how quickly we can drive across the entire expanse of over 2,500 miles to the State of California, where we have the opportunity to see the dreams of the Beach Boys firsthand, experience the sights along the Ventura Highway, take a shot at stardom at the studios in Hollywood, and see what makes Silicon Valley so vainly attractive to Generation X and our entire new social class of computer "techies." Thereafter, if we become so inspired, we can take a trip to our many national and aerospace museums to see what great progress we have made in launching ourselves into the outer atmosphere since we finally ran out of room to explore anything merely mortal once we arrived at the trembling shores of the Pacific Ocean.

The point in all of this is not that we have done anything wrong by making the most of our intelligence, our creative intuitions, our ability to solve problems, and the care we have taken to make human life better for our children and their progeny; for we have made great strides in the fields of medicine and nutrition, public safety, and human development counseling. Our failures have come as a result of our new advancements at the cost of the standard of living of millions of other poor souls who have never been able to deign for themselves. Moreover, we have nurtured a culture of debasement, sex, violence, and wastefulness by allowing our untamed creativity to override our consciences as they are meant to be controlled through the virtues of our faith, integrity, and moderation. This is the true crisis of our American productivity which is reflected quite succinctly in the awful nature of the course of modern history; school shootings, people throwing their enemies out the windows of tall buildings, robbery, rape, arson, and an untold registry of misdemeanor crimes. There was another report released in September of 1998 from the Associated Press, citing a survey from the National Constitution Center, which stated that only 41% of American teenagers could name the three branches of government, but 59% could identify the Three Stooges. And, 74% could name the city where cartoon character Bart Simpson lives (Springfield); but only 12% knew where President Abraham Lincoln is buried, in Springfield, Illinois. There was a little better news, but not very much. Seventy-four percent of those surveyed could say that Al Gore was then Vice-President of the United States; but an amazing 90% knew that Leonardo DiCaprio was the male star of the motion picture "Titanic." Does this not speak to the way we are raising our children and whether they will fully know the priorities with which they will eventually inherit the reigns of governing the United States of America when their generation blooms into fuller maturity? The stage has been set for us to act swiftly in determining what, if anything, we are going to do about reversing these established facts and ruinous trends. Hundreds-of-thousands of Americans have determined that it may already be too late to rescue our country from the national skid toward defeatism which is already hovering above us like a coal-black thundercloud. It may be true that the only other subject that we despised in prep-school more than English literature was history; but only by learning more about how our ancestors fought with courageous spirits will we ever muster the strength to overcome the perils and immorality that time and our own indifference have stacked against us. It is as though we have finally walked out of our American back doors, thrown our hands into the air, and said with a whimper and a tear, "...I give up." Well, this does not sound even remotely like the valor, vision, and strength by which our nation was founded. It has not even the slightest appearance of grace and appeal that made our fallen countrymen once stand with their faces to the wind and vow to never let anyone or anything destroy the great republic for which their fellow comrades had died. Our puny cowardice sounds absolutely nothing like the bombs bursting in air that brought multiple millions of our citizens to fight for their right to bear arms, to stand with equality next to their brothers, to be able to walk into the polls on election day and exercise their right to vote, and to march down the centerline of Main Street in our post-war victory parades to the sensation of ticker-tape glancing off their cheeks. Most all of the great men and women who made America abundant and free may be deceased and resting peacefully in their graves; but their mission and their legacies live-on to this day. If we fail to uphold the inheritance we have been granted to share this freedom with the entire globe, we will have simultaneously brought dishonor to their memory and to the God in whose Arms they now sleep. Indeed, who are these great benefactors of our unprecedented liberties? They have been canonized Saints, authors, pastors, inventors, scientists, public leaders, and countless private citizens whose names are far too numerous to recount. And, sitting quietly in their midst will be none other than U.S. Army counsel Joseph Welch, who will soon repeat his famous question that he put to Senator McCarthy during the Congressional hearings of June 9, 1954. But, this time, while staring directly into the face of our contemporary collective American soul, he will ask of his native country, *"...have you no sense of decency sir, at long last?"* In the next chapter, let us enlist a more detailed overview of those legendary heroes who will someday admonish us for the people we have been, and the nation we have failed to be.

Chapter Six
The Giants of History Shall Return

Saint Augustine, Doctor of the Church
(A.D. 354-430)

The first discernable trend that has made every follower of Jesus Christ a recognizable child of God is discovered in the process and submission of their own humble self-denial. For a man named Saint Augustine, this came only after finally opening his heart to the Holy Spirit once he had renounced a life of secular intellectualism, and through the profound influence of Saint Ambrose, who baptized Augustine to be a Christian of the Catholic faith during the night of Holy Saturday and Easter Sunday, April 24 and 25, A.D. 387. Since the bibliography of all the earlier Saints is public domain by now, it is quite obvious that his life and teachings have been recorded in scores of spiritual textbooks. Augustine was born on November 13, 354 in Thagaste, northern Africa, to a pagan father and a Christian mother; a woman who was later canonized to be Saint Monica. He attended the university at Carthage to study speech and rhetoric, with the purpose of eventually becoming a lawyer. After having dismissed the pursuit, he slowly fell away from his mother's influence and eventually took a woman as concubine, with whom he lived for fifteen years, and who bore him a son. After teaching rhetoric for seven years at Carthage, he relocated to Rome in 383, where he became overwhelmingly impressed by the sermons of Saint Ambrose and avidly chose to avow his faith to the Roman Catholic Church. He was ordained a priest in 391 in Hippo, made coadjutor to Bishop Valerius there in 395, and succeeded him to the See upon Valerius' death the following year. It was during that time until A.D. 427 when he wrote some of the most classical Christian projectuals ever to be revealed to the world. He eventually died in Hippo during the Vandals' siege of the city on August 28, 430. It has been said that Saint Augustine's powerful intellect molded the thought of Western Christianity to such an extent that his revelations shaped the thinking of the entire Western hemisphere for a full thousand years beyond his death. His writings have been hailed as among the most prolific in defending the Christian faith, and include such works as *Confessions* and *City of God*, both of which were his expository philosophies and histories of the early Christian Church. Called the "Doctor of Grace," he is one of the greatest of the Fathers and Doctors of the Church and, with the possible exception of Saint Thomas Aquinas, is the highest spiritual intellect that Roman Catholicism has ever produced. It is for these reasons that he has been cited here in my book as being one of the legends who shall rise again and reproach us all for our ongoing callousness against the Truth of human Love before our weary eyes have yet to peer over the horizon of the immortal skies. Our hearts and families have known our Almighty Creator with a much more distinct perception as a result of the life and legacy of Saint Augustine; and it is in reading his writings that we can best know why.

I have always believed that the tree of Eternal Life is somewhat of an autophyte, meaning that it creates its own food. Love is fed by itself; and it is sustained throughout the world by the way we wield it. When Saint Augustine wrote *Confessions* between 397 and 400, he spoke to the aspects of existence that are inherently exempt from the forces of time. Said he in precise Latin about Genesis 1:1, while speaking directly to God, *"...I find two things which you have made immune to time, although neither is coeternal with you. One of them has been so formed that, without any interruption of its contemplation, without any interval of change, subject to change yet never changed, it enjoys Eternity and immutability. The other was so formless that it could not be changed from one form into another whether of motion or of rest, and thus be made subject to time. But, you did not abandon this second being to remain formless. For, before all days, '...in the beginning you made Heaven and Earth,' those two things of which I was speaking. The Earth was invisible and without order, and darkness was above the deep. By these words you have instilled the idea of formlessness, so that gradually aid might be given to minds that could not conceive complete privation of form without arriving at nothing. From it would be made another Heaven and Earth, visible and set in order, and beautiful bodies of water, and whatever else is recorded as being made thereafter, but not without days, in the creation of this world* (Book XII, *Form and Matter*, Chapter 12 ff.) " In this deeply romantic phraseology, Saint Augustine was saying that he knew that Creation was made not to be an illusion of some ulterior motivation of God, but from His own perceptible Love which He has chosen to make visible to all mortal men, even beyond our death. God has created "matter" out of the "immaterial," and we are the beneficiaries of having been located in its midst. Thereafter, according to Saint Augustine, we can no longer become anything less than eternal since we have already been placed within the context of time, which is a subposition of everything good that will perpetually exist, at least somewhere, inside or outside of its culmination. His key point is quite simply taken when surveyed through its proper epochal context.

It was Augustine's introduction to this metaphysical nature of the presence of humankind which assisted the millions who would discover his works to nurture the seed of Christian faith inside their hearts ever since he penned them. His point is that there is no logical explanation for us to refute the existence of God; and we have no ideological excuse to deny Him. The world today, despite the leanings of many people toward agnosticism and materialism, contains no evidence that the Deity who created it has tossed us over the transom of the universe for someone else to preserve and defend. Do we decline to believe this because our senses have refused to perform their preordained reconnaissance for our spirits? If this is the case, then why have there been so few blind and deaf people burned by fire whose flames they can never see and crackling embers they cannot hear? Is it not the warmth they can detect, an invisible radiation of the presence of another sovereign force, which formulates their own conclusion that they must not be alone? Therefore, in accordance with the contemplations of Saint Augustine, has God not allowed the world in which we live to be neither abandoned nor physically formless? Even after pondering my own studies and having been awarded a Baccalaureate Degree in Physics in 1984, I have come to the conclusion that the laws of action and reaction, averages, conservation of mass and energy, cosines, and gravitation have naturally given-way to the Pentateuch Law of Moses which contains God's intercessory dispensations and His prelude to the Messianic God-Man, Jesus Christ, in whom Saint Augustine ultimately came to believe. And, if Augustine was to preserve the principles of Love which had guided Him by the power of the Holy Spirit to become a priest in A.D. 391, he had to also deduce that it was this same Divine Truth which would continue to hold our feet closer to the torches of faith, the same tongues' afire which have taken the Church nearly 1,600 years further into the future since he first closed his eyes in death. Like him, I had no choice but to surrender my original pursuits in understanding Creation by the quantum nature of its temporal facts and bow in deference to the spiritual Beatitudes which define the unseen world that Augustine proclaimed to be just as immutable as God, Himself. Indeed, in keeping with the theme of our geographical expansion in America of the 19th and 20th centuries, the Louisiana Purchase; which was the territory that the U.S. bought from France in 1803 for $15 million, extending from the Mississippi River to the Rocky Mountains and from the Mexican Gulf to Canada; was to become no more than a makeshift barter that only allowed us greater reason to embrace the "framed world" of rationalism over the highly ethereal Kingdom of God.

Essentially, therefore, the origin of our enlightenment that neither human Love nor faith is an inherent product of our capacity to shape and design the material Earth has been enhanced by the contemplative influence of the likes of Saint Augustine. Are we to additionally assume that the ...New Heaven and the New Earth..." about which he was speaking in *Confessions* would be a resurrected remnant of the first, the one which could not be seen with the naked eye prior to God's manifest alignment of the mortal ground upon which we now walk? This is the one, soon to be glowing in the Light of Divine Revelation, that will be absolutely and irreversibly the pride of Paradise, and seamlessly coeternal with our Almighty Father, His Omnipotent Son, the Holy Paraclete, the Angelic Courts, and the entire Communion of Saints. All reasoned judgement, piety, apparency, hope, and faith tell us that this must be true. Augustine proposes that there is no reason why human life as we know it cannot be restored to its creative pristineness, even though it is still subject to the element of time; such is how he concludes the heretofore quoted passage. Jesus Christ says, "...be perfect as I am perfect." Hence, we are asked to *become* His Love, as He is wholly present in Spirit and Corporeal Species through the Most Blessed Sacrament, and in compliant affirmation with the Immanuel Prophecies of Isaiah (6:3), assembled into such an appropriate acclamation for the Eucharistic Liturgy of today, *"...Holy, holy, holy is the Lord of all hosts! All the Earth is filled with His Glory!"* Therein resides the purpose for offering our Sacrificial Communion to Jesus Christ for surrendering His Life on the Cross; whereupon we reciprocally acknowledge that our mortal souls must become equally as indispensable as the "...created form from God's Hands," which took Saint Augustine to the very pinnacle of understanding the reason why we reside with such custodial dominion upon a planet of soil, air, water, and crawling creatures. This is the beginning of the expulsion of human arrogance and the essence of knowing our righteous God by what He hath covertly wrought.

Saint Francis of Assisi, Stigmatist
(A.D. c1181-1226)

By moving the clock of mortal time forward another 750 years from when Saint Augustine died, we discover thereabout the date of the birth of one of the most austere, humble, obedient, majestic, and pious Saints of the history of all histories; Saint Francis of Assisi. I have taken the liberty to assume that most everyone who is reading my books these days already knows about the life and legacy of Francis; if not, they must be living under a rock somewhere. It is well known that he was born into great wealth, but later denounced it; that he repudiated and disavowed his own father for the sake of his Christian mission; how he was able to spiritually communicate with animals and birds to get them to obey him; he was given the power of prescience and prophecy; and that he is credited as being the designer of the first *creche*, the Scene of the Nativity of Jesus in Bethlehem which we still see during Christmastime to this very day. There is certainly no doubt that Saint Francis of Assisi led an exemplary Christian life; and untold millions have followed him into the faith as a result. Therefore, rather than describe a factually mundane accounting of the synopsis of his years, I thought it would be more appropriate to discuss the offering of Francis' life to God and human Salvation as an actual message from Heaven; not just to the awesome purposes to which Francis, himself, subscribed. He was never ordained into the priesthood, but he was known as the greatest friend of the poor in his age; called the "Seraphic Patriarch" by those who knew him through his angelic presence. His much renowned bibliography that was written by none other than Saint Bonaventure (1221-1274) is perhaps one of the most revealing of any at our disposal to date; for it was he who was cured of a childhood illness by Saint Francis, given the name of Bonaventure, and declared his vows to the Franciscan Order in the mid 13th century. Bonaventure said that Francis' miraculous relationship with Jesus Christ during his mortal years on Earth was unprecedented for his time; and that his journey of faith would lead to a life that would mend sorrowful spirits, heal broken bodies, deliver countless souls who were endangered from certain death, and restore the vitality of an uncountable number of admirers who went to their graves in appreciation for his indelibleness.

The most profound manifestation in the life of Saint Francis occurred when he received the supernatural "stigmata," meaning that the Wounds in the hands, feet, and side of Jesus Christ were physically inflicted upon his own body in reflection of the Crucifixion of Our Lord on the Cross. While there have been many others to receive this series of paranormal impositions, Saint Francis was one of the fewer laymen to have been given it from God. The purpose of my having included him in this particular chapter is to envision how the purpose in his mission was, and still is, a way for Our Creator to tell humanity that everyone can be like Jesus, not just those who profess a religious vocation by way of donning its formal vestments. One of his more personal extractions, as recounted by Saint Bonaventure, was when he was greatly anguished by doubt as to whether he should enter a monastic life, or become a disciple of evangelism; whereupon he turned to his friends and said, *"...Which do you account more praiseworthy; to give myself wholly to prayer, or to go about preaching the Gospel? ...for I, being a poor sinful man, and unskilled in preaching, have received the gift of prayer, rather than speech. In prayer, again, is great gain and accumulation of graces; in preaching, the distribution of whatever gifts we have received from Heaven. In prayer is the purification of the interior affections, and union with the One True and Supreme God, together with an increase of all virtues. In preaching, the feet of the spiritual man are defiled with dust; therewith comes distraction concerning many things and great relaxation of discipline. In prayer, we speak to God and listen to Him, and, as if leading an angelic life, we converse with the angels. But, in preaching, we must condescend to men in many things; and, living among them as men, we must think, see, speak and hear as men. On the other hand, this one thing would seem to outweigh all the rest before God, which is to say, that the Only Begotten Son of God, Who is the Supreme Wisdom, descended from the bosom of the Father for the Salvation of souls, that He might teach the world by His example, and speak the Word of Salvation to men whom He redeemed with the price of His Sacred Blood, washing them therewith in the laver of Baptism, and nourishing them therewith in the Chalice of Salvation, reserving to Himself nothing, but pouring forth all liberally for our Salvation. And, therefore, we ought to do according to the example of those things which we have seen in Him, as in a high mountain set forth before us, so that it seems to me more pleasing to God that I should lay aside my quiet, and go forth to labor."* (*The Life of Saint Francis of Assisi*, by Saint Bonaventure, Chapter XII, para. 1, *Of the Efficacy of His Preaching, and of His Gift of Healing*.) Francis later sent two of his brethren to summon one Brother Sylvester, who was a man devoted to deep contemplative supplication at the summit of a mountain in Assisi, and the holy virgin Clare, who had conjoined with her sisters in prayer; to beseech them to ask God what he should do. The two brothers returned to Francis and reported to him that it was revealed to both Sylvester and Clare from the Throne of God in Heaven that Francis should go forward to preach.

Thereafter, Saint Francis of Assisi lived one of the most mystically iconic lives ever known to a mortal man born under the Supremacy of our Almighty Father. In the brief span of his 45 years, he was a miracle-worker of the highest magnitude; casting out devils, turning water into wine, commanding a stream to flow from a bare boulder in the countryside, and even raising people from the dead. The stately means by which Saint Bonaventure announced the passing of Saint Francis is quite divulging of their age. He said with great eloquence, *"...the venerable Father passed away from the wreck of this world in the year of Our Lord's Incarnation, 1226, on the 4ᵗʰ of October, on the evening of Saturday, and was buried on Sunday. The sacred and blessed body, glorified by Divine grace, began at once to work manifold and great miracles, that the excellence of his sanctity, which during his life in the flesh had made known to the world by the example of true and perfect justice, whereby he had directed and reformed the manners of men, now that he was reigning with Christ, was proved by the miracles wrought by the Divine power in confirmation of the faith by which he was believed to be in Heaven."* (Chapter XV, Para. 4, *Of His Canonization and Translation.)* My secondary purpose hereon is to bring new life to these words by celebrating the intercession of the Saints from their station in Paradise, as has been well documented in the case of Saint Francis by Saint Bonaventure (Chapter XV, Part II, *Of Certain Miracles Wrought after His Death*.) One of his own Franciscan Friars, who had fallen into a sedentary doubt about the stigmatic insignias on Francis' hands and feet after his death, was asleep one night and suddenly awakened when Blessed Francis, himself, posthumously appeared in his room. His feet were all covered with mire, and he had an appearance of discernment on his face. He said to the Friar, *"...And what are these conflicts and vile doubts with thee? Behold my hands and my feet."* The Friar saw the pierced hands, but the feet he could not see because of the bespatterment which covered them. *"Remove the mire from my feet, and you shall see the place of the nails."* So, he took hold of Francis' feet and washed away the mire, then touched the place where the nails had been imbedded with his hands. His face was bathed in tears when he awoke, and he traveled far and wide to proclaim the authenticity of the Stigmata of Saint Francis of Assisi for the rest of his mortal days.

There was a clerk of the Cathedral Church who lived in the city of Potenza, Apulia in southeastern Italy who had been ill for an extended period of time. He went to the church to pray before a picture of Blessed Francis, showing his Stigmata. He, too, had doubtful thoughts about the genuine nature of such a phenomenon, when he was suddenly severely wounded, himself, in his left hand under his glove; at the same time that he had heard the whizzing of an arrow blaze past his ears. He immediately removed his glove upon noticing that his previously unwounded palm was now so intensely writhing from pain that he could scarcely bear it. There was no sign of a hole in his glove, so that the secrecy of the wound in his heart corresponded with the secrecy of the wound inflicted as his penalty. He thereafter professed his belief in the Stigmata of Saint Francis and sought God to purify him through this very miracle. Upon his having made such a conversion, the pain in his palm disappeared, as the healing of his body followed the offering of his faith. According to Saint Bonaventure, this wonderful miracle was affirmed by many witnesses under oath and authenticated by the Bishop's Seal, so that the knowledge of it has come down to us today. Now, for my favorite one of all! In the city of Parmaco, there was a young maiden who died from a grievous illness, and all of her family and friends came together to offer her a sorrowful departing. Her wailing mother was so overcome by the death of her daughter that she was completely oblivious to her surroundings thereafter. Meanwhile, Saint Francis, who was accompanied by a single Friar, deigned to appear to her and console her despondent heart because she was so very devoted to his apostolic mission. Francis said, *"...Weep no more; for the quenched light of thy candlestick, for which thou now weepest, is restored to thee by my intercession!"* At these words, the woman immediately stood and declared to everyone at the funeral what Saint Francis had just said to her, and she forbade them to bury the corpse; but calling upon Saint Francis with titanic faith, she opened her dead daughter's coffin, took her by the hand, and helped her onto her feet, alive and well, in the presence of all the mourners who were there to offer their final obsequies and last goodbyes. There are other such cases where the intercession of Saint Francis has aided in the miraculous raising of the deceased from their terminal fall to human mortality. Why? Because God so wishes us to accept that we, too, are meant to share in the Crucifixion of Jesus Christ; and that if we do, we shall be the miracle-workers of our own contemporary age.

Saint Alphonsus Mary De Liguori
(1696-1787)

Some people claim that the articulate writings of intelligent men are inscribed only to impress themselves; to surmise whether they can put their thoughts onto a page for the sole purpose of inflating their own self-esteem. While this may be the case in some secular quarters, it is not evenly slightly true regarding those who have penned their memoirs about their imminent Salvation in Jesus Christ. The Holy Spirit would never allow Himself to be forever concealed inside the heart of someone who is bound for Heaven before God's message of human redemption is transferred at least to a single other man. As defenseless at it sounds, this is just the way He reigns. Around the time that the framers of the infant government of the United States were working in full swing on the western shores of the Atlantic Ocean, another great man was hailing a more notable cause in Italy, exhorting the Holy Gospel to anyone he could find. Saint Alphonsus De Liguori, who was deeply consecrated to the Immaculate Heart of the Blessed Virgin Mary, was one such celebrated author whose purpose, it seems, was to tell the entire world that the Kingdom of God is at hand, and we had all better accept it quickly. He was loath to be described as "evangelical" because of the term's reference to the 16th century Protestant Reformation; knowing that such a movement was in direct opposition to the institutional authority of the Roman Catholic Church. Despite what he thought of such preaching, however, he compiled a massive collection of Christian apologetics of his own that are still popular reading to this day. There was no question in his mind that God is just and loving, but He is also prepared to administer swift punishment to those who reject Him. It was this type of admonishment which became the central thesis for most all Alphonsus' works; and Jesus Christ is all the more glorified for his having loved Him. He often wrote quite lavishly about the omnipotence of God and the intercessory powers of His Mother; and the fuller virtues of faith, hope and charity; but he was quite intent upon warning humanity that we are practically undeserving of the Fruits of Redemption if we decline to pray to receive them. The Divine Mercy of Jesus, he felt, is reserved only for those who seek Eternal Salvation with a predetermined sanctity.

Saint Alphonsus was born near Naples on September 21, 1696, a day which has been set aside as the Feast of Saint Matthew, the Apostle. He earned his doctorate in both canon and civil law at the University there when he was only sixteen years old, and practiced law for the next eight years.

Finding this to be not of his liking, he chose instead to become a Roman Catholic Priest; joining the Oratorians, and was ordained in 1726. He met a very holy nun, Sister Mary Celeste, in Scala, joined with her in founding the Redemptorines Order in 1731, and organized the Congregation of the Most Holy Redeemer, the Redemptorists, early the next year. For five decades thereafter, he set out to assist the poor through the Hierarchical Church, was personally proactive in teaching in rural precincts and parishes, and increasingly devoted his life to his personal writings. He was stricken so badly with illness and rheumatism that he was forced to resign as Bishop of Sant' Agata dei Goti in 1775, and retired to Nocera. For the last few years of his life, he experienced a deep spiritual depression and went through what Mother Teresa of Calcutta once called, "...the dark night of the soul;" for she had suffered the same affliction before her death in September 1997. But, as in the case of Mother Teresa, Saint Alphonsus' convalescence was found in an almost supernatural period of peace and light wherein he experienced heavenly visions, enjoyed spiritual ecstasies, made prophecies that were later fulfilled, and performed numerous miracles of healing and grace. He died on August 1, 1787, after writing a series of moral, theological, and ascetical manuscripts; including such masterpieces as *The Passion and Death of Jesus Christ, the Glories of Mary, The Holy Eucharist, Victories of the Martyrs, Dignities and Duties of the Priest,* and the volume from which I have chosen to recite in this particular chapter, *The Way of Salvation and Perfection.* It was in the latter that he penned some of his most reproving meditations about how sinful humankind has been, and unappreciative of the kind Love and Mercy that God is showing through Our Divine Lord and Savior. Moreover, what seemed to be most striking about the works of Saint Alphonsus is that he rarely spoke or wrote about Jesus without including The Blessed Virgin Mary in the same oral and literary passages.

I have found it to be explicitly appropriate to incorporate Alphonsus' *Part I, Meditation VIII, The Abuse of God's Mercy,* in its entirety in this brief biography because he has explained what I firmly believe to be true about the seriousness with which we should be taking our spiritual conversion and the gamble we are facing if we continue to ignore the call of Christ to heed His Holy Word. Henceforth is its text, verbatim.

1. *There are two ways by which the devil endeavors to deceive men to their eternal ruin: after they have committed sin, he tempts them to despair on account of the severity of Divine Justice; but before they have sinned, he encourages them to do so by the hope of obtaining The Divine Mercy. And, he effects the ruin*

of numberless souls as well by the second as by the first artifice. 'God is merciful,' says the obstinate sinner to him who would convert him from the iniquity of his ways. 'God is merciful.' But, as the Mother of God expresses it in Her Canticle, 'His mercy is to them that fear Him.' Yes, the Lord deals mercifully with him that fears to offend Him, but not so with the man who presumes upon His Mercy, to offend Him still more. O God! I give Thee thanks for having made me sensible of Thy patience in bearing with me. Behold, I am of the number of those who, presuming on Thy goodness, have offended Thee again and again.

2. God is merciful; but He is also Just. Sinners are desirous that he should be merciful only, without being Just, but that is impossible because were He only to forgive and never to chastise, He would be wanting injustice. Henceforth, ...(Father Avila)...observes that patience on the part of God towards those who avail themselves of His compassion to offend Him the more, would not be compassion, but a want of justice. He is bound to chastise the ungrateful. He bears with them for a certain time, but after that, abandons them. Such a punishment, O God!...has not as yet overtaken me, or else I had now dwelt in Hell, or had been obstinate in my sins. But no: I desire to amend my life; I desire to offend Thee no more. Though I have hitherto displeased Thee, I am sorry for it with my whole soul; I desire henceforth to love Thee, and I desire to love Thee more than others do because Thou hast not shown the same patience towards others as towards me.

3. 'God is not mocked!' Yet, He would be mocked if the sinner could go on continually offending Him, and yet afterwards enjoy Him in Heaven. 'What things a man shall sow, those also shall he reap.' He who sows good works shall reap rewards; but he who sows iniquities shall reap chastisements. The hope of those who commit sin because God is forgiving is an abomination in His sight: 'their hope,' says holy Job, 'is an abomination.' Hence, the sinner, by such hope, provokes God to chastise him the sooner, as that servant would provoke his master who, because his master was good, took advantage of his goodness to behave ill. O Jesus!...such I fear has been my conduct towards Thee; because Thou wast good I have made no account of Thy precepts. I confess that I have done wickedly; and I detest all the offenses I have committed against Thee. Now do I love Thee more than myself, and I desire never more to displease Thee. Ah, if I should again offend Thee by mortal sin!...Permit it not, O Lord, rather let me die! O Mary, Mother of perseverance, do Thou assist me!

Do we, therefore, as 21st century Americans, expect to prevail upon the Merciful Love of Jesus Christ to heal the wounds of our nation while He still knows that we are so offending Him as we make our plea? Are we among the "seeing" who are closing our spiritual eyes to the Truth and continuing to stand in opposition before His unapproachable Light, attesting that we cannot quite envision ourselves ever fully acknowledging the presence of His Divine Sovereignty? Do we not yet know that the Sacred Heart of Jesus Christ is the amulet, charm, and safeguard into which the God of our fathers fully intends to deposit the world someday? If we are to be perfected in the likeness of the hopes of Saint Alphonsus De Liguori, is not the entire universe meant to become the phylactery into which the shining New Jerusalem is to be placed atop the Mantle of God's Hearth in Paradise for Him to adore as the fruitful new beginning of Eternity, without end? Those who have read my first book, *Morning Star Over America*, know that I have been taught about Love and human Salvation by the most chaste of all virgins, the Immaculate Mother of God, to whom Her Sacrificed Son wishes us to turn for prayerful consolation. It is She who is the reflecting resonance of the Holy Spirit in North America and around the world today; for She has stated in Her apparitions to me that this will be the last age in which Her supernatural presence will occur before the end of the material world. I have quoted Saint Louis De Montfort in my first book, as he was so foretelling as to call us in our present-day to enlist Her humble intercession. Indeed, he has stated that those who are consecrated to Her Immaculate Heart and devoutly pray the Holy Rosary will be the true apostles of the latter times; that we who follow Mary to Jesus before the hour of our death will be provided a peaceful mortal passing into the Mansions of Paradise. We will be the "odor of death to the great, the rich, and to the proud worldlings;" and let anyone who ascribes to these things be properly warned. It is through this same premonition that we are asked to anticipate the Wrath of God by Saint Alphonsus De Liguori; for he also came to know Mary, the Mediatrix of all graces from Heaven, long before our post-modern world wilfully chose to abandon our childhood faith in Her Son.

Benjamin Franklin, Colonialist
(1706-1790)

If most present day public servants and common sense thinkers were to ever have a role-model to emulate, the quite pithy and pragmatic Ben Franklin would be their best example. How would this decent man, whom many of his age thought to be stuffy and eccentric, look now upon our American society before which he once stood and uttered so many of his thoughtful orations? While he was a seasoned politician who was greatly interested in the vocations of invention, science, rationalism, and the architecture of the physical world, he was also quite strong in his opinions regarding humanity's dependence upon God, "...the Omnipotent One..." as he was apt to say it. The most notable reference we have to the legacy of Ben Franklin was written by himself in his *Autobiography*, which he compiled from 1771 through 1789. He lived to be an elderly gentleman of eighty-four years, and his understanding of the principles of aging brought him to be quite provincial before he died. He pined to be remembered for much more prophetic reasons than having proved that lightning is also electricity while flying a kite in a thunderstorm in 1752; for he always wished that there would be nothing scandalous in nature which would ever diminish the hope for a newborn democratic freedom in the United States; quite a dashing expectation as time has ultimately revealed. If he were alive today, he would wish to initiate a complete belt-and-suspenders inquiry as to why we allowed the simpler virtues about which he wrote in *Autobiography* to become so unimportant to us now. Indeed, he often quoted from the Sacred Scriptures and the writings of the ancient Roman statesman, Cicero. On one of his more spiritual days, he penned his own supplication and placed it into the story of his life, *"...And, conceiving God to be the fountain of wisdom, I thought it right and necessary to solicit his assistance for obtaining it; to this end, I formed the following little prayer, which was prefixed to my tables of examination, for daily use. 'O powerful Goodness! Bountiful Father! Merciful Guide! Increase in me that wisdom which discovers my truest interest. Strengthen my resolutions to perform what that wisdom dictates. Accept my kind offices to thy other children as the only return in my power for thy continual favours to me.'"* (From *Autobiography*)

Through this succinct reminder, we can detect Franklin's self-disciplined requirement to acknowledge God as the source of our every power; but his purpose was not to narrate an even slightly glowing or authentic treatise in following the Hierarchical Church. He was a more practical man than that; but his logic and human propriety never allowed him to stray too far from the comfort, civility, and mightiness of his Eminent Maker. If anyone had ever asked him to climb over a four-foot fence with the aid of a pair of two-foot soap boxes, he would have been among the only people to suggest that they would be much better used *not* by stacking one atop the other, but to set one at his feet and the second on the other side, so he could just stand on the first and take a step over the rail to the other, where he would be only a twenty-four inch leap from standing back on the ground. While there has never been known to be a literary work entitled, *The Sufferer's Journal*, Ben Franklin would have surely composed it. He understood the problems that make life difficult for people; and he was well principled in how to alleviate them. He was one, like myself, who believed that we are often called to serve both by chance and duty; and we should otherwise not be too adversely affected or overly offended by the innocuous misgivings of other men before taking a greater look at ourselves. The main reason that I referenced him in this book is to assist those who do not believe they can know God very well so they can finally acknowledge who He is. Ben Franklin did it; although he was rather reticent about even broaching the subject. When the president of Yale asked him to write his opinion about Jesus of Nazareth in January of 1790, Franklin's answer was this, "...*I think the system of morals and his religion, as he left them to us, to be the best the world ever saw or is likely to see; but I apprehend it has received various corrupting changes; and I have, with most of the present dissenters in England, some doubts as to his divinity; tho' it is a question I do not dogmatize upon, having never studied it, and think it needless to busy myself with it now, when I expect soon an opportunity of knowing the Truth with less trouble. I see no harm, however, in its being believed, if that belief has the good consequence, as probably it has, of making his Doctrines more respected and better observed...*" Herein, Ben Franklin admitted by innuendo that Jesus Christ is the essence of moral Truth. He also suspected that he might die in this same year, but he was like many other people living today; thinking that hailing our Salvation in the Blood of the Cross is much too infantile and sentimental for such a mature society. Thank God, however, he knows by now that Jesus Christ is the origin of all Eternal Life.

John Henry Cardinal Newman, Priest
(1801-1890)

What in the world would bring any author to include Cardinal Newman in a polemic about the need for greater conservatism in our march toward human Salvation? This is the question that most everyone will ask when they see his name on the top of this brief summary, celebrating his dedication to the Church. What more noble concession can there be than to follow the Guiding Light of God into the vocation of the priesthood, especially for someone about whom we could trace the principle stages of his development from its strongly Protestant roots, all the way to his conversion to Roman Catholicism in 1845? By all means, this is exactly the point in discussing his stature!   To say that his thoughts and writings were controversial would be putting it very mildly; but his intentions and their final effect gave way to a host of common people to be led to the Seven Sacred Sacraments of the Original Catholic and Apostolic Church.   Cardinal Newman's life is an essay, in itself, about how anyone can be transformed by the wisdom and power of the Holy Spirit to arrive at a full understanding of God. While he was a liberal intellect in his individualist approach to formal education, he became quite orthodox in defending the Church as being the indispensable institution for the Eternal Redemption of humankind in the Blood of Jesus Christ. He was born in London to a wealthy banker and, like Benjamin Franklin, wrote his own spiritual autobiography, which he entitled *Apologia*, because he did not really trust anyone else to get it right. Like many others of his time, he took a great deal of effort in penning his thoughts about the future course of Christianity as it was about to enter the 20th century. Having been a maverick member of the Anglican Church for most of his life and taking a stroll around the Oxford lecture circuit, he finally broke-away and studied for the Roman Catholic priesthood, and was ordained at the age of forty-four. He relocated to Birmingham, Warwickshire, where he lived until his death, having been elevated to the College of Cardinals in 1879. Unfortunately, however, he was forced to spend many of his years in Birmingham defending his earlier contumacious orations, although he wrote some masterful works in religious poetry and prose that were hailed as quite defensible before his supporters and detractors, alike.

So, what does John Henry Cardinal Newman have to do with our 21st century western hemisphere? His style is one that is lauded by many people who are presently trying to reinstate the traditions of the Church where many of them have been nearly stripped from existence. He persistently appealed to everyone else's sense of honesty and fair play; a role which garnered him a very sympathetic audience among those who could sense the innocence of the earlier ages slowly slipping away. When we fast-forward to our modern age, this is exactly the same approach we should ascribe for ourselves. He delivered some additional lectures, which were published in *The Idea of a University* in 1852, in Dublin at the newly-founded Catholic University of Ireland, where he briefly served as rector. I offer the following excerpt from his *Apologia*, as it freely stands, so that everyone will know what many of us are hereabout attempting to underscore, *"... To consider the world in its length and breadth, its various history, the many races of man, their starts, their fortunes, their mutual alienation, their conflicts; and then their ways, habits, governments, forms of worship; their enterprises, their aimless courses, their random achievements and acquirements, the impotent conclusion of long-standing facts, the tokens so faint and broken of a superintending design, the blind evolution of what turn out to be great powers or truth, the progress of things as if from unreasoning elements,...the greatness and littleness of man, his far-reaching aims, his short duration, the curtain hung over his futurity, the disappointments of life, the defeat of good, the success of evil, physical pain, mental anguish, the prevalence and intensity of sin, the pervading idolatries, the corruptions, the dreary hopeless irreligion, that condition of the whole race so fearfully, yet exactly described in the Apostle's words, 'having no hope and without God in the world;' all this is a vision too dizzy and appalling, and inflicts upon the mind the sense of profound mystery which is absolutely beyond human solution;...since there is a God, the human race is implicated in some terrible aboriginal calamity. It is out of joint with the purposes of its Creator. This is a fact, a fact as true as the fact of its existence; and thus, the doctrine of what is theologically called original sin becomes almost as certain as that the world exists, and as the existence of God. And, in these latter days, outside the Catholic Church, things are tending, with far greater rapidity than in that old time from the circumstance of the age, to atheism in one shape or other. The Catholic Church holds it better for the sun and moon to drop from Heaven, for the Earth to fail, and for all the many millions on it to die of starvation in most extreme agony...than that one soul, I will not say, should be lost, but should commit one single venial sin, should tell one willful untruth, or should steal one poor farthing without excuse."*

Abraham Lincoln, U.S. President
(1809-1865)

This public hero and noble man, who was martyred for liberty and often recited; who is frequently characterized, and who is the most notable statesman in the history of democracy, certainly requires no introduction from me. The equation between freedom and equality was completed with the stroke of his presidential pen, effectually emancipating an entire race of Americans from the oppression of slavery; this orator who spoke so eloquently about the divinity of God, who took his oath to heart and preserved a nation, who seamlessly reunited a fractured union of states into one country again, is beatified because he so blessed us through the integrity of his life. The mortal shell of Abraham Lincoln, the 16th President of the United States, is entombed in an elegant monument within a five-minute stroll from where I have inscribed this tribute to his legacy; located at Oak Ridge Cemetery, in Springfield, Illinois. My purpose in remembering his life and teachings is not only to reflect upon his administrative service as our nation's chief executive, among which he has few peers; but to certify what every American already knows; that we can spring from quite simple walks of life, with little education, and become among the greatest of all human beings to make a mark not only on history, but to define it; to create it, and to preserve it into perpetual posterity. If anyone wishes to know more about how he exchanged the facts with his advisors so as to render the proper decisions which would define his presidency, I would respectfully submit that you might acquire the best of the record from the quotable likes of Alexis de Tocqueville, Doris Kearns Goodwin, and Haynes Johnson. As for me, I am more inclined to speak to the quality of President Lincoln's heart; that sincere appropriateness which made him both a simple man and a giant among us. Is this not the direction that our major news anchors also took in the wake of the attacks of terror on the same American soil that Lincoln shed his own blood of innocence for the cause of democracy? Did not Tom Brokaw, Dan Rather, Peter Jennings, Brian Williams, and Wolf Blitzer become more inclined to speak to the human side of our democratic experience since the 21st century has already taken its toll on the civility of man? Therein rests my purpose for celebrating the life and heroism of one Abraham Lincoln, the adolescent Kentucky prodigy and Illinois railsplitter.

Mr. Lincoln's self-propriety, sympathetic expressions, and prophetic speeches were not the offspring of an Ivy League diplomacy, but the spoils of a life of human suffering which he not only overcame, but sought to eradicate from the lives of other men. He entered public life in a soul-wrenching way; losing more elections than he ever won; but was victorious when it meant the most to America, as he so aptly served as the communicator of his age; like his successors Franklin D. Roosevelt, John Fitzgerald Kennedy, Ronald Reagan, and William Jefferson Clinton would also become. Who else but the towering minister in the stove-pipe hat could stand at a Gettysburg battlefield amidst thousands of bloody corpses and commend their souls to God in thanksgiving for their having cleansed the earth with the nectar of their veins? On that November 19, 1863, he said to humankind and our Creator, alike, that *"...from these honored dead, we take increased devotion to that cause for which they gave the last full measure of devotion; that we here highly resolve that these dead shall not have died in vain; that this nation, under God, shall have a new birth of freedom; and that government of the people, by the people, and for the people shall not perish from the earth."* Nearly every seventh-grader in America today is forced to memorize this historical oration; but they are rarely, if ever, told why President Lincoln spoke so profoundly about the sacrifice of the lives of those around whose remains he stood weeping. It was not so much about his concern for the record of history that he spoke, but whether America would even have one after that day. Should not a nation perish from the Earth which has allowed a culture of death so great in intensity to overcome it in the past thirty years; from abortion, to capital punishment, to euthanasia? This is a matter not for our generation to decide, or any of our successors; but for God, and God alone. The poised presence-of-mind that was the hallmark of the Lincoln speeches was a premonition of what our Almighty Father might say to us because the suffering of Jesus Christ was reflected in the life of our 16th President. History tells us that he placed a placard on the wall of his office which recounted his ascension to the White House. It was in penned writing, and said that he had failed twice in private business, became a lawyer of the famous Almanac Trial, was defeated for the legislature before he was first elected, lost his sweetheart to death in 1835, suffered a nervous breakdown the following year, was defeated for Speaker, Elector, and for a second term in Congress, was defeated for the Senate in 1855 and for Vice-President in 1856, and lost a bid for the Senate again in 1858. One would have thought that his luck had finally turned around for good once he was popularly elected to the United States presidency in 1860 and 1864, only to have been shot and killed while in office in 1865.

Now, after scores of years have passed, there is a new Presidential Library in Springfield, Illinois to commemorate the many contributions and the great influence that he had upon our nation, our culture, our freedom, and our hopes. It is a permanent record of the many factual characteristics of his life; that he was born on February 12, 1809 in Hodgenville, KY, was reared in Spencer County, Indiana where his mother died, moved to Macon County, Illinois onto a farm, to New Salem near Petersburg in 1831, and to Springfield in 1837 from where he was elected the nation's 16th president. He was a notorious debater, as Stephen Douglas might well attest; and a good husband to Mary Todd, whom he married in 1842; and loving father to his four children, Robert Todd, Edward Baker, William Wallace, and Thomas Lincoln; the latter named for Abraham's father. Any historian or layperson can find the indelible words of President Lincoln chiseled into granite and marble all across America; from the east walkways of the Illinois State Capitol, to the facades of the Lincoln Memorial in Washington, and the hallowed tomb that shelters his body amidst the oak trees in his hometown of Springfield. Any soul can be moved by the closing statements of his extraordinarily brief Second Inaugural Address of March 4, 1865, when the U. S. was so sorely reeling from the ongoing Civil War, *"...With malice toward none, with charity for all; with firmness in the right as God gives us to see the right; let us strive on to finish the work we are in, to bind-up the nation's wounds, to care for him who shall have borne the battle, and for his widow and his orphan; to do all which may achieve and cherish a just and lasting peace among ourselves and with all nations."* With this as America's backdrop, we marched forward to be reunited again as a singular nation. These consoling words from this thoughtful man laid the framework for nearly every inaugural address thereafter; from his immediate successor, Andrew Johnson; to Grant, Hayes, Garfield, Arthur, Cleveland, and Harrison; none of them saw the office of the presidency quite the same beyond the tenure of Abraham Lincoln. He forever redefined it as the "bully pulpit" from which a compassionate leader could speak to his constituents like an advisor, brother, and friend. From William McKinley to the gritty retorts of Teddy Roosevelt, they all looked back in awe at this man who, himself, had surrendered his life in much the same way as those he eulogized so profoundly on the flats of that infamous Pennsylvania battlefield in 1863.

Would Taft, Wilson, Harding, Coolidge, and Hoover be able to shape a nation through the economic perils and political climates of their own ages with the same consummate love that made Mr. Lincoln the best of their kind? We have watched them all come and go; from colonial, to industrialist, to contemporary statesman; but none could compete with the grand composure of the only servant to preserve the Union. As some of the greatest of my own ancestors might say,...methinks I will allow the Honorable Mr. Lincoln to conclude for me here, remembering what he said as he was about to leave Springfield for Washington to take the oath of office on February 11, 1861. *"Friends; no one who has never been placed in a like position can understand my feelings at this hour, nor the oppressive sadness I feel at this parting. For more than a quarter of a century, I have lived among you, and during all that time, I have received nothing but kindness at your hands. Here I have lived from my youth until now, I am an old man. Here, the most sacred ties of earth were assumed; here all my children were born; and here one of them lies buried. To you, dear friends, I owe all that I have; all that I am. All the strange, checkered past seems to crowd now upon my mind. Today, I leave you; I go to assume a task more difficult than that which devolved upon General Washington. Unless the great God who assisted him shall be with and aid me, I must fail. But, if the Omniscient Mind and the same Almighty Arm that directed and protected him shall guide and support me, I shall not fail; I shall succeed. Let us all pray that the God of our fathers may not forsake us now. To Him, I commend you all. Permit me to ask that, with equal sincerity and faith, you all will invoke His wisdom and guidance for me. With these few words, I must leave you; for how long, I know not. Friends, one and all, I must now bid you an affectionate farewell."* If ever there was a mortal man to speak in as supplicating a tone as Jesus Christ, Abraham Lincoln was assuredly him. Could these be the same parting words that the Son of God might have spoken to His Angels before descending to the Earth to be born incarnate in the body of a tiny child from the Womb of His Mother, Mary? And, might a portion of this same beautiful oratory have been lifted by Christ on Ascension Thursday, when He told His faithful flock that He was leaving them, but He did not yet know for how long? Indeed, are we still awaiting His return as we speak? It is not too great a stretch of imagining that the life, death, and memory of Abraham Lincoln was a 19th century model of the Holy Gospel of Christianity, played-out before our nation's eyes. There is no doubt that this is true; because Mr. Lincoln called upon God for help; the same God whom many in our midst today deny as existing, even as they hail Abraham Lincoln as the greatest president who ever lived.

Walt Whitman, American Poet
(1819-1892)

Anyone with a sense for underscoring the invaluable historical skylines of the culture of the Americas will almost certainly turn to the aesthetics of their particular age; to the liberal arts, entertainment, music, theatre, and contemporary literature. Our nation is not shy of great writers and poets who have repainted our social landscape in our minds; from Wordsworth to Shelley, Emerson, and the venerable Carl Sandburg. Walt Whitman is among the most remembered for his patriotic mosaics about the American experience, and is highly regarded for writing an elegy in honor of the slain U.S. president, Abraham Lincoln in 1865, *When Lilacs Last in Dooryard Bloomed.* Lest there be any misunderstanding; most Christians read Whitman while also strongly disagreeing with his evaluation of the Church and grossly detesting his decided corporeal orientations; but his capacity to place the visions of our hearts into comprehensible phrases was, of itself, a rather remarkable contribution. His writings spirited the cause of those who really do not know what to believe about God and country because they have advanced very little toward a divine spiritual life and have refused to allow faith to be their guide in understanding the modesty and purity by which Christians are supposed to live. Whitman errantly predicted, for example, that there would no longer be any priests or even any need for them by 1900; a false prophecy that sprung from his lack of acknowledging the purpose of the Church in human Salvation. Having said this, he was very capable of understanding mortal suffering, as he worked as a nurse for three years in the hospices near Washington, D.C. beginning in 1862. He was a native of Long Island, but also traveled to New Orleans and Chicago, Illinois in his profession as a journalist and writer. He was the editor of the *Daily Brooklyn Eagle* before taking to the road with his literary talents; and is also quite renowned for his famous *Leaves of Grass*, which is a collection of essays and poems that he wrote from 1855 until he revised them for the final time during the year of his death in 1892, in Camden, NJ, where he had lived for two decades prior.

It was in his preface to *Leaves of Grass* where we find his visionary summation of the 19th century western hemisphere. *"...The Americans of all nations at any time upon the earth have probably the fullest poetical nature. The United States, themselves, are essentially the greatest poem. In the history of the earth hitherto, the largest and most stirring appear tame and orderly to their ampler largeness and stir. Here, at last, is something in the doings of man that corresponds with the broadcast doings of the day and night. Here is not merely a nation, but a teeming nation of nations. Here is action united from strings necessarily blind to particulars and details magnificently moving in vast masses. Here is the hospitality which forever indicates heroes...here are the roughs and beards and space and ruggedness and nonchalance that the soul loves. Here, the performance disdaining the trivial unapproached in the tremendous audacity of its crowds and groupings, and the push of its perspective spreads with crampless and flowing breadth, and showers its prolific and splendid extravagance. One sees it must, indeed, own the riches of the summer and winter, and need never be bankrupt while corn grows from the ground, or the orchards drop apples, or the bays contain fish, or men beget children upon women."* So, here, we are able to sense the promise of strength and prosperity that he foresaw before we ever entered the productive industrial and technological ages. What, of all things, would he say about us now? In a later collection of narratives in the wake of the Civil War, entitled *Democratic Vistas*, which are also quite revealing to the American conscience, he wrote *"...In short, and to sum up, America, betaking herself to formative action,...must, for her purposes, cease to recognize a theory of character grown of feudal aristocracies or formed by merely literary standards; or from any ultramarine, full-dress formulas of culture, polish, caste, etc.; and must sternly promulgate her own new standard, yet old enough, and accepting the old, the perennial elements; and combining them into groups and unities; appropriate to the modern, the democratic, the west, and to the practical occasions and needs of our own cities, and of the agricultural regions; ever the most precious in the common."* As Whitman envisioned it, the greatest device that would separate future Americans would be the particulars of their own wealth and their power to hold it hostage from others, as though we are all lords of our own segments of the Earth which have been, somehow, bequeathed to us from God. As for those modern democratic cities and farms, the ability of Whitman to know where we were going was quite prescient, after all. Are we the nation to which he said, *"...all truths wait in all things...,"* and *"...whoever degrades another degrades me...,"* in *Song of Myself?* Let us see whether this, too, plays to the favor of the legacy of Walt Whitman and the deliverance of America to a more spiritualized community of political states.

Albert Einstein, Physicist
(1879-1955)

There would be new realists and practical reformers, mathematicians, scientists, and physicists; without whom the material world and human history would be a far different prospect. Where do these great intellects belong in the development of civilization and the shaping of the political lairs of the rest of the world? Albert Einstein came to America in October 1933 as a refugee from Nazi Germany, and made some of the most profound discoveries in the history of modern man; from matter, to space, energy, and nuclear physics. He had once abandoned the concept that our Creator could be confined to a written page, although he was born to a Jewish mother and father in 1879. It was not until he published his own work in 1950, *Out of My Later Years*, when the world actually discovered what he thought about life in general; particularly to the point of supporting his indigenous people and addressing the plight they suffered during both the First and Second World Wars. Why is his inclusion in my book so important to America today? Because Albert Einstein represents so many other philosophers and scientists who made the conversion from transient indifference to spiritual awareness and actuarial participation in defining the struggles of human existence, recognizing that there must be a higher Being who has placed the logical majesty into position over which they pored so profoundly and gave the utmost of their intellectual labors and years; garnering Einstein the Nobel Prize for Physics in 1921. His lack of Christian conviction was not because he rejected it, but he had never truly been exposed to its tenets. If he had, one might wonder whether his theory of relativity or the fact that he wrote the historical letter to U.S. President Franklin Roosevelt while trying to persuade him to look at nuclear warfare as a means of national security would have been so important to him after all. He maintained quite explicitly that he was never much of a political operative, turning-down an offer to be the president of the State of Israel in 1952.

What Einstein would say about his convictions and beliefs, his theories of the purposes and usefulness of science, time, space, and gravitation, would give way to a new perception of public affairs which he shared with the world in *Later Years*. Some of those whom he said to have had a great impact upon his persuasions were Isaac Newton, Johannes Kepler, Marie Curie, Max Plank, Paul Langevin, Walther Nernst, Paul Ehrenfest, Mahatma Gandhi, and Carl von Ossietzky. Why? Because they seemed to agree with his theory that God cannot be found in any fixation with a religion of the masses, but within each individual conscience. What he also wrote about himself is quite the poignant passage when commemorating his contributions toward a world of lasting peace. *"...of what is significant in one's own existence, one is hardly aware; and it certainly should not bother the other fellow. What does a fish know about the water in which he swims all his life? The bitter and the sweet come from the outside, the hard from within, from one's own efforts. For the most part, I do the thing which my own nature drives me to do. It is embarrassing to earn so much respect and love for it. Arrows of hate have been shot at me, too; but they never hit me, because somehow they belonged to another world, with which I have no connection whatsoever. I live in that solitude which is painful in youth, but delicious in the years of maturity (p. 5, Self-portrait.)"* Could it be true that a man of such pragmatism knew that the human heart has its own protective shield and that the world to which he dedicated his entire intellectual deposit was void of all meaning without a comprehensive perception of what it looks like from the other side of life? If so, we should be hailing Albert Einstein not only for the accordance of his temporal genius, but for posing the proposition that our feelings are our guide to fully understanding the concept of escaping the perils of Earth by a decision *we* can make; one which will deliver us to an unconditional trust in the reality we cannot yet see. *"The further the spiritual evolution of mankind advances, the more certain it seems to me that the path to genuine religiosity does not lie through the fear of life, and the fear of death, and blind faith; but through striving after rational knowledge. In this sense, I believe that the priest must become a teacher if he wishes to do justice to his lofty educational mission (pp. 29-30.)"* Henceforth, through the Sacraments of the Catholic Church, particularly the Holy Eucharist, humanity is not so blind anymore; there is no longer any reason to be afraid of life or death; and the Son of God, who is Healer and Teacher of all mankind, is glorified through the hands of his priests who consecrate His Body, Blood, Soul, and Divinity upon the Altar of Sacrifice, having carefully been conscripted into participating to the elation of Albert Einstein's postulate; that our rational knowledge of the Creator of life is related to our individual conversion, purification, and beatific understanding; i.e., the local effects of a gravitational field and of acceleration of an inertial system are identical.

Pope John XXIII, Supreme Pontiff
(1881-1963)

When the world grows cold and the winters come, the trees shed their foliage and bare their primal nature before all Creation; and such was the hollowness that met the Church during the modernized expansion of the United States in the decade of the 1950s. Americans were leaving the cities in droves for western suburbs, countertop gadgets were being invented to take the place of our mothers' handiwork, and automobiles the size of small ships were being rolled out of the doors from the factories in Detroit. This was the scene just after World War II, when the Catholic Church and the entire world required a sense of new union because people were beginning the horrible route which would embroil them in materialism and the advancement of the self. Our great God Almighty knew that His Church was in need of the "good pope" who saw fit to beget the recollection of its "separated brethren," those who had strayed too far from the Truth through the influences of such distractions; from Protestantism, to politics, the spoils of battle, and an outright disingenuous thrust toward the artifices of fads and motion pictures. This timely giant would be none other than one Angelo Giuseppe Roncalli, who was elevated to the Roman Papacy at the age of 76 years by a conclave of his peers on October 28, 1958. What was the Divine intention of the Holy Spirit for having this humble man serve during these particular years in the history of Creation? It was quite obvious, as he was described on June 3, 2001 by his modern successor, Pope John Paul II, *"...he was extremely docile to the action of the Spirit and an admirable witness of God's love. He let the Spirit mold him day by day, seeking with patient tenacity to conform himself increasingly to God's Will. This is the secret behind the goodness with which he conquered the people of God and many people of good will."* These are pretty high remarks from John Paul II who, himself, will be remembered in history as the greatest Roman Catholic Pontiff to ever succeed Saint Peter to the Papacy. He knew that his predecessor, John XXIII was inspirational for having convened the Second Vatican Council in 1962, about which John Paul stated, *"...it took the form of a renewed Pentecost. Even in our time, the Church is passed through by a strong driving wind. It is experiencing the Spirit's Divine breath, which opens it to the evangelization of the world."*

There is a list of all the Popes to have served the Church in Chapter 12 of this book, where we see that John XXIII succeeded Pope Pius XII, who saw the world through the perils of WWII. And, it was Pope Paul VI whose service from 1963 to 1978 that allowed the fruits of Vatican II to come to pass; fully approved and published into canon law by John Paul II in 1983; recalling that John Paul I served only a brief 33 days between them. These were among the memories which consoled the world so well when the venerated remains of Pope John XXIII were exhumed in January 2001 from their resting place in the grotto at the Vatican so they could be relocated to the main level at St. Peter's Basilica at the altar of Saint Jerome. Before he was buried in 1963, his holy body had been laid inside a cypress casket, a lead container, an oak crypt; and all three of them entombed inside a marble casing. Thousands of admirers stood in line for hours to see the late Pope on the 38th anniversary of his death, June 3, 2001, the day when the Holy Father, John Paul II celebrated the Church's Pentecost Mass, just prior to relocating the body of John XXIII to its final resting place. His predecessor's apparently incorrupt remains were laid inside a new crystal transparent coffin, his hands folded in prayer, his body dressed in a white laced tunic over a white cassock, with a short red velvet cape, and red hat trimmed with ermine; his head resting upon two scarlet pillows. This was an appropriate way to commemorate the man who saw fit to reunite the faith of millions under the cloak of the Mother Church, to reach-out to Jews and the unchurched, alike. After the Holy Mass was ended, the half-ton, shatterproof crystal and bronze coffin was delivered into the Basilica by 16 white-gloved pall-bearers. He was previously beatified by John Paul II, putting him in line for sainthood, as a miracle had been attributed to his direct intercession; an Italian nun who had recovered from a grave illness. So, the short four years and seven months of the pontificate of Pope John XXIII is remembered for the distinction which made him the catalyst for the reunion of the Church in the latter 20th century. We honor him for this, and for acknowledging that the world of his day had been drifting from understanding that the traditions of Christianity have little to do with modern ingenuity. He did nothing to diminish these traditions; and, in fact, it has been the action by thousands of rogue opportunists who have attempted to take advantage of his sacred vision which has introduced many of the unwelcome alterations to the Church that we see now; the redesign of new buildings, the errant revision of some of the liturgies, and the call for a new tolerance for arts and vices that have nothing to do with the Will of God for us to remain one people under the Cross of His Sacrificed Son.

Padre Francesco Forgione Pio, Stigmatist
(1887-1968)

It is time to speak about miracles again; ones which will not go away through the force of any book or broom, conflagration, or attack from the nether world. Father Pio was a humble Franciscan friar who was given the same Stigmata that was heretofore impaled by God upon Saint Francis of Assisi, September 20, 1918, the date of my own birthday in 1961; which he bore for exactly fifty years, until three days before his death on September 23, 1968. The story of the life of this priest almost transcends the imagination of human logic; for he was one who was forced to fight against evil spirits that he could see with his own eyes from the very day he was ordained on August 10, 1910 in the Cathedral of Benevento, Italy, which was named by the Romans for the term, "good wind." Twentieth-century authors, Fathers Rumble and Charles Mortimer Carty of Radio Replies Press, Inc. and also Tan Books have both published biographies about the supernatural aspects of the life and priesthood of Padre Pio; and most all the revelations which appear in their books have been substantiated by first-person accounts of those events. Padre Pio was given the gifts of emanating the aroma of perfume and the powers of healing the sick, the bi-location of his mind and body, the discernment of spirits, and prophesying the future. He could read the hearts and consciences of those who asked him to hear their confessions; and before dispensing absolution to some of them, he was apt to say, *"...you forgot to tell me something;"* such was his desire for them to lay bare their entire souls during this Sacrament of Penance. In addition, there are multitudes and thousands who were converted to Christianity because of his faithful teachings; and hundreds-of-thousands more have been welcomed into the flock of Jesus Christ since his mortal passing. Why? What did this holy man possess which was of such great attraction to the people who hunger and thirst for God? First and foremost, it was his dedication to offering the Holy Sacrifice of the Mass in the most pious, humble, and sacred way that he could evoke. His belief that the bread and wine which he was offering to God upon the Altar was, indeed, removed from Creation and replaced by the Body and Blood of Jesus Christ; so much so that sometimes tears of joy and affection for the Cross would roll down his cheeks during his consecration of the host. This was a heart who knew that Divine Perfection was being placed into his unworthy hands; and yet, he carried-on as well as his faith in the Lord would allow.

Once he held the Body, Blood, Soul, and Divinity of the Savior of the World before the hungry eyes of his communicants, he knew that the wounds which had been stigmatized into his own hands and feet heralded the reason why the Last Supper and Crucifixion of the Son of God became transferred from the Upper Room and Mount Calvary to the very sanctuary in which he was standing. It was for this trust that he was so despised by Satan and the other enemies of the Church; but it is also why he never surrendered the fight to take the Sacred Heart of Jesus to the rest of the world; for the millions who would seek his assistance in their conversion to Christ in the most profound and excruciating way. How could such a Franciscan friar with only God and humanity to serve create the strength from within to survive the decades which he proffered Paradise in exchange for his own Salvation as well? God has since revealed to us through the very aforementioned miracles that are only now beginning to become known worldwide that the priesthood of Padre Pio is a citation in the elements of human obedience. We must understand that the Almighty Creator works in the same mystical ways that we see Him in life and nature; that there are certain people among us who are His mortal devices; those who reflect the Passion of Jesus, the incarnation of the Sacred Beatitudes, who personify the apostolic lessons of the Holy Gospel to the point of seeming almost supernatural in form. This was the essence of Padre Pio because he knew that God wanted something more of him than just his birth, adolescence, priesthood, and severance from the temporal world. Padre Pio was to be a messenger and sign of the times during the early and middle 20th century that the statutes and decrees of Heaven are yet alive, to the tune of 2,000 years since they were dispensed, and beyond the passing of the First Apostles; particularly of Simon Peter, who was Rock, upon whom Christ has chosen to build His faith-Church on the Earth. There are few who could look someone in the eyes as did Padre Pio and tell them the very day upon which they would endure their natural death; but he did it without ever stopping to ask God why. His presence was almost of the divination of our own urgency to seek the purging of our souls from anything that separates us from God; corporal, temporal, and intellectual. He did all of this, and yet was proclaimed to be one of the most jovial of all of God's disciples; happy to be alive in the Holy Spirit, and confident of the culmination of the entire universe under the concise direction of the Messiah on the Cross; that he would eventually set everything perfectly aright by the alignment of our temperament with the effectuation of his Holy Will.

It is worth quoting the evaluation of Father Carty in his book, *Padre Pio, The Stigmatist*, with regard to extraordinary manifestations. *"Miracles are a part of our supernatural gifts; they are free gifts which God gives to man as a manifestation of His omnipotence, of the divinity of Jesus Christ, and the Holiness of the Roman Catholic Church. I have said that a supernatural act is manifest to our senses. Well and good; but it must, however, have aspects which stupefy us with wonder, that strike us forcibly, and make us acknowledge Divine intervention. A miracle accepted by the Church must be instantaneous, such as; to resuscitate a corpse, to cure a sickness on the spot, to restore a missing limb, to restore sight, to multiply loaves and fishes, etc. I believe and maintain that in miracles, as in all things, there are varying kinds and degrees. Miracles are of the first degree when neither science nor natural law can be agencies, either in the present or in the future. They are, however, of the second degree when either science or natural law might, over a prolonged period, have accomplished the act, which in a miracle occurs instantaneously. There are also so-called intellectual miracles, such as true and sudden prophecy of the future, the knowledge of one or more languages that have never been studied, or the revelation of an unknown doctrine. Padre Pio has predicted events which have occurred. Speaking Italian, he has been understood by persons who spoke only some other language; he has answered questions regarding any speculation or school of philosophy. I will say, again, that the Father has brought about unexpected conversion of sinners. He reads their thoughts, for if they do not tell him the truth, or if they have forgotten some fact, or some circumstance, he describes it exactly, to the amazement of him who has come to him. I don't know what to call the action of keeping a person dry while it is raining in torrents, of warning him by means of his perfume or by his presence if he fails in his devotions; by predicting an approaching event, such as the sex of a child about to be born; by asserting that the finest water one could desire would be found by digging a well five meters from the new monastery of Pietrelcina, although he had never been to the site; of stating that he had aided by touch, the hand of a surgeon who was operating upon a cataract of the eyes to restore the sight of a woman blind for twenty-eight years...Enough, for if I continue to cite examples, I should never end."* (Chapter VI, pp. 120-121) Through this dissertation, Father Carty is asserting that the miracles which are attributed to Padre Pio meet the criteria both in the first and second degrees to satisfy the faith of the Roman Catholic Church. Indeed, the facts and the evidence speak quite profoundly for themselves. I have incorporated Padre Pio into this book of legends because his spirit is the inner-miracle that we should all be seeking; without having to summon the judgement of our inferiority to do it. What we make of our own faithfulness is assuredly found in the fact that we continue to trust in Jesus Christ without our ever walking into a mortuary and raising someone from the dead, or touching a dying patient in a hospice and having them ask to race us to the front door. The true miracle God is wielding through the likes of Padre Francesco Forgione Pio is that our trust and faith yields an equally miraculous fruit for ourselves; that of the power of the Holy Paraclete to intervene into the world through *any* venue He elects to employ. The greater gift from Heaven is not whether someone has the foresight to determine what sex a child will be prior to its birth, but to be given children in the first place. In reflection of the serious demeanor through which Padre Pio accepted his vocation to the priesthood, we become just as faithful and demanding of ourselves to accept the role that God has given us to play as followers, authors, and advocates in defining His Reign before the rest of humanity.

Father Carty stated it as plainly as anyone might regarding the special revelations that have been made to the Saints, *"...belief in them is not required by the Church, even when She approves them. By this approbation, She only intends to declare that nothing is to be found in them contrary to faith or morals, and that they can be accepted without danger and even with advantage...When the Church approves revelations, they are merely received as probable and not as indubitable. They are to be used as is customary in deciding questions of history, natural philosophy, or theology; which are matters of controversy between the doctors. It is quite permissible to differ with these revelations, even when approved, if we are relying upon solid reasons, and especially if the contrary doctrine is proved by unimpeachable documents and definite experience."* (*Declaration*, pp. xiii-xiv). This is the strict adherence by which Fathers Rumble and Carty observed, evaluated, and accepted the miracles surrounding the life of Padre Pio; placing their own reputations on the line to maintain their faith in everything God performed though his lifelong vocation. If these two holy men were willing to risk the fabric of their own esteem to ensure the good standing of Padre Pio before the mortal world, surely we can bow our heads before our Almighty Father and thank Him in-kind.

Dietrich Bonhoeffer, Prisoner
(1906-1945)

I generally maintain that if a person believes in God for the furtherance of seeking immortal life, it is better to allow them to become the best they can in that religion and not make too great an attempt at proselytizing them into my Roman Catholic faith; except in cases where someone goes completely out of their way to denigrate it. The writing of Dietrich Bonheoffer, the young German Protestant pastor who was imprisoned and executed by the Nazis in World War II, is one such extraordinary example. He was a very self-confident organizer of his thoughts who often examined the traditions of the Roman Catholic Church out-of-context and perverted their meaning before the rest of the world. However, in doing so, he allowed us to see that the living faith of Catholicism is more in communion with the Truth than the dimensionless assumptions of the Protestant Reformation.   For whatever reason, Bonhoeffer and his like thinkers refused to accept that human Salvation is a Holy Mass of Sacred Mysteries; holding-out instead for something more tangible they could grasp or see with their eyes. He was held inside a German prison camp during most of the war that was named the Tegel Detention Center, from where he wrote his many *Letters and Papers from Prison*, which have become quite the reading for millions of Protestants around the globe. The 1970 edition of the book, edited by Eberhard Bethge, to whom Bonhoeffer penned many of his letters about Christianity, includes most of his final philosophies about the mortal dilemma of human suffering. His reflections speak to the prospect that the Protestant Church often places an inordinate amount of emphasis upon how humankind is affected by the material world, as opposed to how we are called by the Holy Spirit to shape it into the likeness of Heaven, ourselves. Hence, he does not acknowledge the Divine presence of God in our everyday lives in the way that more charismatic Christians do. *"...God would have us know that we must live as men who manage our lives without him. The God who is with us is the God who forsakes us (Mark 15:34.) The God who lets us live in the world without the working hypothesis of God is the God before whom we stand continually. Before God and with God, we live without God. God lets himself be pushed out of the world onto the Cross. He is weak and powerless in the world, and that is precisely the way, the only way, in which he is with us and helps us. Matthew 8:17 makes it quite clear that Christ helps us, not by virtue of his omnipotence, but by virtue of his weakness and suffering."* (pp 360-361). This passage indicates that Dietrich Bonhoeffer did not fully understand what Jesus meant when He said that the world was seeing the Almighty Father when it saw Him. Christ was never weak or powerless; but, rather, He relinquished His Holy Will before our Divine Creator so as to be the likeness of humankind in its most perfect form. This is what He taught us through His example, and what He continues to expect from us today.

We must always try by whatever means at our disposal to accept that our initial responses are generally the most accurate in determining the conscience of our hearts; and this maxim holds true as we stand beside the universal Catholic and Apostolic Church of the original Disciples of Christ; the Apostles who became the first ordained Bishops. When people like Martin Luther and his Protestant followers, such as Dietrich Bonhoeffer, tried to intellectualize the mortality of man inside the parameters of some tangible definition, they discovered that God was unwilling to allow them to determine the conditions by which they would be saved or the characteristics that He requires from our faith. In essence, they wished not to allow God to *be* God. Oftentimes, there are so many misconceptions which distract our consciousness that we are too frail and tired to recognize the Truth when it hits us right in the face. Such is the dilemma of the observations, objections, and teachings of Bonhoeffer's Protestant Church. Therefore, his *Letters* are part of the greater error of the anti-Catholic movement at home and abroad; but he is a legend of human piety anyway because he was martyred for what he *did* believe. There was never a question that Christ would accept him into Heaven beyond his death; but there is also no doubt that He would assuredly ask Bonhoeffer why he stood-out in protest and opposition to His universal Church; which He knew all along would be led by sinners. The Protestant Reformation of the 16th century could boast of no members in their ranks who were absent of this same imperfection. I have included Bonhoeffer in my book because he had such a profound impact upon encouraging the persuasion of other people in simple Christian virtues, his recognition of the suffering of man, and those he led to the Cross who would otherwise have had no other venue in submitting to the judgement of God at all. Most non-Catholics do not even know what they are protesting anyway; they just realize that they do not understand all of the facets of living inside the Holy Arms of the Mother Church that well. Others, however, have chosen to be wilfully disobedient, citing the fact that there are six-billion people on the Earth and are not enough names to go around, so they choose one by which they can remain anonymous at the end of time, when Christ will ask those to stand forward who have persecuted, abandoned, and crucified the Catholic Church for hundreds of years before. Too bad for them though, because He will recognize them, nonetheless. The defeatism of the Protestant Church constantly keeps their heads lowered in hopelessness, unable to comprehend what it really means to live inside the fulness of the Light of the Paschal Resurrection. Why? Because not all of them wholly embrace the Cross, since they reject its presence in the Holy Sacrifice of the Mass. In the words of Bonhoeffer, himself, *"...the decisive factor is said to be that, in Christianity, the hope of Resurrection is proclaimed, and that that means the emergence of a genuine religion of Redemption, the main emphasis now being on the far side of the boundary drawn by death. But, it seems to me that this is just where the mistake and the danger lie. Redemption now means redemption from cares, distress, fears, and longings, from sin and death, in a better world beyond the grave. But, is this really the essential character of the proclamation of Christ in the Gospels and by Paul? I should say it is not... The Christian, unlike the devotees of the redemption myths, has no last line of escape available from earthly tasks and difficulties into the eternal; but, like Christ, himself ('My God, why hast thou forsaken me?'), he must drink the earthly cup to the dregs, and only in his doing so is the crucified and risen Lord with him, and he crucified and risen with Christ."* (pp. 336-337).

Here again, Bonhoeffer taught an entire generation of Protestants that it was useless to expect to be able to sip from the Cup of Eternal Salvation while still in mortal flesh. If only he would have taken his blinders off, he would have seen that this Chalice of Divine Peace and Joy is hoisted from the Altar of Sacrifice by the priests of the Catholic Church everyday, containing the Blood of the Crucified Son of God. The Holy Eucharist and the Cup of Jesus' Blood are both the past and the future; Good Friday and our everlasting life, having been conjoined by God and delivered to humankind during the Mass. If Bonhoeffer would have accepted this Truth, he would never have written with such despondence or lack of hope about what the anticipation of our immortal Resurrection really means. In rejecting the Seven Sacraments of the Catholic Church, Protestants refute in hapless decadence the command of Jesus to *"...be perfected as I am perfect;"* saying quietly to themselves, instead, "...I will never make it, so why should I even try?" And, yet, they are the first to deny the Sacred Heart of Jesus Christ as being the infinite source of Divine Mercy; as though it were some sort of violation to stand in contrition before His Altar and ask for forgiveness now. Our Lord is directing them into the confessional for the Sacrament of Reconciliation, but they keep turning a deaf ear to His call. Bonhoeffer's greatest lack of trust is revealed in these words. *"...I'm still discovering right up to this moment that it is only by living completely in this world that one learns to have faith. One must completely abandon any attempt to make something of oneself, whether it be a saint, or a converted sinner, or a churchman (a so-called priestly type!), a righteous man or an unrighteous one, a sick man or a healthy one. By this worldliness, I mean living unreservedly in life's duties, problems, successes and failures, experiences and perplexities. In doing so, we throw ourselves completely into the Arms of God, taking seriously not our own sufferings, but those of God in the world; watching with Christ in Gethsemane."* (pp. 369-370). Herein, he believes that only an inanimate faith will suffice and not our participation in proactive Love; the dispensation of the charitable Works of Mercy, attending Marian cenacles, praying the Holy Rosary, and the offering of thanksgiving alms. With all due respect to Mr. Bonhoeffer, Mother Teresa of Calcutta would have asked him to take a second look at the plight of the suffering poor before he decided not to perform the holy labors of a righteous man.

Some of the last remarks that Bonhoeffer ever made were whether we can scribe the destiny of our own faithful standing, asserting that we are not honest with ourselves if we presume to beseech God to make it greater through our metaphysical intentions, *"...We cannot, like the Roman Catholics, simply identify ourselves with the church. This, incidentally, explains the popular opinion about Roman Catholics' insincerity."* (p. 382). This is from the same Protestant who said that nothing we despise in other men is entirely absent from ourselves, and that we often expect more from them than we are willing to afford. Could it be that he was angry at God when he wrote his letters from his cell, ignoring the fact that Roman Catholics recognize the entire world to be a vast prison of horror and indifference before the Holy Paraclete who is trying to bring it to completion? Bonhoeffer should have remembered that the entire of humanity *is* the Church, Christ's Mystical Body; and this is what Catholics know to be in need of conversion. There is not a hint of insincerity in bringing this to pass. Indeed, it was by taking-up his own cross of suffering and imprisonment that Bonhoeffer was able to see more clearly how Jesus purifies the world; and millions of souls around the globe, including the very Catholics he disdained, will be forever grateful.

Thomas Merton, Author
(1915-1968)

I walked into the rectory of St. Augustine's Catholic Church in Ashland, Illinois on September 12, 1978 at the invitation of my pastor, (the late) Reverend Father Joseph Timothy Murray, and he asked me to take a seat in one of the guest chairs in the livingroom. We had been reflecting upon the recent death of Pope Paul VI and wondering what the Papacy of his successor, Pope John Paul I, would be like by comparison, since he had been elected only about two weeks prior. Father Murray handed me a paperback book entitled *A Thomas Merton Reader*, about a Trappist monk from Kentucky, which was edited by Thomas P. McDonnell. After telling me he would be right back, Father left the room and I opened the book he had just presented to me at random to page 182, where I read the following passage, *"...If ever there was a country where men loved comfort, pleasure, and material security, good health and conversation about the weather and the World Series and the Rose Bowl; if ever there was a land where silence made men nervous and prayer drove them crazy, and penance scared them to death, it is America."* The paragraph went on to say that in spite of these things, there are certain people in the United States who are willing to enter the religious vocation of becoming Trappist monks and living an otherwise austere mortal existence. Merton pondered why this might be the case by saying, *"...when you ask them why they have done such things, they may give you a very clear answer or, perhaps, only a rather confused answer; but in either case, the answer will amount to this;...the Trappist life was that which least resembled the life men lead in the towns and cities of our world. And, there is something in their hearts that tells them they cannot be happy in an atmosphere where people are looking for nothing but their own pleasure, advantage, comfort, and success. They have not come to the monastery to escape from the realities of life, but to find those realities; they have felt the terrible insufficiency of life in a civilization that is entirely dedicated to the pursuit of shadows."* It certainly did not take me long to figure out what Thomas Merton and Father Murray were both trying to tell me and the greater world through a not-so-subtle means at that very moment. I vowed thereafter that I would someday treat humanity to the impression that Merton had about America; and now, 24 years later, I have finally kept my promise. I hope and pray that he and Father Murray are looking down from the bounties of Heaven and realizing that our nation has not really changed that much from the materialistic approach we take to human life; if not factually having even gotten worse through time. There is no need to enter a biographical sketch of the life of Thomas Merton here because most everyone who knows anything about Christianity has either heard of him or read his spiritual works. He died in 1968 as the result of a rather bizarre accident in Bangkok, Thailand.

It was what Merton wrote for the rest of us that truly matters in the end, anyway; from his declarations against our strange penchant for materialism, his admonitions about the outright apostasies against the Roman Catholic Church, and our unsavory approach to morality and faith. As McDonnell put it; Thomas Merton wrote about everything from war, love, peace, Eastern thought and spirituality, monastic life, art, the Psalms, contemplation, and solitude. Therefore, we should remember him for teaching us that it is not uncivilized to address the agnosticism of our fellow humans and teach them through the powerful Wisdom of the Holy Spirit that the purpose of life is not the pursuit of fiscal wealth and temporal power. There has been no one yet to this day to say it as candidly as Merton, himself, *"...the fact that men spend so much time talking about nothing or telling each other the lies that they have heard from one another, or wasting their time in scandal and detraction and calumny and scurrility and ridicule shows that our minds are deformed with a kind of contempt for reality. Instead of conforming ourselves to what* is, *we twist everything around, in our words and thoughts, to fit our own deformity. The seat of this deformity is in the will. Although we still may speak the truth, we are more and more losing our desire to live according to the truth. Our wills are not true because they refuse to accept the laws of our own being; they fail to work along the lines demanded by our own reality. Our wills are plunged in false values, and they have dragged our minds along with them, and our restless tongues bear constant witness to the disorganization inside our souls(ff)."* (Chapter 7, p. 121, *Sincerity.*) It has been my prayer ever since, especially through the series of books I have written about post-modern Christianity, that more of us will acknowledge and accept the vision of such good souls as Thomas Merton; even though we do not have to become Trappist monks to do it. Did not Jesus tell us that it was for "sinners" that He came to the Earth to be Crucified? With all the justification we are trying to falsely claim before Him that we are living a righteous course in America today, would we not do better to walk a more selfless path toward the enlightenment of our own spiritualism?

Reverend Dr. Martin Luther King, Jr., Pastor
(1929-1968)

There is absolutely no way to confine the story of this legendary hero, the Reverend Martin Luther King, Jr., on a single page any more than it was possible for anyone to prohibit his indomitable spirit for freedom and love from escaping the parameters of his bountiful heart into the rest of Creation. This giant among men lived generations ahead of his time, and his stature has already complemented that of U.S. President Abraham Lincoln, Sir Winston Churchill, and the great African President, Nelson Mandela, as servant and statesman who championed the cause of human civil liberties around the globe. He lived in a 20th century which was steeped in bias, bigotry, and racism; but he challenged it head-on and became triumphant because he was a genius in the parables of God and implemented them to the purpose of setting not only those of his own color free, but also eradicating the blindness of those he was forced to confront along the way. He was awarded the Nobel Peace Prize in 1964 not for inciting riots or inflaming the rhetoric of an already divided American society, but by teaching that we are all worthy in the eyes of God through his placid expressions and exemplary love; rendering him a living disciple of Jesus Christ in the United States during the 1950s and 1960s. He was martyred by those who despise human decency and equality; so that the name of Martin Luther King has become equated with civil rights because he broke the back of our nation's own haughty arrogance. He was a catalyst who called for Americans in every state to live-out the meaning of our Constitution and our faith in God, alike. Up close, he was as gently benign as were his many pleading and eloquent speeches; from the pulpit to the secular platform, and from the prayer room to the outdoor theatre. Dr. King is remembered most for his *I Have A Dream* speech, which he delivered before the Lincoln Memorial in Washington D.C. on August 28, 1963 because he referred both presently and to the future with hope and with the promise that he knew that our great nation would become all it was meant to be from its very foundation in 1776. He was a masterful communicator and orator because he spoke from the depths of his soul; he saw clearly, beseeched humbly, prayed profoundly, loved dearly, and suffered deeply. How else could a single man inspire a nation of such pride to bow before the Truth and set the sights of its people on the newer horizon of social justice thereon?

Reverend King walked arm-in-arm with those who only wished to break free from the chains that bound them into class-slavery, those who wanted to breach the loathsome imprisonment of hatred which kept African-Americans from realizing the true meaning of our Declaration of Independence and the First 10 Amendments' Bill of Rights. Indeed, there would be world-wide repercussions in the wake of the vision of this elegant man, as he inspired other international republics to review the decency and civility of their own judicious poise. He advanced the freedom of millions of black Americans who could thereafter pursue their own dreams in the aftermath of a national nightmare of hatred because he owned the strength, wisdom, and perseverance to hope for them when they had all but given up for themselves, and even for those who were yet too young to know the traps that the earlier decades had set for them once they came into their age. His desire was not to make a mark on history, but to set it free from the bigotry and dire straits into which the progeny of his entire race were being birthed. The indignity and injustice that held America captive for every generation theretofore was ended because this holy man saw fit to engage the traditions of an uninformed U. S. public through the effective amendment of our earlier laws and the enactment of many ameliorative new ones. President Lyndon Johnson signed the Civil Rights Act of 1964 because of the direct service, intercession, and optimism of Martin Luther King. His approach was toward prioritizing and implementing a peaceful transition of equality inside America by appealing to our senses of decency and trust, both of which finally betrayed him by failing to protect him from being assassinated at the hands of a disgruntled rifleman on April 4, 1968. But, before he died, Dr. King seized every opportunity to speak some of the most prophetic words ever uttered by a mortal man, telling us what a great nation we were, and what a better one we ultimately had to become. His poetic phrases and inspiring dissertations brought tears to the eyes of those who had a desire for peace and an intrinsic obedience to the Will of God. He stood on the right side of human history because he was inspirited by the sovereign Love of Jesus Christ; not by a brash defiance, as his movement was so often errantly described.

If there would be violence and unrest amid the peaceful persuasions of Dr. King, it was certainly not of his part and nothing of his doing. Many were the times when his Southern Baptist churches were set afire and burned to the ground; but their charred remains would only cause his movement to become the new phoenix of its age. Hundreds of Negro people were taken hostage, tortured, and killed because the other races in America refused to love them; not knowing all along that the God of Abraham was on the side of those who were being persecuted, maimed, and impaled. The presence of these things only made the righteousness of Reverend King all the more attractive to pious people everywhere, and to the millions who were fortunate to hear his words in person, via television and radio waves, and in the printed medium. Perhaps the most endearing of all these were stated from the pulpit of the Ebenezer Baptist Church on December 24, 1967, which would be the last Christmas that the world would ever see the likes of Dr. Martin Luther King. It is from the excerpts of this speech that we sense the loving dignity and powerful holiness which made him, through his own clement determination, one of the seminal visionaries of all modern history. *"...How can one avoid being depressed when one sees with one's own eyes evidences of millions of people going to bed hungry at night? How can one avoid being depressed when one sees with one's own eyes thousands of people sleeping on the sidewalks at night? More than a million people sleep on the sidewalks of Bombay every night; more than half-a-million sleep on the sidewalks of Calcutta every night. They have no houses to go into. They have no beds to sleep in. As I beheld these conditions, something within me cried out; 'Can we in America stand idly by and not be concerned?' And, an answer came; 'Oh no!' And, I started thinking about the fact that right here in our country we spend millions of dollars every day to store surplus food; and I said to myself, 'I know where we can store that food free of charge; in the wrinkled stomachs of the millions of God's children in Asia, Africa, Latin America, and even in our own nation who go to bed hungry at night. It really boils down to this; that all life is interrelated. We are all caught in an inescapable network of mutuality, tied into a single garment of destiny. Whatever affects one directly, effects all indirectly. We are made to live together because of the interrelated structure of reality."* This is the same unavoidable truth which hits us in the face today; but too many of us turn away, pretending that such conditions no longer exist anymore. It was Dr. King's concern for the poor that led him to speak in such an admonishing tone in 1967, and we should continue to heed his words in the 21st century. We disliked the message back then, so we killed the messenger outright in order to silence him. Is this not, too, what we did to Jesus Christ? This Divine Love is what made Martin Luther King and the Son of God almost inseparable before the eyes of the world; for in that same speech, he said, *"...the Greek language talks about 'philia,' which is another word for love, and philia is a kind of intimate love between personal friends. This is the kind of love you have for those people that you get along with well, and those whom you like on this level you love because you are loved. Then, the Greek language has another word for love, and that is the word 'agape.' Agape is more than romantic love, it is more than friendship. Agape is understanding, creative, redemptive good will toward all men. Agape is an overflowing love which seeks nothing in return.*

Theologians would say that it is the love of God operating in the human heart. When you rise to love on this level, you love all men not because you like them, not because their ways appeal to you, but you love them because God loves them. This is what Jesus meant when he said, 'Love your enemies.'...I've seen too much hate to want to hate, myself; and I've seen hate on the faces of too many sheriffs, too many white citizens' councilors, and too many Klansmen of the South to want to hate, myself; and every time I see it, I say to myself, hate is too great a burden to bear. Somehow, we must be able to stand-up before our most bitter opponents and say, 'We shall match your capacity to inflict suffering by our capacity to endure suffering. We will meet your physical force with soul force. Do to us what you will and we will still love you. We cannot in all good conscience obey your unjust laws and abide by the unjust system, because noncooperation with evil is as much a moral obligation as cooperation with good; and so throw us in jail and we will still love you. Bomb our homes and threaten our children, and, as difficult as it is, we will still love you. Send your hooded perpetrators of violence into our communities at the midnight hour, and drag us out on some wayside road and leave us half-dead as you beat us, and we will still love you. Send your propaganda agents around the country, and make it appear that we are not fit, culturally and otherwise, for integration, and we'll still love you. But, be assured that we'll wear you down by our capacity to suffer, and one day we will win our freedom. We will not only win freedom for ourselves; we will so appeal to your heart and conscience that we will win you in the process, and our victory will be a double victory."

Herein, we listened to the modern imagery and Passion of the Love of Jesus Christ aboard the Holy Spirit from within the heart of Martin Luther King. We are blessed to have known him as our example of such perfection; not only that he summoned it from himself, but that he also humbly sought it from others, as well. While the expulsion of racial segregation will be the hallmark of our tribute in remembering him, it was his Christian love that made his commission from God complete. He ended his speech that Christmas Eve in hoping for Jesus' return by saying, *"It will be a glorious day, the morning stars will sing together, and the sons of God will shout for joy."*

Robert Francis Kennedy, Servant
(1925-1968)

"...The great challenge to all Americans—indeed to all free men and women—is to maintain loyalty to truth; to maintain loyalty to free institutions; to maintain loyalty to freedom as a basic human value, and above all else, to keep in our hearts and minds the tolerance and mutual trust that have been the genius of American life throughout our history." With these prophetic words from a speech he delivered to the National Conference of Christians and Jews Dinner in Cleveland, Ohio on December 3, 1961, Robert Kennedy took a stance which he would never compromise; that the United States has the responsibility to maintain the consistency of honesty and integrity by seeking the Truth of God; a vision that would take him on a vast journey across America and around the globe. When Lou Rawls, Gary Morris, and Bette Midler sang their individual renditions of the popular song *Wind Beneath My Wings*, they surely could not have known that they were unwittingly telling the story of Bobby Kennedy, brother of the 35th President of the United States, John F. Kennedy. Bobby produced the picturesque wisdom and protocol behind his brother, and served not only as his chief advisor, campaign strategist, and Attorney General; he was also his counselor, comrade, companion, and friend. There would have been no Kennedy to have ever been elected to the White House without the unparalleled talents of RFK; for it was his calculatingly cool and studious labors that allowed his brother to defeat Vice-President Richard Nixon in November 1960. Indeed, as close as that election was, Nixon would have won if not for the "Bobby factor" that JFK wielded from his camp. However, Bobby Kennedy was more than a keen intellectual planner, he was also a servant to the American people, to the departments of our government, to the poor, and to Almighty God. He stood the day after Martin Luther King, Jr. was assassinated in April 1968 as he was seeking the Democratic nomination for president in his own right before another crowd gathered in Cleveland and stated the obvious, *"...no one, no matter where he lives or what he does, can be certain whom next will suffer from some senseless act of bloodshed."* And, while there were undoubtedly several anonymous and less-heralded people shot and killed from that day forward, he would become the next national figure to be murdered in front of a national audience after having just won the California primary election the following June.

Bobby Kennedy will forever be remembered as the fighter for the rights of the impoverished, for social justice, for world peace, and for the restoration of decency and civility in public discourse; in the arts and entertainment, and in our responsibilities to one another before God. Many were the times when he and Martin Luther King, Jr. would accidently encounter each other at an airport, engaged shoulder-to-shoulder in the same battle against the evil and complacency that was trying to bring America to its knees. But, in no more than a flash, they were both dead and gone, and our nation continued down its perilous course to arrive at the brink of a new century much the poorer for facing their loss. They were near equal in their prose and eloquence; and they both spread a legacy of humanitarian love all across this land, alongside the pools of blood they shed by assassin's bullets in their efforts to prove it. One might say that Bobby Kennedy owned a better venue for taking his message to the people and into the world because he had served in his brother's national government, he was elected to the U.S. Senate in 1964; and he would assuredly have been the Democratic nominee for president in 1968, had he not been gunned-down so soon. But, Bobby accomplished plenty during his brief span of years, and left a profound message that most wealthy people in our country cast-off as being unworthy of their valuable time. But, the poor, the outcast, disenfranchised, and minorities heard what he said to the depth of their beings. If they could not find a way to come to hear him in person, he would travel to be with them. He saw the world with intense scrutiny for what humanity had made of it; and he wanted to bring change where there was social intolerance, starvation, and disease. He was the 1960s version of former President Jimmy Carter; circling the globe seeking reconciliation between enemies, aid for the indigent, and new beginnings in nations grown stagnant by latent civil wars, tribal disputes, and state-sponsored terrorism. There is no doubt that his most popular speech was given at the University of Capetown, South Africa, for their Day of Affirmation on June 6, 1966; precisely two years before he died. It was so popular locally and around the world that his sole surviving brother, Senator Edward M. Kennedy, made it a part of his funeral eulogy during the Roman Catholic High Requiem Mass at St. Patrick's Cathedral prior to Bobby's internment in Arlington National Cemetery on June 9, 1968.

To place his speech to the South African students into perspective that day in 1966, Bobby Kennedy told them, *"...in a few hours, the plane that brought me to this country crossed over oceans and countries which have been a crucible of human history. In minutes, we traced the migration of men over thousands of years; seconds, the briefest glimpse, and we passed battlefields on which millions of men once struggled and died. We could see no national boundaries, no vast gulfs or high walls dividing people from people; only nature and the works of man—homes and factories and farms—everywhere reflecting man's common effort to enrich his life. Everywhere, new technology and communications bring men and nations closer together, the concerns of one inevitably becoming the concern of all. And, our new closeness is stripping away the false masks, the illusion of difference which is at the root of injustice and hate and war. Only earthbound man still clings to the dark and poisoning superstition that his world is bounded by the nearest hill, his universe ended at river shore, his common humanity enclosed in the tight circle of those who share his town and views, and the color of his skin. It is your job, the task of the young people of this world, to strip the last remnants of that ancient, cruel belief from the civilization of man."* I submit that speeches such as this should be required reading for memorization in every schoolroom in America today; and not the liberal arts of skewering the sacred images of religious icons, not teaching adolescents how to safely have sex, and not preparing them for inevitable interpersonal competition and international secularism. It was for teaching unprecedented human responsibility that Bobby Kennedy lived and died; and we are desecrating his legacy if we refuse to carry-on the fight against greed and avarice in his stead. He spoke far and wide about ending the war in Viet Nam, challenging children and adults, alike, to see the world through the eyes of the suffering and less-fortunate. He said that he was unilaterally opposed to Marxism and Communism because it exalts the state over the individual and the family, and because of its lack of freedom of speech, of protest, of religion and of the press; which is characteristic of all totalitarian states. He also said that the best way to oppose it is to enlarge individual freedom; a struggle that ultimately took him to his death—because he saw the lack of freedom in more than just Communism—but in the United States as well. To him, anyone who had no food to eat or anyplace to sleep in America was not truly free. He once complained that we collectively purchased eight million cars a year, and then drove past ghettos where people were unable to afford any shoes. Let his words be our guide to a new beginning for which he and thousands of others have died.

"There is discrimination in this world, and slavery and slaughter and starvation. Governments repress their people, millions are trapped in poverty while the nation grows rich, and wealth is lavished on armaments everywhere. These are differing evils, but they are the common works of man. They reflect the imperfection of human justice, the inadequacy of human compassion, our lack of sensibility towards the suffering of our fellows. But, we can perhaps remember,

even if only for a time, that those who live with us are our brothers, that they share with us the same short moment of life, that they seek as we do nothing but the chance to live-out their lives in purpose and happiness, winning what satisfaction and fulfillment they can. Surely this bond of common faith, this bond of common goals, can begin to teach us something. Surely we can learn, at least, to look at those around us as fellow men. And, surely we can begin to work a little harder to bind-up the wounds among us, and to become in our own hearts brothers and countrymen once again. The answer is to rely on youth, not a time of life, but a state of mind, a temper of the will, a quality of imagination, a predominance of courage over timidity, of the appetite for adventure over the love of ease; for the cruelties and obstacles of this swiftly changing planet will not yield to the obsolete dogmas and outworn slogans; they cannot be moved by those who cling to a present that is already dying, who prefer the illusion of security to the excitement and danger that comes with even the most peaceful progress. It is a revolutionary world we live in, and this generation at home and around the world has had thrust upon it a greater burden of responsibility than any generation that has ever lived. Some believe there is nothing one man or one woman can do against the enormous array of the world's ills. Yet, many of the world's great movements of thought and action have flowed from the work of a single man. A young monk began the Protestant Reformation, a young general extended an empire from Macedonia to the borders of the Earth, a young woman reclaimed the territory of France, and it was a young Italian explorer who discovered the New World, and a thirty-two-year-old Thomas Jefferson who claimed that all men are created equal. These men moved the world, and so can we all. Few will have the greatness to bend history, itself, but each of us can work to change a small portion of events; and in the total of all those acts will be written the history of this generation. Each time a man stands up for an ideal or acts to improve the lot of others, or strikes-out against injustice, he sends-forth a tiny ripple of hope. And, crossing each other from a million different centers of energy and daring, those ripples build a current that can sweep down the mightiest walls of oppression and resistance. Few are willing to brave the disapproval of their fellows, the censure of their colleagues, the wrath of their society. Moral courage is a rarer commodity than bravery in battle, or great intelligence. Yet, it is the one essential, vital quality for those who seek to change a world that yields most painfully to change. And, I believe that in this generation, those with the courage to enter the moral conflict will find themselves with companions in every corner of the globe. For the fortunate among us, there is the temptation to follow the easy and familiar paths of personal ambition and financial success, so grandly spread before those who enjoy the privilege of education; but that is not the road history has marked-out for us. Like it or not, we live in times of danger and uncertainty, but they are also more open to the creative energy of men than any other time in history. All of us will ultimately be judged; and as the years pass, we will surely judge ourselves on the effort we have contributed to building a new world society, and the extent to which our ideals and goals have shaped that event. Our future may lie beyond our vision, but it is not completely beyond our control. It is the shaping impulse of America that neither fate nor nature, nor the irresistible tides of history, but the work of our own hands, matched to reason and principle, that will determine our destiny. There is pride in that, even arrogance; but there is also experience and truth. In any event, it is the only way we can live."

These words flowed from the sincere heart of a person who could sense the wide chasm between the present condition of the world through the blindness of humanity and the Earth as it might have been with the fuller vision of a more benevolent people. The tone of his voice was one of a beggar, almost weeping to get us to focus our attention on the needs of the ignorant and those who had only little to claim. He was his own best critic; someone who knew that Creation had to be challenged to be better, because that is what God has called us to do all the way from the summit of Mount Sinai to the foot of the Cross on which His Only Begotten Son laid-down His life to save us. There is no doubt that the same Holy Spirit who lived inside the conscience of Martin Luther King also guided Bobby Kennedy; to shape his thoughts, to choose his words, to inspire his devotions, and to place him head-to-toe before crowds of thousands to hear what he had to say. From the Berlin Wall to the streets of San Francisco, Bobby Kennedy's main purpose seemed to be the search for social justice and personal equality among all men. When he lost a primary election in the Pacific Northwest in 1968 and was asked why it may have happened, and what it felt like to be the first Kennedy to lose such a race, he said *"...it was because I just did not do well enough; I have no one else to blame but myself,"* refusing to criticize his opponents or adopt any pretense that would somehow shift the burden of responsibility to someone else. We recall the scene at the August 1964 Democratic convention when he was asked to speak for the first time since the assassination of his brother, the President, the previous November. He stood before a cheering crowd of tens of thousands of admirers who knew him for who he was; holding his head with such humility that the walls in this largest convention hall of all time even seemed to take a bow before the platform upon which he was standing. The ovation lasted almost fourteen minutes before he was forced to begin the opening remarks of his speech anyway; trying to be heard amidst the clapping palms and hailing voices of those who loved him. He stood for almost a quarter of an hour while the convention delegates had *their* say about the life and legacy of Bobby Kennedy and the late President for whom he was now asked to speak; and for all the goodness they both brought to the poorest of America's poor; its senior citizens, the mentally impaired, and racial minorities. In their own particular way, the delegates that night played the part of God's angels in lauding this humble prince of peace, whose life and likeness of Jesus Christ was almost too uncanny to describe. Like any other mortal man, he was a sinner who had his faults; but he was also a monumental hero to those who espoused human dignity and the renewal we celebrate in the Resurrection of Our Savior at Easter Sunrise every year. He thought we could surely do something to bind-up our nation's wounds, even as he stood before a massive convention center while still grieving the loss of his older brother and an heroic leader of everyday working men.

     Can we rediscover this new America that the likes of Bobby Kennedy saw for the future? Do we possess the proper combination of realism and hope to make our country united again? The problems that confront us in the 21st century are a great deal like those from 40 years ago; for we still have people sleeping on the downtown sidewalks and eating out of restaurant dumpsters. African-Americans are still denied equal access to the voting booth, as we saw in the 2000 presidential election. The elderly are being forced into deeper poverty because the suppliers of their medication have decided that billions of dollars is not a sufficient amount of profit for them to retain for themselves. It is a mystery that the Cold War ended without a single brick being knocked down in America by those with whom we disagreed; and yet, September 11, 2001 will forever be the dividing line between what we previously thought to be domestic security and the wariness by which we must now live. As Bobby Kennedy would say to us now; "...go make peace with your enemies, and you will live in peace again." As Edward Kennedy said at his brother's funeral, *"...that is the way he lived, and that is what he leaves us."* This must be what kept ringing through the hearts and minds of the millions of Americans who mourned his loss in June 1968, just like they agonized over the assassination of his brother. Soon after he was shot, the coffin containing Bobby Kennedy's body was placed inside a railroad car with glass windows and taken from New York to Washington for his memorial services and burial. While many of us were yet young people at the time, we can still remember the camera shots of that sleek blue locomotive making its way ever so carefully through the downtown depots and burrows where he used to stop and speak so kindly to his constituents there. As the train quietly disappeared into the distance where the tracks seemed to conjoin, it was as though our hopes vanished almost as inexorably into oblivion as did the car bearing his remains. People stood by the thousands alongside the rails, waving American flags; veterans saluting, women holding their children in tears, Boy Scouts standing at attention, and the poor souls for whom he had lived holding their faces in their hands and weeping unashamedly at the loss of one of their dearest friends. When we ponder that it was only two months prior that America was forced to part with another of its greatest civil rights heroes, Martin Luther King, Jr., and now having to say goodbye to one of the most compassionate Christians to ever draw the breath of life, we wonder whether the essential agony and violence of America had finally bitten two of the greatest outspoken patriots to ever stand up and fight. The irony of all ironies will always live inside America; as we produce men of good will and sound vision, only to see them stalked by their fellow citizens, hate-mongers, and deranged villains who cannot see past their own bigotry to hope for a better world. We can always pray that we did not inter our better future into the graves of such American heroes as Abraham Lincoln, John and Robert Kennedy, and Martin Luther King, Jr.. Does it seem too inappropriate to say that they were all martyred because they possessed the inherent decency that is still lacking in this world? Would it be too much to ask an American society and the rest of the nations to remember what these thoughtful men stood for, when they could have just as easily spent their lives comfortably sitting at their own tables at home and reading the news of the day, instead of making it? Were the *Pieces of April* that Danny Hutton, Chuck Negron, and Cory Wells of Three Dog Night sang about in 1972 all that was left of the hopes of our African-American friends when Martin Luther King was killed during that month just four years before? Bobby Kennedy knew all too well that hope springs from keeping our aspirations alive; a noble task which has been espoused by only a few since him, not the least of which has been the Reverend Jesse Jackson. But, we do not seem to hear much about such social values anymore. Our leaders seem to be more interested in taking office for the purpose of enriching themselves, effecting a new career for their children, and for making a mark on history that elevates their own legacy in the minds of the affluent. Back when Bobby Kennedy was running for the Democratic nomination for president, he was no stranger to the ghettos where he visited because he had been there before to lift-up their people many times. He never once made an appearance someplace to feign some false affection or to get a photographer to take his picture for the cover of *Vanity Fair*. He simply wished to hold office so he could make the laws of America more equitable for those they disavowed. He once posed a poignant question to a group of white people during a speech by asking, "*...who among us would be willing to change the color of our skin?*" In essence, who would be willing to walk in the shoes of those who were sent away from institutions of higher learning because their parents could ill-afford to send them to the private preparatory schools that made most white people more competitive for entry into their doors? Bobby Kennedy wished to know which ordinary Caucasian citizens would volunteer to be scorned and ridiculed as being somehow personally and socially deficient because they were different from everyone else in the neighborhood. This was a war he was willing to wage; and one that we need to prosecute in our own time.

When speaking about our international neighbors and our participation in foreign conflicts, he referred to our indignance by saying, "*...I'm not blaming them; I am blaming myself, and I am blaming you,*" as he stood before a crowd of undecided Americans as to whether we should fight the reigns of the dictators who were continuing to oppress their peoples. The point he was making, and one we should consider today, is that we should not enter a war in a foreign land just because it is convenient for our own political gain or to protect only the nations with whom we are allied; we should fight for the freedom of every individual who lives on the same earthen planet he looked down upon from that airplane on his way to Capetown University that day. Indeed, his vision was as elevated as the ship in which he was flying. Our task in remembering his service to the lands he left behind is to make the difference he could not make, and knowing that his sad departing was not a tragedy in vain.

Thomas A. Lock, Humbly His
(1928-1996)

One could travel to the most contemporary libraries in the largest cities in America, search through the National Archives, study the World Almanac, and even scour the files at the Library of Congress, and he would likely not be able to find the works of Thomas A. Lock; who lived his latter years in a public housing authority senior citizens' highrise in Springfield, Illinois. He was an ordinary man who paid his rent on time, performed his societal courtesies promptly, said his prayers faithfully, and went to bed at night in hopeful anticipation that he would see the Face of Jesus Christ before the dawn of another day. This was him; a man who was asked by God to walk with crutches in order to perambulate, who placed it all into perspective through the purview of the Cross, and practically pleaded his heart-out for our Divine Creator to finally purify and cleanse the Earth, once and for all. The most compelling aspect of the life of Thomas Lock was that his commonness was exemplary, that he had worked in community service most of his life, and he was a quiet author and poet of some of the most profound and beatific Christian apologetics of anyone who ever lived. Someday, the entire world will recognize his name alongside the Frosts, the Poes, the Hawthornes, and the Longfellows. It may be 50 years in coming, but our great-grandchildren's children will someday study the rhythmic meters of Thomas Lock; and they will revel his name in every literature class and amphitheater from Stockholm to Peoria. Historians will try to find the home of his birthplace and wish to spend millions of dollars restoring it for future posterity. Why? Because this prayerful soul left in his absence a gift that not many men bequeath to the rest of the world; a collection of personally inscribed spiritual sentiments which serve to glorify Jesus Christ the way He was always meant to be praised.

A good friend of mine and writer of the *Preface* for this book, Timothy Parsons-Heather, met Thomas Lock while he was working as an apartment manager for the Springfield Housing Authority in 1995. And, it was through Timothy that I met Mr. Lock. We were sitting in Timothy's administrative offices one day and Thomas came in to make sure his financial records were accurate for the paying of his rent; since the amount was based on a percentage of his income; and he wanted to ensure that he reported every penny of it so as to pay his fair share of the bills. Once a year, each tenant is required to visit the office for the reassessment of their rental payment, to recalculate it for income adjustments, and the like. Mr. Lock was quite prompt to appear, even before he was summoned, so as not to leave any hint of impropriety on his part in the mind of anyone else. For his honesty, sincerity, tranquil humility, the respect he showed to those he knew, and even to perfect strangers now and then; and for caring enough about God and humanity to compose the meditations of his heart onto the written page, Thomas A. Lock will always be a legend and a giant of Americana, a noble representative of Christian faith, a teacher of compassion and discretion, and a gentleman to the tee. It was quite easy for me to recognize these traits of perfection in him, and they shined brightly that cool autumn day while we were sitting in Mr. Parsons-Heather's office. He was holding some sort of a tablet in his hands when we saw him, and asked if we would like to have a copy of his poetry. He knew that Timothy and I were about to release a couple of new books on our own in the not-too-distant future. We casually responded that we would be honored to have a copy of his writing, just to be nice to him at the time. We thought it might be the kind of amateurish work that older people usually scribble onto a stenographer's pad or the end of an old envelope. But, when he showed us what he had done, we were taken far aback and pleasantly by surprise. Thomas had typewritten his poetry and prose neatly onto sixteen plain-bond white pages, with all the margins just right, the punctuation in order, his paragraphs perfectly formed, and each piece signed underneath with his trademark, "HUMBLY HIS, Thomas A. Lock," making certain that the former was always in upper-case letters. He even had a hand-drawn picture of his crutches on the cover which were shaped into a "plus" sign, and a shadow of the Cross of Jesus Christ on the surface behind them as though there was a bright light shining toward them or rays from the sun hitting them on the top of a hill. This was his metaphor for telling the world that he had accepted his portion of human suffering in the image and likeness of the Son of God who was Crucified to redeem his mortal soul.

There was also a heading on the front of his booklet which was a verse taken from the Holy Bible, Romans, Chapter 8:37 which said, "...*We are more than conquerors through Him Who loved us,*" written in his own layman's penmanship. He also cited the Book of John 6:63,64 on the bottom of the cover which he had carefully inscribed with his typewriter, "...*It is the Spirit that gives Life; the flesh profits nothing. The words that I speak to you, they are Spirit and Life. But, there are some of you who do not believe.*" Thomas did not seem to be feeling very well that day, although he was not reluctant to tell us how he felt. He handed his pretty poetry to us without a lick of pride; only seeming to hope that we would in some subtle way show him that we approved. It was what he did next that nearly broke our hearts. He said that he would not live long enough to ever get them published, and could have never afforded it anyway; and he knew that we had done a great deal of such planning on our own. He asked us in the most childlike demeanor if we would tell the rest of the world what he would never have time to reveal; wishing that we would someday share his writings with humanity at large, and hoping it would lead just one other soul to the Blood of Jesus Christ. I thought to myself when looking upon this humble man that if everyone on the Earth would approach the Altar of God with the same beseeching love that was pouring from his heart, there would never again be a single soul ever pass through the gates of Hell. I shall not forget it; that day of October 19, 1995, because it was one of the few times in my life I had ever felt like I was in the direct presence of a living Saint; except this particular Thomas was certainly no "doubting" one, and never had to place his hands in Jesus' Sacred Wounds to recognize Him through his faith. So, the opportunity arose for me to keep my promise to Thomas Lock that day when I planned the outline for this book; as I knew that I would place him in this section where I have honored some of the greatest men to ever live; and this one was very special to me. I have not yet been able to trace-down his surviving family members or to work-out the copyrights for his citations, but I hope to do so someday soon and, with their assistance and blessing, compile a separate booklet entitled, *"The Complete Poetry and Prose of Thomas A. Lock."* I have placed one of his poems hereafter, just as I told him I would in October 1995.

On Milton's Sight!

"They also serve who only stand and wait"
Who serve The Lord with Holy Love so great,
Who understand The Word in Spiritual measure,
Who thank The Lord for His Heavenly Treasure,
For life, Love, and hope eternally born
To rise above conditions others mourn
To find a purpose in all worldly stances
Through Spirit-filled prayer The Lord enhances!   8
Some see the handicapped through eyes of pity,
Hopeless without a place in society;
Yet, strengthened by the soul's Holy Fire,
We meet the tests that Heaven does require,

Humble, faithful, Loving each worldly day,
Giants among people the Eternal Way,
Living by faith in life's barricaded road,
Adjusting life's problems to Heaven's Sure Code!   16
If the way seems so impossible to tread,
Remember the words that Jesus said:
"Love the Lord with all your heart, mind, and soul,
And love your neighbor as yourself," Loves Goal!
In this way, you acquire self-worth and respect,
A place in the world all persons expect!
According to our means, serve the Lord
And others! The Lord shall bountifully reward!   24
Maybe all you can give is a soul's sweet smile
Of Love and concern along life's weary mile!
Yet, give, and it shall be given to you
By the Lord, for His promises are true!
By giving, a blessing you shall receive,
And others' problems you shall truly relieve!
Accept His Love, and then you shall know
Heaven's Treasure of Love within you shall grow!   32
The Lord's greatest gift of success
Shall be yours, your own life to bless
And flow to others, a Christian Light,
A beacon to some poor soul's blind sight:
The miracle of salvation for one to attain,
The reconciliation in Christ Jesus without one stain!
Holy Lord and God Above,
Bless this soul with Holy Love!   40

Thank Thee, Lord,
For Thy Word!

HUMBLY HIS,
Thomas A. Lock

Part Three
The Universal Mandate of Christ

Chapter Seven
Forgiveness, Harmony, and Reparation

After having briefly recounted the lives of these great many legendary heroes, we discover that everything they had in common revolved around God and His infinite goodness; and specifically their allegiance to His Triune Deity. Their desire for the restoration of the dignity of each individual person on the Earth stemmed from their own inclusive perception of humankind as a whole; rich and poor, foreign and domestic, friend and enemy, alike. They knew that this would eventually become the universal mandate of Christ for all men. It made sense that they suffered in His likeness because, like all other Christians, they espoused the same highly apocalyptic virtues; and, in this particular mortal world, there is a peculiarly high price to pay for such precocious foresight, intense benevolence, and receptive faith. Hardly any two of the religious icons whose memories were celebrated in the last chapter came from the same walk of life; and yet, each of them took great strides toward the unified goal of perceiving their Creator as He truly is; through the Most Blessed Trinity and, more specifically, within the embowering protection of the Calvarian Cross. The expanse of the centuries and generations of everyone who has accepted Christianity as their chosen belief is as timeless as the mission of perfect love of those who aspire to profess it; apparent in our actions, teachings, writings, oratories, and posthumous legacies. Do the greatest among us, therefore, not require that everyone embark on our own personal relationship with God this same way; by fusing our distinct and charismatic pathways into one supreme excellence? If we generate a massively spiritual and theological catholicity which is in full alignment with the Mother Church, does this not make us apostles, too? If we emulate the greatest love that any mortal could ever muster from the center of our hearts and live-out every waking moment in synchronicity with the wishes of the Pope in Rome and the Magisterium, will we not also be granted admission into the same Heaven to which he and each of the legends I have heretofore mentioned so uniquely ascribed? There is no doubt that, if we do, God will hail us as being geniuses in their lineage; for we will become the new poets, contemplatives, presiders, visionaries, and spiritual doctors of the 21st century Messianic movement; taking-up where they left-off in ensuring that the entire message of human Redemption in the Cross of Mount Calvary never pales.

This is what I have tried to accomplish in the ensuing chapters of *Part Three* of this book; to attempt to make the case for Jesus Christ through my own distinctive means, while praying deeply and devotedly for the guidance and wisdom of the Holy Paraclete to give me strength to provide the imagery I need to succeed and mold my message into a synopsis of parables and phraseologies that will help America better understand what is expected from us by God. There are countless ways that nature and our intrinsic intelligence try to wheedle us into a more concise understanding of the mysteries of Creation, but we inadvertently do our worst to keep them at bay, holding-out instead for a life which is filled with empty promises and reclusive meanings. This is why Christianity seems so opaquely theoretic, rather than socially advantageous and materially practical. It is also why the tenets of our faith defy nearly every sense of capitalistic logic by which we live in the free world today. We speak about the relentless pursuit of the origin of life's defining meaning, but often scoff at the God-like perception required to allow us to discover it. Therefore, I have made it the purpose of this chapter as another step in explicating the thesis of where I think our hearts and emotions should go next; not that it will make all that much difference in determining who we are amid the contextual societies of the Earth or from whence we may have earlier been conceived, but as a precursor to our transfiguration from our blandly pragmatic rituals to our more refined spiritual calling. The evolution of our interpersonal relationships upon which Christ has placed so much emphasis is centered around how we perceive one another as third-millennium people; articulate, honest, sincere, advanced, and telegenic. Can it really be true that we have arrived at the brink of creating another human person through the cloning of an existing one, as though we can somehow replicate what God has already done? The larger question to which we are directed is neither how nor when, but why? Have we so relinquished our hope for God to heal us that we feel forced to develop an expendable bloc of identical *Homo sapiens* to do it ourselves? Let us consider such larger questions while responding to our desires for societal advancement, extreme mortal longevity, and our endless search for Truth; remembering well the caution we have received from the greatest mortal beings the world may have ever known; not the least of which are those whose biographies appeared in the preceding chapter. It was not through the ancient philosophers or our Precambrian ancestors that our modern-day world has come of age, but through the officious revelation of Divine logic found inside the Sacred Heart of Christ. If not for His lessons and teachings, and the Blood of Redemption from His Veins, we would still be beating our tunics on rocks to clean them and pulling our female companions around by the hair.

Aristotle, Socrates, and Plato knew only what the stars and the physical Earth allowed them to discern, and nothing about the God-Man who would eventually ratify their immortality and free their souls from the grave. Unlike them, we must realize that human existence is not as unscientifically abstruse or metaphysical as our philosophical counterparts would have us believe; for they did not know to turn *toward* one another instead of against each other to achieve an ideal purpose between men. This is why the countless imageries, metaphors, allegories, parables, and colloquialisms are pertinent to our final understanding. Our basic instinct is to become entertained by strained mental concepts and malapropos correlations, which we often call puns, such as trying to catch a mouse in the kitchen by putting a collar on the cat made of cheese, or saying that the telephone is "running over" when it is ringing in another room. While such nonsense may be humorous for a time, it is only an end in itself, and rarely provides a more transcendental message. The focus of the Holy Spirit, however, is to employ the detectible aspects of the ordinary world to elevate our awareness past our casual senses. Thus, a human heart becomes the invaluable equivalent of precious gold; our souls are the priceless diamonds in the Crown of Christ the King, and our faith holds an equity unlike any currency ever before known to man. There is an entire language and dialect which is attributed to the specific imagery of holiness that we are meant to envelope within the scope of our Christian consciousness; and the most prevalent matter of importance is our interdependence upon other people to reveal their truest motivations on a higher plane, defined by an artistic reality. Therein, we discover that the circumference of our mutual trust is altogether like a sunbeam because you can see it with your eyes, although you cannot touch or walk upon it. If we are not careful, however, through the slightest breach or hesitation, we can quickly sever it completely in two. This is how we perceive our expressions of Love toward one another because they so often tend to be conditioned upon factors over which we still wish to maintain absolute control. If our allegiance to our brethren were to be seen like a spigot, there is no doubt that we wish to continue to wield our autonomy to turn it off and on at the temperance of our hearts. It seems as though we are constantly making adjustments and evaluations upon human life, while crafting our motivations and designs to best suit our own personal advancement; calculating our reactions and responses so as to prohibit our neighbors from rendering our memories too archaic before we die. The human spirit is comprised of a collection of emotions which are so diverse in nature that it is nearly imponderable for us to decide how so many feelings can be contained inside a single personality. Whether we know it or not, we bear an entourage of trepidation within us when we first wake in the morning that mirrors our innate impulses toward self-survival and curiosity, along with a smattering of discrimination which helps us define who we are in the midst of the foreign nature of the rest of the world. All of this is sustained by the way we are treated by those with whom we interact during the occasions of the ordinary day.

Our proprietary conscience is not an ordinary aspect of our mortal constituency, but is a supernatural facet of our potential to be Divine in the likeness of our Almighty Father. We gain a newer sense of purpose by listening to the advisory counsel of our Christian peers and their fond affections through the Holy Spirit living inside their hearts. We wallow and mesh, lurch, jolt, embrace, constrain, and interact all through the refinery of absolution we are granted by those whom we have offended. The noticeable absence of their pardon is the begetting of the deterioration of our own self-respect. The question of why we allow their misgivings to be transformed into an inaccurate reflection of ourselves is the basic error we must overcome in our search for understanding how God views our individual souls. We have long forgotten that Jesus Christ sees us as the flowering blooms in the New Cornucopia which He gave us from the Cross and founded through His Easter Resurrection. There is no need for us to blend-in with the greenery of the bushes or embosk ourselves inside the grape arbors along our backyard fences anymore because the hues of our faith keep growing us beyond the shadows into the sunlit skies. The seemingly obscure and enigmatic definition of the personal "self" is, indeed, quite elusive because we fail to incorporate the rest of humanity into our contemplations when we dictate the terms of whom *we* wish to be. There are no longer any bars to cross on our journey toward spiritual enlightenment because every origination and development of our nature has been borne inside the suffering we have endured and the full adaptation of our more sincere and genuine charities along the way. There is no such thing as someone having to remember to forget something because it mysteriously seems to occur on its own. This is the same auto-charismatic honesty through which we must forgive those who have trespassed against us. We keep confounding ourselves with the question of how we can possibly write-off the transgressions of our enemies when there seems to be no penitential nature in them. Christ did not condition His Love upon whether His foes ever approached Him to apologize. Indeed, it was not the ability of the criminal who hung at Our Lord's side on Good Friday that reversed his own error, but his recognition that Jesus had the power to expunge it at the whisper of His Sacred words. Calling upon the Savior of the World *is* our confession, because we fully recognize our own helplessness to ever eventually acquit ourselves. Hereafter, we cannot expect to stand before the Son of God and tell Him that we have failed to forgive our trespassers because they did not search us out or bow in contrition at our own whimsical feet. We are expected to Love them unconditionally, nevertheless. And, what about our own rapprochement with His Eternal Justice? Now, we fully acknowledge the reason for the Sacrament of Reconciliation. We realize the sensitive nature of having to muster the desire to forget the sins of those who have never said they were sorry to our face; and we likewise never want our Lord to feel this same way toward us. He has given us the Sacrament of Confession to take away every venue through which we might indict ourselves of any unmitigated hypocrisy at the end of mortal time.

   Therefore, let us utilize the ropes within our grasp to pull one another back from the precipices over which we have cast ourselves in shameless disregard, instead of attempting to hang our estranged conspirators out to dry. We will discover in time that true frustration comes not in what the world may do, but in our own disbelief that the Covenant of Christ has already mended our ways. Ancient tribes and Indians formerly knew many false "gods;" not the least of which is the one they called "fire." They harbored a kindred need to honor their pyrotechnic friend because "he" kept them warm when it was cold outside and allowed them to transform their combustible wares into invisible fumes as though they were spirits somehow having drifted aloft. In Truth, we do not own the right to condemn those who are our enemies just because they do not yet understand our Love. In knowing God, Himself, we fully comprehend that *we* are the flames of righteousness who must emit the Light of Truth to every man; not for the purpose of turning his hopes into ashes, but to help him find his way through a world of darkness, back to the reason for his birth. We own the dominion of conciliatory Blood in Jesus Christ, which is our consanguinity with God, because His Crucifixion has made it so. Our ancestry and kinship with Heaven are conserved by His Passion and Death; and this is the true funeral pyre of our wretched foes for which we have longed since the early days of man. For all the agonizing we do in life about our role and purpose in society and the world, we often shed more tears as a result of our lack of understanding and our own blindness to "reason" than we do by the misfortune of outright sorrow. If our feelings are somewhat heavy at times, it is ironically from the void that has been left in our hearts by the strictest omissions of other men. But, if our efforts are always directed toward the goal of filling ourselves up with infectious goodness, then we will also simultaneously enhance the maximum capacity of our brothers and sisters to be nothing-less than the absolute Love we have always hoped them to become; but somehow never really quite knew how to evoke. It seems as though we have always employed the coldly generic measure of trying to balance our own attractive nature with our expectation that any person of sound judgement could not resist being drawn toward our subtle overtures, while we were appearing to be greater than we really are. There is an immensity of assumption in this prospect, perhaps even a sliver of pride and envy, too; but this is how we survive in a world where there is such competition for the respect and affections of our peers, even when we do not think very highly of the way we have turned-out as adults. We somehow believe that if we are worthy of being noticed, we are also important enough to justify the price of the sacrifices of others to make our lives more compatible and complete. After all, everyone would rather hear the sound of guitar strings being plucked in the background than the blasting of a trumpet in their ear at point-blank range. Unfortunately, however, only few among us ever bother to listen to any romantic melodies in the distance, so we are forced to resort to a more assertive concert of flares.

If our designs were always meant to be a state-of-the-art compulsion, we would never bother to practice them because so much daily effort is involved in finally getting it right. We are constantly required to hone the edges of our civility and smooth the roughness of our admirable character to make higher societies stoop to hear what we have to say. We often recall the souls who are now at rest in Christ, and how each of them tried to be their best for somebody, even if only for a single significant other. It is in this struggle that our potential is fulfilled, whether we finally succeed at achieving it or not. The point is, if we could employ this same desire to be known on our journey before our unseeable God, we would be dressing ourselves in His grace because such a motivation can only come from within His power. Thereafter, we can know the full reason for those indelible sunbeams; that they are the epilogues to His priceless daily repertoires; that we can look beyond them and see the Hem of His Garment by which so many of us have been healed; and we can know that our urging to look upward preludes the elevation of the human heart and the spirit of interior harmony. It is in this response where we discover the genesis of our hope and anticipation; and nothing beyond that moment can ever hold us down again. We are raised, ourselves, when we dignify both the existence and necessity of human life at large; knowing full-well that we cannot dismiss either one as being someone else's albedo or their platitudinous product of chance. Everyone whose soul is bound for Salvation eventually learns that Love is the source of all immortal reparation; and we are the catalysts who must procure the refinement of the world on God's behalf. Jesus Christ will vouch for us if we set our own self-interest aside; at least until the moment we see His Face and ask Him to deliver us from death. The sense of longing in our hearts is our question of when to begin this process of change; and why, where, and how. The intrinsic continuation of everything that is decent is nourished by the calling of the same conscience of civility Who has given us the breath of life. In knowing this Truth first-hand, if we cross one another's path and fail to collide in Love, then we are paying too close attention to where we are going in the physical world. Let us be assured that life is no accident, and neither is the pristine excellence that lives in us now; just begging in the wings to come out and play. Should we choose to wait an instant longer to effect it; or even a moment, or a breath; we might procrastinate too long for our most exhilarating valor to pour-over the falls of our impending ecliptic joy. When God first said that He is with us, He did not imply that He is somehow only perceiving us from above the clouds or past the canyons of the mountains. He is living in and among us as the purpose of our "being;" and our lives are the undeniable evidence. We should seek His presence before all who suffer because we have yet to accept Him without stopping to ask why. Those who need us to be His comforting peace are always more than willing to direct us toward His reputable cause.

Therein, we have found not only our justification before our Almighty Father, but also our admonishment to replicate His Son as being our benign deliverance, too. After all, it is His pain we are personally chosen to emulate, and whose healing we are to administer to other men. Sadly, we are impeded not only by our own fear, doubt, and animosity; but by the lacking of our faith for which we are as equally responsible to pray. Our Lord gives us plentiful time to protect us from failing to recognize Him in all those we cannot meet in the expanse of a single day. So, let us make the most of the hovering sun; let us look toward the solar spires and tell them that we finally understand why they have lept so proudly into Creation and beyond for so long, never once wincing from emulating their cosmic beauty that is our own souls' flight back to the glistening catacombs of Paradise. We should allow no hint of inhibition to cast a silhouette on our midnight musings because we are now emboldened to lay our heads on our pillows at dusk and proclaim to the world which is still trying to conquer us, *hasta manana*, "see you tomorrow!" Just as we can touch our cheeks with the tips of our fingers, we can also feel the visage of the invincible Love of God by turning to humanity in compassion and admiration as though we are Our Creator, Himself, preparing to address their every need; always reaching to restore the goodness that is lost and the best in what our stale indifference has stolen away; never once turning our backs on the reasons to celebrate human life again. If a rose has the courage to bloom in the midst of such a treacherous world, then so do we have the might to spring-forth with all the majesty we can muster to conquer any force that may try to tear our righteousness down. We have the thorny Crown of Christ to protect us from our predators and the scent and beauty of Love to attract those who have only now chosen to seek His ambassadors on the Earth. It has been said that there would be no need for fortitude if there were no such thing as fear. By all means, there would be no berth for being enlightened if not for the Wisdom of knowing that Heaven is going to judge our actions when we hand-over our souls in death someday. We are required to acknowledge that God not only exists, but that He is still living and thriving, despite all we have done to refuse Him in the past. Every soul we ever knew who has now slipped into immortal history is trying to tell us this Truth from beyond their graves. We shall never really be free from culpability until we listen intently to them, calling upon their intercession, and responding with the crucible of Justice flowing from our lips as the Holy Spirit shapes our every whimper in renewing the Earth. We look to one another for advice on how to deplete the day, but the greatest issues are resolved in the inheritance we have received in the Sacred Heart of Christ before we are barely old enough to state an audible word. If we search for our Redemption before the end of mortal time, we will know that everything about life has led to this; all the dreams-awash and new awakenings; all the ravishing ruins that held our souls at bay; and every grief which accompanied our stateliness that kept trying to tell us that victory was only one prayer away.

No one among us with a firm sense of reality is going to concede that any of this is as easy as it seems because we often turn to each other with our consciousness aghast and wonder when the first miracle is going to fall into our lap. Do we believe that such an expectancy for the *supernatural* is the origin of our faith; or is it truly the other way around? Will not God advance the cause of the things in which we believe if we prove our loyalty to Him first? Do we have reason to proclaim that the Birth of Christ into the world was the result of those who were calling for the Messiah to come to the aid of their souls? With the lack of any substantial opposition by anyone who owns the favor of His Father better than us; Jesus took to the Flesh and lived among us as the answer to their prayers. Why, therefore, do we refuse to believe that

He will also respond to ours? If we succumb to the ritual of continuously questioning His sound objectives in shaping His Creation into anything He wants, we will also be foolish enough to conclude that we were never supposed to be a portion of the mix. Christ cannot succeed without us because we are His Mystical Body for whom He has lived! How much strength He is able to garner by the collection of additional souls under the Cross of Salvation is still a question to be known. He wants to be strapping in numbers; and that part is apportioned to us. Somehow it seems that by the time we are old enough to function in accordance with our basic instincts, society has changed so much that they are no longer relevant anymore. So, we are constantly having to perform penance for the mistakes that we impose upon ourselves. If only others could see that there are no such barometric variables in the Kingdom of God because Jesus has been perfect all along! The Holy Bible states that He is the Way, the Truth, and the Life. What else on the Earth or anywhere beyond it could we possibly require? If we have the means to return to the personification of our own being, why would we wish to turn away and find only death? Since we believe that most people will try to deceive us for their own personal gratification, why would we disavow the blessings of the Truth? If we have gone in every direction we can possibly travel in striving to discover the meaning of human life, why would we turn any other way? We respire involuntarily because our Divine Creator has exercised His Will to give us life. If there is no positivism in that, let someone deliberately stop their lungs from functioning and see how long they can keep from passing-out. Loving in the image and likeness of Jesus Christ is one and the same life-sustaining naturalness because He keeps everything about us from descending into the Abyss. The relevance we should be seeking is the permanent blessing from His Hands so that all the nations in the world can know that only He is the sustenance of their capacity to live unmolested by any other force. We should all hope to see such security, especially in our personal lives.

We must pray that God will have Mercy on those who make it their day's labor to direct the rest of humankind away from His Reign. It is quite easy to see our error in most any direction we look. If it is not the search for the elegant satisfaction of our appetites, it is our insatiable desire to look down on the rest of the world that keeps us from becoming the children of Light. Why? What is it about the mortal man that makes him so blind to the Truth of his own Absolution through the universal equity of the Omnipotence of God? Are we more afraid of losing our handle on the comforts of life than we are the destiny of our souls, come the end of time? How intelligent must someone be to finally grasp the lesson that Jesus Christ will not allow us to continue to pervert His purposes for much longer, despite our bland intentions to somehow reverse our course? All the high-flying speeches in the world about inclusiveness and a charitable spirit will do nothing at all if we do not place our words into discernable action. We can say "I Love you" until the cows come home, but we will be lying to each other's face if we do not live it from the depths of our hearts! There is no conceivable way that we will ever talk God into believing that we are worthy of being Redeemed in the Blood of His Son if we do everything we can to avoid becoming converted to Christianity while we live on the Earth. Oh! We can hear Him laughing disdainfully at our haughtiness now! Are we to pity those who have poignantly criticized our faith who will stand beside us on Judgement Day and tell God that we refused to tell them the Truth? We can stand upright with a look of confident assurance on our faces if we have done all of these important things well because our reluctance to impress our own willingness in reflecting the power of God will be expunged before the vastness of Creation. In our resolute dissertation, we will learn that spiritual responsibility is the true Love from which all life and holiness ultimately spring. What, then, is to be said about human intuition and our desire to continue dredging the past from under the present and hypothesizing about a future that is still quite uncertain to the majority of the people in the world? We discover the direct path toward the perception of Truth only by following the lessons and teachings of the God who has created us, i.e., His Holy Presence Incarnate, Jesus Christ. Faith in His Gospel is, indeed, independent from any process of rationalization which inquisitive men apply to most other propositions in these modern times. The Holy Spirit gives us an immediate, keen, and unimpeded insight about the Will of God for every soul who has ever lived on Earth; and it is through this definitive process that we cast our personal interests aside and allow for the greater advancement of the Kingdom of Heaven to assimilate the mortal globe into its Divine parameters again. The triaxial alliance that we share from within ourselves toward God and with humanity as a whole is contained inside the Dominion which Christ holds over us at the service of His Father and the collection of individuals and societies with whom we live today.

The forces of Paradise cannot be diminished by anything we do to oppose them; but we can certainly enhance the prospect of their success if we join in their immortal purpose. Faith, charity, righteousness, devotion, and service are all seeds which have been formed inside the perfect Fruit of Love; the same Love who is God and is the reason for the transparent nature of our lives to those who have already died. There is nothing we do that they cannot see if He so chooses to reveal it to them. Do we surmise that they can also perceive our lack of willingness to cooperate with them in ascribing the synthesis of the universe to our Almighty Father and fighting to make the best of His dreams come true? There is a great deal of work to be done toward that end; but many among us cannot see where their efforts can best be deployed because they refuse to look through the focus of the Cross. It seems as though we grow older and exchange our candy-canes for intoxicants, wondering all the while why our best oratories and poesies do not grant us the benefits of their inebriating consolation anymore. When we take the oath to become one of the Christian elect, we fully expect to be delivered to Heaven someday; and this self-assurance is the quietus of every anxiety that could ever try to haunt us again. There is no wonder, therefore, why we properly boast that we are given life in the Blood of Jesus because His Paraclete has left us incapable of perishing this brand of hope for very long. We are like children at His feet again; all leaping at once in beckoning Him to take us into His Arms. All existence hereafter is only a suffix to the completion of our lives which He finished during the Holy Week of His Passion, Crucifixion, and Resurrection from the Tomb almost 2000 years ago. If we evince these mysterious tenets of Christianity before those who have yet to embrace them, will they not see that we are part and parcel of God in ways that they have never thought to achieve? What other prophet is said to have conquered death by crucifixion and rose to tell it to his chosen seers at the crack of daylight on the morning of the third day hence? Only God in Human Flesh could ever make such a proclamation and know it to be true. There is but one Messiah who has ever been Anointed by the Almighty Father as the Savior of the world. This "Christ" is Jesus; the same Child who was conceived by the power of the Holy Spirit without sin in the Womb of the Blessed Virgin Mary. Now, we know what it means to truly allow our Divine Creator to bloom into life inside us. Jesus is this new Life; and Mary is our Perpetual Mentoress. Should we ever become like this Handmaiden from Nazareth, would we not, too, be looked upon by the Kingdom of God as those who nourish what is good and right in His perfect sight and Judgement? In the words of our Redeemer, Himself, *"...Amen, I say to you, no soul who is alive or passed beyond the sepulcher shall ever know a greater grace than to be called an offspring of the Mother of their God."* So, let us not be so meandering in our chosen profession to live-out the mandate we have gained through our acceptance of Her Son. There is nothing nondescript about Love or absolution; and the glasswort of our righteousness which blooms beside the seashores of our faith is sufficient for God to know that our hearts are now His crystal chandeliers, just waiting for His Holy Sacrifice to come and light us up again.

We remember the fateful and miraculous Aramaic writing on the wall which was interpreted by Daniel as foretelling the destruction of Belshazzar and his kingdom of, *mene, mene, tekel, upharsin,* "numbered, numbered, weighed, divided." (Daniel 5:25-31) Is this not also a prophecy of the days in which we live for those who have so long ignored the arrival of the hour when the Son of Man will bring an end to the material world? Those who are not in favor of God are most decidedly against Him, whether they are aware of their station of error or not. We are forced to choose of our own accord if we shall ever walk into the Gate of Paradise or succumb to the legions from Hell. Christ has told us in the parables of His speech that we, too, should be capable of seeing the handwriting on the parapet because our days are numbered, our souls will be weighed against the righteousness we have known, and we will be divided from those who will be saved and discarded with the goats, the chaff, and the weeds to be condemned if we do not convert to His Blood dripping from the Cross. For lack of a better word, "slothful" is a term that best describes our approach to Christianity these days. We know what is right to do, but we are not yet sufficiently disciplined to make it all come true. When we have seen enough of the Wrath of our Almighty Father in Heaven, we will finally act. He knows as well as anyone else on Earth that it is just a matter of time. So, when we feel slighted because life seems to be so evasive, we should realize and remember that He is still trying desperately to reach us; and it is ourselves who are attempting to elude our own justification in Him. When it appears as though our friends are giving us the slip and our enemies begin to charge the gate, then Our Creator will always be there to tell us that we should have turned to Him long before. If our souls were to be an individual corporation of their own, one would wonder whether they would advertise for patrons because they need the present tender, or just to see their names put up in lights. Such is the pride which continues to keep us separated from the humility, pardon, and peace that is ours inside the circumference of the thorny Crown worn by the best of all Creatures, Our Savior Jesus Christ, who has suffered the Passion required by His Father to belay our inner spirits to the Cross, asking that we salute His Kingship with the same valor as the Roman gladiators who said to their Emperor upon entering the public arena, *morituri te salutamus,* "we who are about to die salute Thee!" In doing so, there will be nothing expendable left in the pockets of our souls to reveal to the failing Earth how wealthy we have become through the new immortality we have inherited in the very Father who once cast us from His side.

Recessional
1897

God of our fathers, known of old—
Lord of our far-flung battle-line—
Beneath whose awful Hand we hold
Dominion over palm and pine—
Lord God of Hosts, be with us yet
Lest we forget—lest we forget!   6
The tumult and the shouting dies—
The Captains and the Kings depart—
Still stands Thine ancient Sacrifice,
An humble and a contrite heart.
Lord God of Hosts, be with us yet,
Lest we forget—lest we forget!   12
Far-called, our navies melt away—
On dune and headland sinks the fire—
Lo, all our pomp of yesterday
Is one with Nineveh and Tyre!
Judge of the Nations, spare us yet,
Lest we forget—lest we forget!   18
If, drunk with sight of power, we loose
Wild tongues that have not Thee in awe—
Such boasting as the Gentiles use
Or lesser breeds without the Law—
Lord God of Hosts, be with us yet,
Lest we forget—lest we forget!   24
For heathen heart that puts her trust
In reeking tube and iron shard—
All valiant dust that builds on dust,
And guarding calls not Thee to guard—
For frantic boast and foolish word,
Thy mercy on Thy People, Lord!   30

Joseph Rudyard Kipling (1865-1936)
Nobel Prize for Literature, 1907

Chapter Eight
A Mere Temporal Inoculation

———————————

There is a great deal more to engaging our relationship with Paradise than telling the rest of humanity that we wish to have no more to do with secularism because we have chosen to restrict our conversations to matters solely to do with Christ, while ignoring the mutual communication which will help our friends understand why we have decided to work for God. We cannot become entirely segregated from other people if we expect to effectively communicate the Holy Gospel to those who are living-out their vocational missions to the best of their talents. Loving God and our fellow human beings does not imply that we are forced to relinquish some of the activities which bring us peace of mind; such as hunting, fishing, appreciating the fine arts, and just casually relaxing alongside a stream on a midsummer's day. It would be nice if we could live inside the same folksiness by which we remember a Prairie Farms Milk truck rolling over the hills and through the valleys of the narrow country roads on his daily delivery route, and the wildflowers which blow freely in the wake of the breezes he leaves behind. Somewhere in our hearts will always reside the feeling we have when we smile before the face of a little baby and hear him laughing aloud back at us. When God sent humanity into mortal exile on the Earth, it was not for the single purpose that we needed to be purified because of our sins, but also to learn how to be holy by employing the pleasant demeanor which will make it all come true. We are to become imbued and indoctrinated with immeasurable pleasance and good will so that we can recognize the friendship of the Holy Spirit of Christ when we seek Him at morning's light. If our weeks have somehow become drab and boring, it is only because we have decided to cease achieving the objectives that will take us closer to His Grace. It is true that life will suffer great persecution upon us when we embrace the Cross, often leaving our consciousness rubbed raw to the bone and our interpersonal relationships splintered almost completely in two. But, these are not the things which should cause us to cease our efforts in continuing to secure a positive relationship with everyone we meet, even those who oppose what we choose to espouse. Indeed, Christians are often visited by rejection and disdain, and subjected to the outright horrors of violent evil. This is no reason to quit the fight just because it may be a little uncomfortable at times or because those who surround us might grate against our nerves once in awhile. If we did not know better than to surrender to such duress, most of those who follow Christ would probably dig holes in the ground and crawl into them like some religious factions in foreign lands have done.

Our reasoning is justified in knowing that we have been implanted into the world for the purpose of rendering ourselves immune from the perils and distractions that have caused others to eventually abandon their faith or never accept it from the start. We must, therefore, look for the identifiable contrasts which help us remember why we were born; not that life is the ending of a journey, but a way for our souls to learn the difference between right and wrong, propriety and error, and spirituality and apathy. We achieve these things by becoming one with perfect Love, while we concurrently welcome the Holy Paraclete into our hearts and consciences to aid us in choosing the proper courses of action. There can be no true goodness, healing, proper confession, peacefulness, and no Christian conviction unless we live Love in the way of the Son of God. Period. Anyone who professes to believe in the Apostles' Creed and does not approach all humanity with unconditional Love is committing a moral vice which is tantamount to high treason against the Kingdom of God. Too many of us are worried that the Bible is sending mixed signals because we are trying to dissect our human experience inside the boundaries of time. How can we admonish our brothers and sisters to become near-Godlike in conduct and have the clear vision to lead them away from their transgressions while simultaneously needing to remove the wooden beams from our own eyes? Just because there may be seeming-contradictions in what Jesus has asked us to achieve does not imply that there is also hypocrisy there. We are required to be self-penitent in our struggle for purity and righteousness at the same time we must care enough for the souls who live around us to spiritually and corporally offer them our merciful counsel and advice. If they choose to ignore it or confront and accost us for our efforts, we are simply asked to shake their dust from our shoes and walk another way. But, declining to leave our influence upon them should be a last resort because their souls are far too important to Christ than to have us simply cower beneath their rancor and crawl away like scolded dogs.

Those who are following Jesus to their Salvation already own the vision to know the distinguishable differences between the faith which gives us life and remaining camouflaged amidst the ordinary world. There can be great accomplishments made in some of the most mundane circumstances at times. Who would have guessed after the decades of the 1960s through the 1980s that a leader from Russia, President Putin, would come to America to ride around in a sport utility vehicle with U.S. President George W. Bush on his ranch in Crawford, Texas, just to see what the weather and landscape looked like? Oh, yes, it is important to remember that they also discussed the dismantling and elimination of about 5,000 nuclear warheads from their military arsenals at the time! Such opportunities are lines of demarcation in the continuum of history; and ones which should not be taken lightly or cast aside as being just another occasion to piddle away. During *any* instance when humankind avails himself to the elimination of weapons of war or the imminent rumors of war, or works toward bringing accord between former enemies, or says by subtle implication that they should dissolve their prior animosities, we can be quite confident that the Spirit of God is between them. It is the same principle as when we implore our children to be more responsibly selective in what they choose to watch on television in the confines of their bedrooms at night. What pummels their impressionable nature through such an uncontrolled medium sets the tone for how they behave and what choices they will make for the future. It is not necessary for us to stand over their shoulders with the "hoot" in our hands or install a V-Chip in the TV because we cannot trust them to refrain from watching such corruptive channels. If we can only show them that not everything they see is beneficial to their personal disposition or the advancement of their judgement, then *we* will become the instruments of that same Spirit of God who guides those international heads-of-state. Believe it or not, there are numerous times when our teenagers wish to become like little children again, once they have been abandoned or betrayed by their circle of friends or, perhaps, committed an act which has left them feeling alone, guilty, and afraid. This is precisely when we should become better parents than either ourselves or our sons and daughters know we have the capacity to be; for these are our descendent citizens who should learn that human decency comes from open understanding and forgiveness, not punitive scorn and rejection. If we hold them close to our breasts during their times of greatest temptation and inter-relational strife, they will also seek us out for advice when searching for the truth about personal decency and responsibility as well. Whoever said that it is impossible to be both parents and friends to our maturing offspring did not know exactly what they were talking about.

  I once attended a Koinonia where the sponsors handed-out a newsletter which had an article in it that I thought was rather profound. It was about an event which occurred at the SS. Peter and Paul Church in New Braunfels, Texas; saying that there was an eight-year-old boy who wrote a very interesting and amusing letter about what God does with His time in Heaven. He penned the following thoughts on his own. *"One of God's jobs is making people. He makes new ones to put in the place of the ones who die, so there will always be enough people to take care of things on earth. He doesn't make grown-*

ups, just kids. I think its because they are smaller and easier to make. That way, He doesn't have to take up His valuable time teaching them how to walk and talk. He can just leave that up to Moms and Dads. I think it works-out pretty good. God's second most important job is listening to prayers. An awful lot of this goes on, especially in church and at bedtime. God sees everything, hears everything, and is everywhere, which keeps Him pretty busy. Jesus is God's Son. He used to do all the hard work, like walking on water and doing miracles, and trying to teach people about God who didn't want to learn. They finally got tired of His teaching and crucified Him on a Cross. He told His Father 'forgive them,' and God said O.K. The Father liked everything Jesus had done...so He raised Him up to Heaven and told Him He could stay there. So, Jesus did. And, now, He helps His Father out by listening to prayers. You can pray anytime you want and they are sure to hear you because they've got it worked-out so at least one of them is on duty all the time." Is this not the same innocuous simplicity with which we are supposed to carry the maturity of our faith into Eternity, even if we live to be a hundred years old before we die? The end of our innocence often arrives when we try to become barn-busters for accumulating material assets and amassing a stash of corporate wealth. What do our hearts say, however, about which of these Our Divine Lord prefers; the sentiments of that eight-year-old child, or someone who has arrived at the age of forty years, wears a suit and tie to see the glitter and lights of Hollywood Boulevard every evening, and checks his standing on the New York Stock Exchange on his laptop computer while flying from one coast to the next?

All of this seems to be too technologically advanced for those of us who grew-up sitting on our backyard porches while looking at the garnet sun setting on the western horizon, thrilled to the gills that it was kind enough to cast a silhouette of the corner latticework onto the rear of the house. We knew then what people should accept now; that the telling sign of human decency blooms amid the fruit of our own good works, the structure of our reinforcing motivations, our approach to the suffering of others, the generosity of our spirit, and our willingness to diminish ourselves for the advancement of those who have no way to endow themselves. We peer into the distant past at times with somewhat of an implied disdain for the addlebrained way our parents did things, but hindsight shows us that they did as well as they could inside the constraints under which they lived. Today's baby boomers and Generation X are none the lesser for their having to struggle to feed us and send us through school. We saw a common faithfulness in those days that has yielded a lesson of simplicity by which we should always live; and our identification with their genuineness reflects the benign aspects of our own resourcefulness. It is true that our hearts are filled with countless memories, the good and the bad; so we therefore know that our past is a direct determiner of who we have become today. So, if America is to be a land of decency and peacefulness in the decades of tomorrow, the change for good must begin with us; for we have to initiate the concordance which will sow the spiritual healing that our land so desires to retrieve. In effect, we must inoculate the future against ever having to suffer the diseases of inequity and moral turpitude again by becoming the antithesis of everything which suborns evil in and around our midst. Forget about those who maintain that the conquest of the human spirit somehow contradicts the giddy adolescence which becomes our new vitality thereafter because we can nurture their peaceful coexistence inside our souls; for God will undoubtedly corroborate our trust in Him by protecting us from our more malevolent foes. Did Jesus not tell us that He is our Strength and Refuge in times of trouble; and that He is our shield, rear guard, armament, advocate, and the sword of every facet of our immortal defense? Disbelieving these certitudes makes most people shun His mightiness sometimes; often mistaking the Christian Gospel for a doctrine of shallower inhibition, rather than the imperishable confidence which gives us Divine power no matter how long we live; per diem, per centum, by fortnight, or by score. The world is altogether different than it was during the decades we studied about in our history books; it is more perilous to our individual safety; our stockpiles of offensive weapons are scattered into more lethal hands; our religious animosities are becoming evocatively more pronounced; especially in light of the jihads and holy wars in the Middle East, between the nations adjacent to China, in Northern Ireland, and in some extremist circles right here at home.

There can be no true global unity unless we adhere to the protracted principles of shared respect, the elimination of economic sanctions that only hurt the poor, disavowing violence and vengeance as the means through which to redress our mutual grievances, restraining ourselves from deploying force over diplomacy as a venue for ending our public disputes, and envisioning the entire world as being one society of a species of human creatures under the guardianship of God as though we have already seen it from the perspective of His Throne. Has not every astronaut and cosmonaut who ever saw the Earth from outer-space in his oxygenated capsule returned to terra firma and said that he could not understand what we are all fighting about? Humanity is too much a compilation of emotions, inconsistencies, insecurity, collateral ignorance, inherited discrimination, and trepidation for the unknown. Balladeers and lyricists have been trying to tell us this for centuries, but we continue to turn a deaf ear to their words. If we are searching for heroes and heroines who have left us subliminal messages in their wakes, why not look to the likes of Princess Diana of England as an example? She deposited a legacy of charm, charity, and charisma into the annals of history through her concern for the helpless poor before her death in late August 1997 that would make any Christian evangelist proud. And, what about the final remarks that former Beatle George Harrison bequeathed to his followers prior to his death in November 2001 as a noble remembrance of his evaluation of mortal life? *"Love one another,"* is the epitaph he chose to impart. His challenging bequest to those of us who survive can be no clearer than this. The fact remains, we belong to a priceless age of advanced knowledge and shared values; and if we are searching for a means of catharsis to purge us all of our interior regrets and paranoiac anxieties, then the life of stability we discover in Jesus Christ is our only true way to regain our national composure from the senseless deterioration of our social morals of the last thirty-five years. When we look at the bottom of a fine painting or underneath a rendition of a work of art, we will often find the word *fecit* after the inscription of the name of the person who brushed, forged, or crafted it. It means, "he made it," so as to give a Latin accreditation to the artisan of the piece. In a like means, there are multiple-thousands of people who continually travel around the globe climbing to the highest peaks, diving to the oceanic depths of the salty seas, dismantling forests, overturning boulders, exhuming the shrouds of deceased Pharaohs, scrutinizing the unseeable universe through sonar equipment and microscopes, and even transforming the atmosphere into tangible liquids and back again; all in an effort to rediscover the identity of the Creator of everything that exists. They refuse to accept the fact that God is the genius who constructed the physical aspects of all Creation through the self-deifying Omnipotence which has always been His.

Christ is that Alpha for which men of every century have pined to know, whether they thought it would eventually be Him they would discover or not. In the timelessness of His dominion and by learning the origin of life in His Most Sacred Heart, we also uncover the secrets of how the galaxies will end; for His Supreme Reign is the perpetual Omega over everything to eventually survive the culminating conflagration He is about to ignite upon the Earth during His Second Return. Jesus is the Wise Counselor who knows best how to wield His power with both serenity and compassion atop the elements of Judgement and Justice. He realizes full-well that the exterior architecture of human life is often grossly overstated for what it truly is, and that we often make more of our reactions and impulses than we should; forgetting that our progress is a fruit of our own hard work, rather than a product of chance or the result of some random opportunity. Our best-laid plans are often modified by the harsh reality that most people do not really care what we think or do, as long as they are not adversely affected, or unless it benefits them in some way for which they are not required to make recompense. We tend to forget that the greatest expression of the "self" comes from the inside; that what we wear and the color of our skin, hair, and eyes does not contribute in any way to who we are. The center of our "being" is the concentration, composition, and combination of our intellectual, psychological, and sentimental attributes. People wish to know whether we can read and write, or if we are Western, European, Democratic, Republican, Libertarian, or apolitical. This is the unfortunate way by which most of us determine the value of someone else's worth, believing most of the time that they cannot be our friends or share the same forensic ideals if they envision our Republic through a different set of eyes. We cannot always determine whether a sartorially elegant man has spent his life's savings on the clothes on his back, or if an elderly gentleman wearing a pair of bib-overalls has concealed a million dollars' cash inside his mattress at home; let alone try to reckon the eternal standing of someone else's soul before the judgement of God just because he might make different secular choices than we choose to endorse.

However, we can always be defined by how we treat other people, the tenability of our arguments, the integrity of our proof, whether we say what we really mean, and all the other outward signs that can only be a product of our inner-constitution. This is why Jesus said that the heart is the origin of all goodness, and that everything we become unto ourselves and openly to other men is defined by the characteristics of our own moral scrupulousness, sincerity, kindness, honesty, and trustworthiness. It is usually possible and oftentimes inevitable that insecure people live the entirety of their years while lying to themselves about who they really are and fabricating a pretense in their identity before the rest of humankind. This is the self-delusion which causes their mental frustrations to turn into physical bloodbaths and keeps them from realizing their greatest potential to enhance the truth for the elimination of aggravated error inside the pool of their peers. It also prohibits them from purging themselves of anything that impedes them from becoming one with the larger population which has heretofore surrendered its fears in exchange for a more sustainable approach to societal problems. While I am obviously no psychiatrist, I still suppose that such interior pathologies lead to many other irregularities which keep the process of crime and punishment so evident and apparent in the public debate. I also believe that any sovereign country which has a majority population of such citizens becomes, in itself, quite rogue and disenchanted with the community of nations in which they perceive themselves as being fodder amidst a school of hungry piranha. Is there any wonder why so many of our impressionable youth balance a boombox on their shoulders these days or put a set of stereo headphones over their ears and crawl inside one of their favorite songs to get away from it all? Understanding how other people endure the battle against their enemies is the only means by which we will ever be able to protect ourselves and our neighbors from forces that are so sinister in nature that the security we hope to achieve might never be able to see past them into the full light of day. The amendatory conversion which will help us better comprehend one another's sorrows rests in the decisions we make to offer our sympathies, consolation, and affinities when they are steeped in the throes of private devastation or facing the many catastrophic events which too often send our spirits tumbling to the ground. There has been a long-heralded understanding by those who believe in God that the Holy Spirit will provide the proper words to say when such occasions arise; known in most religious circles as *afflatus*, which is compassionate inspiration through the Divine communication of knowledge. How many times have we listened to the record of someone's mortal life as they are about to be inducted into an organization while at the brink of death, or after they have recently passed-away?

Perhaps it would be appropriate to take a pause at this juncture to understand what that really means. Are we saying that we are willing to elevate the dignity of the rest of humanity only when their longevity is found to be endangered? Is it true that the quarterback we traded-away looks much better in hindsight than the one we got to replace him, or that our lame-duck public officials' poll numbers often skyrocket because they are unable to serve another term? Is there evidence that this is the only way we are willing to compliment our acquaintances and fellow Americans, as they are walking out the door? If we are really going to make a difference in remolding the Earth into a planet of tranquilness and decency, there is no doubt that we must begin with our own lives. The Greek term *gnothi seauton* means, "know thyself," and we have been reminded about it from the B.C. philosophers to William Shakespeare, and to most all the prominent psychologists of the 20th century. But, do we actually know what criteria we should employ to fully comprehend the complexities that make us such distinguishable individuals? How can we discover who we are if we have absolutely no control over our mental and emotional development for the first fifteen years of our youth? We are a product of our environment during those formative times; and we must often cast them aside in favor of a more modest and moderate way of living as we mature into adulthood. Our youthful indiscretions will almost always be transformed into global conflicts if we do nothing to become more reasoned into principles of tolerance and sharing. It takes quite a sacrificial community spirit to accomplish this most often; one which many among us are unwilling to exude. Mending our social breaches does not mean going home and sewing the holes in our pants, for they are breeches of another kind. If we are going to make a difference in repairing the divisions between our not-so-united states in America today; its racial divides, subcultures, and economic inequalities; we are going to have to compose our best speeches and devise our most benevolent plans; for we have a long distance to travel before most of us are willing to walk hand-in-hand with perfect strangers again. We are far too great a nation than to become united only after we are attacked by foreign legions; and we are perhaps too blind to see that we have some equally as divisive rancor within our own borders to ever allow us to stand as the perfect example of a gentle democracy before the rest of the world. Our informal inheritance from the most influential writers, orators, and leaders on Earth is to realize that we can do better by a diverse population of countrymen who do not know very well how to speak for themselves. Their grandest communication comes through silence when they are satisfied, by physical aggression when they are up-in-arms, and by a bland indifference during the moments in-between. This, however, is not the time to become any of the three; for we are turning our backs on the plight of millions of people on the way to the bank as though we share no responsibility before God to nourish them back to their physical, spiritual, and intellectual health.

We can best galvanize our interpersonal relationships by assuming what it would be like to stand inside other people's shoes once in awhile and by identifying with the circumstances that have created the conditions in which they live. Most Americans have heard of the great minister, Rabbi Alexander M. Schindler, a man of God and president of the Union of American Hebrew Congregations, who has written quite prolifically about our need to assist our fellow citizens in their times of great strife. An excerpt from a commencement address which he delivered at the University of South Carolina in May 1987 appeared in *Reader's Digest* shortly thereafter under the heading of "Hold fast, and let go: understand this paradox, and you stand at the very gate of wisdom," echoing the sentiments of the quotable Mr. Schindler. The paradox about which he spoke is that life lures us to pursue the many possessions and artifacts by which we are distracted, and yet we will never be able to take any of them with us when we die. The absolutely profound way that he envisioned human existence can be put into words no better than how he said them to those Carolinian graduates that day, *"...Surely we ought to hold fast to life, for it is wondrous, and full of a beauty that breaks through every pore of God's own earth. We know that this is so, but all too often we recognize this truth only in our backward glance when we remember what was, and then suddenly realize that it is no more. We remember a beauty that faded, a love that waned. But, we remember with far greater pain that we did not see that beauty when it flowered, that we failed to respond with love to love when it was tendered."* Inside these eloquent reflections resides the secret of true effectiveness in the purpose of restoring the dignity of the lost, forsaken, scorned, and abused. It is obvious that we cannot reverse the element of time, but we can prevent the future from slipping beyond our grasp before we have an opportunity to alter its course, to avoid breaking those hearts who might be imminently fractured, to resist avenging the losses we have suffered before, to place a sleeping-pallet underneath a little child before he yawns the first time, to offer him a loaf of bread prior to ever hearing the first growl of hunger pains from his stomach, and holding him so close to our hearts that he would never think of taking his leave, let alone having to bow his head again in defeat and come crawling back through our door in the likeness of the prodigal son.

We will never have to retrieve our lost brethren if we take the proper measures in advance to prevent them from slipping-away. Never again will we have to deliver a funeral eulogy for a fallen soldier if we can make the Earth a place where war is not welcome anymore. There will be no tears shed over spilled milk if we make sure that every last ounce of it is poured past the lips of our starving babies. Indeed, we will be able to allow our carnations to grow unmolested in their fields, rather than having to pluck them to place alongside the caskets of our murdered young sons who all died much too quickly in vain. It was when the sunlight hit Mr. Schindler's face as he was being transferred to another room in the hospital after having suffered a heart-attack that led to his new awakening about the fragile nature of our time on Earth. He said, *"...here, then, is the first pole of life's paradoxical demands on us: Never be too busy for the wonder and the awe of life. Be reverent before each dawning day; embrace each hour; and seize each golden minute. Hold fast to life...but not so fast that you cannot let go. This is the second side of life's coin, the opposite pole of its paradox: we must accept our losses, and learn how to let go."* If we take this noble man's advice to heart, will it not be true that we will stop chasing after material possessions and personal wealth like that young man sitting on the jet airliner checking his laptop computer for the daily stock market report? Will we not realize that the world around us is boiling-over with injustice and outright carnal corruption? By heeding the new awareness which splashed into the face of Alexander Schindler from above, will we not also see his experience as a metaphor for our overcoming the very paradox about which he is speaking? The world may call us into a deeper relationship with its temporal nature, but this does not mean that we are forced to comply. We can thank Almighty God and Alexander Schindler, alike, that he experienced this miraculous event because it stands as quite a remarkable monument to his divine conscience and the goodness in his heart to share it with the rest of the world. The thesis of the earliest chapters of my book are in distinct agreement with what most holy men and women believe about our keeping guard against becoming too deeply involved in the "materiel" and living solely for the purpose of pursuing them. The sunlit rays which blessed Reverend Schindler that day were his sign from Heaven, and one that most of us are not privileged to receive during our mortal lives. This is why we should accept his words as though he is a messenger from God to the rest humanity about seeking only what is truly worthy in His sight.

The last paragraph of Mr. Schindler's 1987 speech, I believe, is the most visionary of all. It speaks to my own desires for a unified world of cohesive societies, which begins within our own thoughts, families, and cities,... *"Add love to a house and you have a home; add righteousness to a city and you have a community; add truth to a pile of red brick and you have a school; add religion to the humblest of edifices and you have a sanctuary; add justice to the far-flung round of human endeavor and you have a civilization. Put them all together, exalt them above their present imperfections, add to them the vision of humankind redeemed, forever free of need and strife, and you have a future lighted with the radiant colors of hope."* There can be no doubt that these are the building-blocks to regaining the lost stature of decency we once espoused in the United States of America. We took prayer out of the classrooms of our children's institutions of learning and they became battlefields of carnage and disgrace. Secular newspaper editors have reserved increasingly more column-inches for corporate advertising and the glorification of violence, instead of speaking directly to the effect of God-like virtues on the American style of life. They thereafter have the gall to publish cultural analyses which bewail the shame of our general population straying too far from the font of civilian decency. The news is not too good to be true that the very God who allowed the sun to shine on the inspired visage of Alexander Schindler is going to bring an end to it all through the effectuation of His Holy Justice. And, by the time He is finished, the blast of Truth which will hit us in the face will make most Americans think that our entire stockpile of nuclear weapons which are encased so clandestinely in their silos will have somehow supernaturally been raised from their depths and simultaneously detonated from their launch pads across the very domestic Republic they were intended to protect.

Chapter Nine
Numbering Our Holiest Sacrifices

———————————————

It must seem almost amazing to God for Him to see how many of us are still counting the passing days as if to somehow be able to enhance or detract from their numbers, while many others have already gained the capacity to envision the totality of Eternity through the purview of their undying Love for Christ. How several are the times when we have turned away from our brothers and sisters with grimaces on our faces because they could not see their way clear to saying the simple, yet utterly profound words, " I Love you." Can we not do more to protect ourselves and those we hold so dearly from people who have yet to give their lives to moral decency? It seems as though everywhere we look these days, tens-of-thousands of unsuspecting children are being molested and shorn of their innocence by predators and violators who lurk to steal what little purity and dignity they have left after having encountered the allegedly-reasoned mainstream world everyday. The horrors we all suffer from an unconverted humanity are the same reason why life seems to be so gruesome to those who take the time to view it from the vantage-point of the poor and unprotected. Where is the decency that we hail as being so important in American life today? The element of time, the factual evidence, and the Truth itself bear-out the virtue that all Love is one; and is fully nurtured by the Supremacy of God, the predestined unfolding of the expansive universe, and the premonition of the inevitable desire of humankind to chase his own curiosity around the corridors of the globe long enough to discover everything that God eventually wants us to know. It is in this seemingly cyclical process where we discover that there is always a certain degree of assessment and relevance which must be applied to every aspect of our spirituality as it relates to what we have done to own-up to the record of our errors on the Earth. Every objective evaluation, the development of social policies, the determination of righteous conduct, and the conclusions we draw about the value of life are all products of the conscience we gain only through our union in the Holy Spirit of Christ.

The question remains to be answered as to whether we have allowed Our Father in Paradise to engage us in His power as we place our souls within striking distance of His Dominion. In Heaven and on Earth, there is no such thing as imperfect Light as it is defined by Love and given to us by His Holy Son. We want our days to unfold both dramatically and explicitly on our own terms, not knowing all along that the metaphysical status of our

individual souls is irrevocably amended to the Truth once we have placed
them inside the Sacred Heart of Jesus. If we allow Him to do so, the Holy
Spirit will give us a new reign, a higher command, and better control over our
inner-personality and outward actions that not even death, itself, could ever
dethrone. Unfortunately, however, there are still millions of people who
believe that God is not sufficiently apparent in the material world to warrant
their concern in being delivered to immortal perfection in His Grace; and *we*
must assume the responsibility for failing to set the record straight on His
behalf. Our focus is woefully inadequate for us to ever make a difference if
our faith continues to be as weak as it has been in the past. If we will only
look at the profile of a crucifix, we can see the way that the future of
humankind used to be impaled against the wall of mortal Creation by the
horrid nature of our grievous transgressions. It was only after Jesus was nailed
to the Cross and eradicated death once and for all that we were finally set free.
He was killed so as to bring an end to our eternal sentence inside the grave,
to stop the loathing which first cast us alongside the pails of the lost from
whence Adam and Eve first walked the Earth, and to instill in us the capacity
to be restored through His Blood and fit for reinstatement within the
unfettered Glory of Heaven once again. If only we would recognize that
hatred manifests itself both in the spiritual confinement of our souls and
through the physical imprisonment of our bodies, we would know that
indifference, lust, and greed are also the offspring of this scowling beast which
strives to keep us at war, one stranger against the next. Again, the answer is
to recognize the reasons why we are not yet united as a family of man, and
then set-out to do something about it. Most of us do pretty well at describing
a problem or putting a face on the nemesis of our hearts, but we are seemingly
helpless on our own to *prescribe* a proper solution that will take us to being
reconciled as one faithful lot once again. This is why we must continue to
reach-out to one another in any way we can, not only to advance the healing
of those we love, but so as to absorb the pain of the countless souls who are
still too timid, reserved, and reticent to agonize in public on their own. Did
not our Dear Lord suffer and die on the Cross so that everyone who ever lives
would clearly see Him there? Indeed, He is still our Teacher, in good times
and in bad; and we must realize that our trials are the doorstops which keep
our avenues of opportunity to do better from being blown shut by the gales
of our own defiance. We must make sure that our loyalties are not given to
an uncertain fate or some disfigured emotion, and recognize that our victories
lie not too far ahead to be seen in advance nowadays. We are oftentimes the
enemies of our own destiny by our unwarranted shyness and unfounded lack
of hope.

Our lives would be sheer bedlam if we did not recognize the little signs that God places in our midst as the receptacles of His Love in which we must place our fullest trust. There is a greater world of nobler virtues which keeps knocking on our doors and asking to come in. Answering them is of the greatest importance as to whether we will ever allow God to heal us in our own contemporary day. Some people just cannot accept the fact that miracles do exist; and these are the ones who never seem to outlive the grief with which they have chosen to cope until the day they finally die; somehow inadvertently passing it along to their succeeding generations. There is no question that we must all set goals that serve to make us a better people. By all means, our existence revolves around our remembrance of our spiritual dreams and the secular heroes whom we have all struggled to become. When referring to the art of reeling-in daily life, most of us seem to be unmoved by the passing commentary of our collateral friends or the circumstances that are bred by others because the veil before our eyes keeps us from seeing their hearts that well. Our human body is a biomechanical composite of cells and organs, made-up of mortal and emasculative flesh, and is a physiological mass of fragile contusions which we have borne through confronting the rest of the world from the moment when we were first slapped on the buttocks in the obstetrics ward; and most of us have grown-up far too fast to suit our minds, moods, fashions, and whims. Many others have never begun the process of their spiritual maturation at all. Indeed, it is true that death may own the night; but the dawn of our decency belongs to the Resurrection of Christ. Evil may have been the first arsonist in the conflagration of our better days; but it is God, Himself, who is about to set the world aflame with the firebrand of the Cross. Our Almighty Father knows that there are continental quarters which house some of the most hard-hearted extremists, coldly-calculating minds, dead consciences, and hate-mongers that the world has ever seen in the annals of history. But, the judgement of His Justice and Peace will assuredly prevail over them all upon the last ticking of the clock. Most of us are unsure about how profound this day will really be because one thing we rarely, if ever, do is accurately predict or anticipate the consequences and aftermath of our own overt actions; be they evasive, preemptive, traumatic, or well-designed. God will place them all into proper perspective when He knows the time is ripe.

We are not the immortal ones who have already gone to the fullest Light of Heaven because God's Will is continuing to succeed. He tells us outright, *memento mori*, "remember that thou must die;" but we all seem to be too preoccupied by our own synthetic gizmos, flying contraptions, inexcusably lame deceptions, and deliberating distortions to pay Him any mind. Titans and gladiators pass not so gently when they are finally faced with the ferocity of death; but we must be like Christological warriors when it comes our time to take to the spiritual air and leave our quiescent flesh behind. It is true that we must learn when to hang-on with the grip of glaziers and when to let-go and forget. Let us remember in the interim that the freedom to procure does not always infer the right to possess. We are given a human will so as to acknowledge the Holy Gospel, but Jesus reserves the right to determine how well we have accepted it and have complied to our noble best. Religious opportunism is not always seen as a precedent to the success of the destiny of our soul if we are not sincere in our Love for humanity as a whole. Once we have begun the process of learning what life truly means; physically, spiritually, and intellectually; we will understand that our existence can never be an end in itself. By every measure, we must strive in earnest to reach those Pearly Gates that so many of our peers have only mused about over the passages of time. Do we recall the little boy who said that he once dreamed about capturing a cyclone while nobody else was watching and hid it beneath his bed? With the child-like faith that Jesus asks us to live, we should assume that his dream was real until God tells us anything otherwise. He will cause the visions of little children to come true and then some; making their nightmares disappear for good. If we are His innocent flock of sheep in this same innocuous likeness, we too will know what it means to conquer Creation by storm. Jesus Christ is the Supreme Doyen to humanity and the caretaker of us all; and He knows which of His people are those who are given to His Love. The time for our concession to His Justice is nigh because all of the signs of the ages are becoming parallel to the Revelation which He etched into time, some 2000 years ago. However, many philosophers and theorists continue to hold that humankind would have somehow restored the world back to peaceful order even so, and that the Son of God would have never had to die in order to effect it. But, the Almighty Father knew that even He would have grown too impatient while waiting for us to bring righteousness into such a brash and incendiary globe. If something was to be done to restore us to incorruption, it had to be done by Him, and through the Divine Providence of the Most High Trinity.

So, let us trust and believe in those miracles that the Holy Bible tells us about. It is time for us to confess our naked aggression to God and man, alike, so that no one will cower in fear anymore that their doors may be stormed by the ravages of sweltering hatred and the throes of a cultured revenge. Let the world be more than the implication of greatness for the modern ages to come; for this is the moment when all heroes shall come to the fore and pull together, one and all, for the movement of the catastrophic stones of social injustice to be cast forever into the depths of the final Abyss. Jesus is reigning freely over the home of the brave; and it is we who should be hailing Him as its Savior and King. He may not yet be tossing pillars through our livingroom windows in the middle of the night, but we can still acknowledge that He has arrived in Spirit and Truth in His own particular way. How so? I once opened the morning newspaper at my home in Springfield, Illinois in May 2001, and took a quick look inside. When I removed the rubber-band that was keeping it curled, three little millers flew out into the room and suddenly disappeared. They fluttered away so rapidly that I never did discover where they eventually went. I then opened the paper to the City/State page and found a huge photograph and an article about a local junior high school class having recently made over 150 paper butterflies in remembrance of the children of the Nazi Holocaust in the 1940s. I just kept thinking what a wonderful sign of the Most Blessed Trinity this had been for me. Could I have guessed that this would be a miracle for which someone might ever pray? Indeed, I attended the Holy Sacrifice of the Mass at our local Diocesan Cathedral of the Immaculate Conception at 5:00 o'clock that very day, and the first thing I saw before the Sacred Mysteries began was a singular butterfly; fluttering freely around the Altar and Baptismal Font as we were celebrating the Season of Easter. I had never in my life seen a butterfly inside the Sanctuary before; and I have yet to see one since. I trust that this was the subtly of God at His best; and I will continue to believe it to be.

There are too many sordid trails that are luring us to take their lead into another pose and purpose; those which will never guide us toward the purified goodness which will eventually overtake the Earth at last. Let us hold to the Wisdom that lives so cunningly in our hearts, and make life's years an experience in awesome genius; for there is no such thing as personal defeat or a lack of perspective on the journey of Holy Love. We may be somewhat distracted by the noncommissioned missteps of our brothers at times, but they shall also see the Truth of goodness with the aforethought of voyagers someday. Forgiveness must always be our goal because it is never too late to amend what we have inscribed upon the surfaces of life, no matter what Pontius Pilate may have said about the writing of his own official edicts. If we focus our energies and every waking moment upon becoming *Divine Love*, there will never be another instant to be given to despair or ever lived in vain again. The august recollections to which we cling day after day are more than just a repertoire of our fondest memories now; they are prophecies that we hold toward the culmination of our often elusive dreams. We used to perceive the years as though we, ourselves, somehow occupied them like a child in a meadow or ravine; and the seasons seemed to be so broad and expansive back then. But, they pass-by so quickly now, while the days come too suddenly and are congested, as though we have grown to become a steed in a cattle stall somewhere. It is true that no single man has a fix on what the ages can do to the greater societies of the world; but we are all still subject to their effects, no matter what our calling or occupation was really intended to be. In light of our helpless nature and less-than benign demeanor, do we adapt to the scurrying of the years that are always beyond our control? Are there some among us who actually retreat in submission into the wild so as to remain anonymous to other noble men? It is true that our words, either spoken or written, are only symbols; no matter in what language we choose to speak; and their only service is to communicate the sentiments of our hearts, or at least our intentions and our needs. Let us also remember the raw and natural capacity we own to see things well, to hold to the extraordinarily pious and distinct character that the Holy Paraclete has bestowed upon us to ward-off the jinns who keep trying to take our spirits into the pit of despondence while we search for the Truth of God in every thought and action that we ultimately commend. It was the Austrian-born musical composer, Wolfgang Amadeus Mozart (1756-1791), who is credited with having said, *"Neither a lofty degree of intelligence nor imagination, nor both together, go into the making of genius. Love, love, love; that is the soul of genius."* And, so it is, that we hold fast to the scores and melodies which he inscribed for the rest of humanity to hear; his own language of Love that brought such solace and peaceful composure to the aching in our hearts. We can heed his spiritual architecture still by understanding the passion that made him collect those magical notes into the workings of strings and horns, keyboards, cellos, harps, and kettle-drums bellowing through the air.

Whatever it is that makes men sit with feathered-pen in hand and scribble their feelings on a page, this is the same tenderness with which the rest of us must approach the caverns of life through the talents that God has bequeathed to each and everyone. There is nothing in the course of our existence that can stop the ingenuity of an inspirited heart once it has finally taken flight. We can go forward and backward through time, transcending the elements of distance and space, and predict how our fortunes might arise through this same genius that even Mozart saw in his day. It is the identical and timeless profundity that causes us to raise our heads and say to ourselves and to the rest of the world, "We are a dignified people in the Kingdom of Heaven; and we do not have to take the scourges of mortal life laying on our faces anymore." It pains us to see so many marriages ending in divorce, separation, and annulment these days; and we wonder what rippling-effect they have on our families and circles of friends. It is almost too agonizing to see a photograph of a divorced couple from years-passed as they are seen walking in the park with their firstborn child holding each of their hands between them in a union of familial love. Now, that same toddler has grown to be a bitterly-scarred adult living on his own who looks back at that picture while weeping and pondering to himself; if only he would have clutched their hands a little bit harder back then, maybe his mommy and daddy would never have broken apart and shattered his life into shreds. He was the conjoining link whom they forgot to remember from those days when he would raise his feet high above the surface of the ground and swing his tiny legs through midair while clinging to the sweaty palms of his greatest friends on Earth. We may not have the prescience to predict what difficulties we will encounter as the years continue to pass; but we can certainly ensure that they will never be able to tear us down again or pepper our joy to the point that we will not be able to muster a smile in a crowd for another snapshot for history to record. We are still the glistening violets in the flower patches of the ultimate Reign of God; and He will never allow us to feel too broken-hearted for very long. Our souls are the animated crystal and priceless sterling that make His treasury complete; and nothing can ever steal us from under the guard of the Angels whom He has so kindly dispensed to protect us from now on.

While we rarely take the time to look at each other as we pass-by in the corridor, the followers of hatred are perched to steal us from under the nose of those who are closest to our hearts. They are like ferocious jaguars hiding beneath the bushes to see whether we might be the ones to whom our parents turned their backs and let go. Are these images enough to teach us what it means to take our affection for one another more seriously now? Can we write our own sonatas and symphonies with the brilliance of the greatest composers who ever lived by simply turning to our brethren on the street and asking them to listen to our spirits until they do not writhe in pain anymore? It cannot be too much to ask that we might cast-away the secular cloak of isolationism long enough to know that our lives matter to somebody once in awhile, at least for a second longer than our worst emotions might have us comprehend. All of this speaks to the necessity for us to be quite wary about what influences we allow to affect us, and how we react to the barnstorms that blast against our consciousness all the time. We must erect a shield of righteousness to protect us from the harrowing elements of the material world; but it must not be one which holds us sequestered from the rest of humankind or keeps us from reaching-out to them in faith. Indeed, we should never be so callous that we prohibit those who need us from asking for our aid. Our gentle guard must be not unlike those transparent nimbuses we often see around depictions of the heads of the Saints and other pious people in paintings and in print. They carry a hallowed aura about their faces which keeps their inhibitions in check, while allowing their holier selves to flourish and pour forth. What would we be today if not for the letters and papers they have left us in advance so we can know what it means to become exemplary in their paths? Our gratitude must consist of our emulation of their deeds as we walk toward the horizons of the Earth. We must allow their imitation of Christ to hold our future hostage until we come to understand why they sacrificed even unto their deaths to usher His Kingdom through time. If we do these things well, there will never be another Holy Matrimony that will ever perish again; not another unborn child will be aborted from a mother's womb; no living being will continue to be stricken by the atrocities of famine or disease; and not a single soul will ever lack the consolation that might bring him to fight for another day before choosing to take his own life in the stark desolation of a prison cell. Hereafter, can there be a new beginning for a world that seems bent on finding its greatest hour to be the hollow stroke of midnight, rather than the Paschal Dawn? The answer is an unequivocal "yes," with the caveat that the refinement of our modesty should also find a home inside our willingness to go forward in the Passion, Blood, and Resurrection of Our Savior on the Cross.

There is a certain transfiguration which must overwhelm us if we expect to have this almost supernatural existence survive in our present-day world. Our minds often play tricks by having us believe that certain tragedies in life are unavoidable, that our deja vu experiences are a premonition of something horrible yet to come, that the images we conjure are the result of some automatism or our exploitation of the effects of chance, that coincidences are just random juxtapositions and not truly signal graces from God, and that our religious articles and holy relics do nothing to enhance our spiritual faith. Indeed, there may be an infinite number to the collection of our holiest sacrifices, but we should never be satisfied until we have amassed so many that it would take the Dominion Angels the rest of Eternity to count them. There should be no limit; we should not keep score, and none should be considered too great in magnitude to offer to the most despicable wretches in our midst. If we are to discover a sound mutual affection inside the prismatic depths of one another's soul, we must be willing to dive headlong into their agony and try with all our might to deliver them intact to the shores of reconciliation. Moreover, this must be done as a desire of the heart and not by some calculated cost-benefit analysis to see what we might profit in return. While collegiate sociologists talk about our capacity to own-up to our public responsibilities, loyalties, considerations, and casual predictability; which are notable enough in themselves; Christian faith goes even further by examining our conscience before the virtues of piety, servitude, humility, and eternal Love. Intellectuals seek to expound upon an environment where their peers are conscientiously approaching well-structured tasks for the purpose of evaluating their own eccentric and experimental postulates. There is far less control in the real world than what most of us profess to believe, and such models are much more difficult to find without their subjects being somehow previously forewarned. In other words, one cannot rehearse to be a Christian in a sequestered society of wary individuals who already know what is expected from them. We must encounter reality in the same way it approaches us, with anticipation for the unforseen and not-so-obvious, and willingness to take our feelings off of our sleeves and put them where they cannot be so easily crumpled. If we attempt to decipher human life through a petri-dish approach to comprehending the massive numbers of actions and emotions that exist in the world, we will have the same feeling as the middle-school student who looked up the meaning of a word in the dictionary and was more confused by the definition than he was before he ever opened it. There is no substitute for maintaining a simplistic approach to interpersonal love and anticipating that the multi-dimensional problems of our peers are much better solved by offering it to them, rather than somehow trying to inversely wrap their twisted logic around our spiritual understanding of the meaning of life.

There will be people approach us as we greet them at daybreak who will have just exited their laboratories and ask us how we can be so content while living inside a Christian faith which has such intangible boundaries; believing that what we contend must be the result of some anomaly in their generally accepted assumption of periodic growth. We should turn to every one of them and ask whether the study of psychoanalysis fields a definition for human love other than a fixed relational reference to someone's blind infatuation, cyclical dependencies, or quantified expendable perception; which ought to send them retreating right back into their chambers to take another look at the works of Sigmund Freud. Love in the way it is defined by Jesus Christ is much more sublimely apparent and sensible than any philosophical practitioner has the capacity or mechanism to define. Love is the invincible and transparent Truth because no one who identifies with it ever wishes to keep to himself. It is a Divine power so intense in nature that it can scarcely be placed into words; but rather best be known by its expression through our silent prayers, audible words, and identifiable deeds. And, we do these things without regard to how much we think of ourselves. Whether we feel inferior or superior to others has nothing to do with the final outcome of the element of time; for the true measurement of our success is ultimately tallied in accordance with the record of how we make *others* feel in light of our shared devotions and whether we overcame our own imperfections and weaknesses. If the clinical Myers-Briggs Type Indicator (MBTI) psychological examination that is used as an analytical tool to determine the mental stability and composure of certain individuals is in any way a reasonably authentic landmark of who we are as private citizens, what can we say about those who undergo it that are not forthcoming in their responses to the various hypothetical conditions and interrogatories which are put to them? There has hardly been such a study in which the examiner did not ask the question, "...do you hate your mother?" or something similar to this. An entire gamut of emotional ties often exists between family members that human development counselors would like to get their hands on to decide whether there may have been some seed of dysfunction or irrational animosity implanted in our subconsciousness from long ago which affects the way we are today. Can we not see that all of this gobbledygook runs contrary to the doctrines of Christianity because we are healed of the effects of the past through the reinvigorating intercession of God? He is our new health, clear vision, and the wisdom we need to overcome our instabilities; so there is no need to ever look backward again.

This is how we should embrace those who once betrayed, abused, or abandoned us; by sitting-down to dine with our captors, making peace with our detractors, extending our hands in fellowship to those who have tried to destroy us, and uniting in Holy Communion with people from all walks of life in whose company we would never before have allowed ourselves to be seen in the pit of night, let alone stand beside them on a street corner in the broadness of midday. Living the spiritual Truth of comprehensive Love allows us to get beyond all of this; not by gerrymandering around certain people whom we may always disdain until the moment we die; but shooting straight to the heart of our own inhibitions and idiosyncrasies to say *yes* to every man, woman, and child of any color or creed who may look our way with a face of pity, need, or even an unwarranted callous expression. It is a sacrifice to be able to accept them all in the same way that we freely devote ourselves to those we have long admired; but time is not on our side if we choose to decline too long before we make amends. If we never allow our determination to grow as thin as our patience sometimes does, we will be successful in becoming the perfected lovers of all God's creatures; young and old; red, yellow, black, and white; rich and poor, faithful and estranged, and friend or foe. Jesus has commanded us to forgive our trespassers not just seven times, but seventy multiplied by seven times. So, why can we not absolve those whom we perceive to be our enemies at least once in our lives? There is no doubt that He knew we would not really keep count, but suffice it to say that His intention is for us to never show-up at death's door with a grudge against somebody else in the palms of our hands. Sometimes it seems as though the Holy Spirit is keeping a more accurate accounting than we do ourselves about how we guard our conduct through the years. What a shame it would be for any one of us to stand before Jesus Christ in Final Judgement to see that our faults have been highlighted in flourescent orange, rather than having been erased altogether by our previous acceptance of His Blood on the Cross. If we continue to abdicate our duties before Him for very much longer, we may die hereafter with no way to retract the past or retrace our steps through a more admirable poise.

However, by embracing the proprietary dignity of our Christian values now, and in advance; we will arrive at our mortal parting to see that the Cross has been the eradicator of our every wrongdoing as though God's promise to turn the world upside-down has been fulfilled and His resulting Etch-a-Sketch approach to our absolution has given us a new slate on which to begin. These are more than just philanthropic images of hope from His Paraclete on High; they are parables to help us understand what complete forgiveness is. Why? Because, as I have said before, there are no words to describe the indelible pardon we receive in the presence of God if only we will accept the Crucifixion of His Sacrificed Son now. He does not dissect our lives into certain instances or crescendos the way we often do because He has already seen them in their entire length and breadth. To Him, our mortal existence is a full reflection of His generative purpose and infinite Will; so our decisions and reactions rarely take Him by surprise. We are the ones who are charged with formulating our compliance with what He wishes us to do; and we have both a compass and guide in the Holy Spirit for finding our way back to Him in the wilderness of our own obstinance and deceit. If there is a falsehood still lurking somewhere on the back of our tongue, we can be sure that He will purge it from us before we ever see His Pristine Face. We are a purified people in His Divinity; and that is why we are capable of serving-out the charge of our most honorable sacrifices without fear of being rejected as hypocrites to the rest of the world or as false prophets before our acquaintances back home. They may still not believe what we are telling them, but at least they will know we are trying. All Truth and power springs from the center of our hearts; and no one can steal it from us if we share it through the fulfillment of our faith.

Chapter Ten
Our Savior, Prophet, and King

———————————

How many times have we heard someone say that when we find the Perfect Cup, we should let it fill us up? This has been the clarion call and heralded advice from our elders and sages throughout the generations; but their opinions have differed on the definition of what is "perfect." However, the profoundly wise man will eventually tender his focus upon the only preeminently Sinless Human Male to ever walk the face of the globe; Jesus Christ, the Son of God. He is not some mysterious or unknowable stranger from an ancient proverbial myth, He is the reason we are alive today and approaching the presentation of the ages before the Deity of God. As His faithful people, we are supposed to move markedly and precipitously into a communicable understanding of the meaning of human existence; and we discover it only in the Truth in which Christ is born, and that He also purely exemplifies. How else could God have taught us to become the likeness of the immaculate Garden of Eden if He had not sent its most Holy Relic into the mortal world to show us? It no doubt takes our submissiveness to believe it, but faith is also a gift from Heaven that He gladly dispenses if only we will step from behind the obstruction of our egos and humble ourselves to ask. Preachers and evangelists have stood in public arenas and private sanctuaries for centuries now; quoting from a Bible of Scriptures that probably two-thirds of their listeners could not muster the strength to believe-in. Even so, this same New Testament is as much the Truth as Christ, Himself; and is the code of ethics from which we must procure the procession of our actions if we expect to accompany Him when we die. His Holy Spirit speaks in parables to our consciences because our haughty intellects refuse to listen to the Will of God, spoken quite plainly through the intonation of His phrases. Our mortal souls seek something more poetic in discovering the mystery of how we were created because there is a certain pageantry which attends our desire to know. After all, are we not taught that there is romance involved in the begetting of all new life? Our spirits pine for the comfort that helps us anticipate our impending return to a home about which we have often heard, but have never truly seen; and we somehow inherently feel as though there is great solace and majesty there. We are quite fond of autumn when the trees blush and their foliage falls deeply in love with the ground below, and enters its billets and bunkers beneath the snow, while the Springtime cannot be far behind. Then, too, we enjoy the aroma of burning leaves on a clear Fall afternoon with just a whisper of a breeze aloft, as though the entire block on which we live has become a cup of incense for the day. This reminds us of a welcome funeral pyre for everything invisible in life we could not incinerate of our own accord; such as hatred, madness, jealousy, and loneliness; almost like smelling the fragrance of a fine cigar that God might be smoking while watching us from His Throne in Heaven, happy that we are thinking about His Eternity for at least a little while.

What has been spoken and recorded about such poetic imaginings from practicing scholars and laymen, alike, is that our hearts are contrastingly filled with pious wit, epigrams, ambiguities, ironies, the paradoxical harmony of dissonance, and our individual perceptions of a single orthodoxy called the "personal conscience" about our relationship with all Creation. It is our own responsibility hereafter to somehow greet one another in that same singularity as a united people worldwide; but it looks hopelessly obvious to many of us that it may never be in our span of life. If we postulate that human Love is the perpetual existence of the Truth to which I have previously referred, and that all immortal reasoning is soundly founded upon its base, then should we not also understand that anyone who wishes to share it will ultimately be either forced or led there by supernatural powers the likes of which we have never previously seen? Is this not the most appropriate axiom upon which we should position the purpose of our spiritual faith; that we intrinsically "know" about the future of our veritable immortality as if it is a forgone conclusion, even though its source rests beyond our immediate sight? We communicate over the medium of an acceptance of mutual comprehension; which is produced by the trivium of grammar, rhetoric, and logic; but none of these seems to be any aid in our search for the meaning of life when we do not utilize them in our struggle to adhere to the Truth. All conformity, actuality, reality, principle, accuracy, factualness, plausibility, and inevitability are the ripened fruits of this same Omnipotence by which we have been given the gift of life; and *from* which we are errantly estranged. If we would only willingly acknowledge that our Divine Creator is this essential vessel through whom we can discover and determine every aspect of our human origin, sustenance, advancement, and culmination; we will become one Body of Love under the Godhead of Triune subsistence which He has always hoped we would be. Therein and by, we have discovered the Supreme Person of all the universes, Jesus Christ; who is the exemplary nature of human idealism, set before us by our Father in Heaven whom we are required to emulate. The all-encompassing veracity of immortal Love on the Earth is a product of our obedience to Him in all desires and in every way; by our essential "being," and in everything we do. It is in Christ Jesus that we have uncovered the secret of our interpersonal deportment; for He is not only our example for life, but simultaneously our purpose for living, too. Beyond anything He might Will or Command us to do in which we may find ourselves otherwise engaged, we would surely be existing only for the sake of the proverbial vanity of vanities.

Every time a shaft of light or revelation cuts through the darkness of our everyday world, or we finally arrive at the verge of discovering who God really is, it seems as though some scientist, pragmatic philosopher, or existentialist finds some way to pooh-pooh it or tries to frighten the infant faith of millions of spiritually-hungry people away. Why is this so? Because the more the Divine Truth becomes apparent in the material world, the less relevant their musings seem to be. Such people live only by assumption, while casting formal religion aside as something else for those who are only clinically introverted and weak-of-mind. They will often say something like, "...there is a likelihood or probability," that some transcendental purpose may be linked to certain unexplainable circumstances or undertakings; but this mere questioning lends too much sedentary doubt to those who may have previously chosen to lean in the direction of accepting the presence of God in the universe, but suddenly discover themselves teetering back into the physical world while falling to the temptations of uncertainty with a bang of their heads on the ground and a huge question mark coiled above them in midair. There are millions of people who hold to the proposition that, "...if it looks like a duck, walks like a duck, and sounds like a duck; then it must be a duck." But, as soon as someone tells them that God has sent one of His angels into the world from Heaven in the form of a feathery bird with a bill and webbed-feet, that quacks and floats on the surface of a pond; they will be the first to say that the little specimen is definitely *not* a duck because they refuse to believe in God. While there are several factors that bring some individuals to refuse to accept the overtures of their Maker, not the least of which is some pent-up childhood frustration, or their infatuation with carnal lust, or an addiction to physical objects and mind-altering substances; the main culprit keeping them from believing is their own conventional pride. The highest and chief good that any mortal can achieve is to acknowledge without inhibition that we live inside a manifested Creation which is the subsequent product of the predestined and deliberate architecture of an Omnificent King; not the inordinate rendering of some inexplicably humongous explosion or a remainder of an invariable accident. God may not have positioned a visible pronoun before our faces which would allow us to research His Holy Name in a telephone book; but He has certainly left us with sufficient details for deducing the reasons why we are among the living, where we are located in time and space, and when we should expect to be transposed into the fullness of His presence. As for the latter, we are told in no uncertain terms that His Kingdom is nigh at hand.

The entire perceptible world we see everyday has been placed into the status of receivership by Jesus Christ from whence He claimed it for His own upon His excruciating Death on the Cross; and it is His final adjudication that will determine our fate. Were it not for our own reckless abandon, we would have already recognized this as being the Truth long ago. And, how does this apply to our contemporary world? The examples are almost too innumerable to envision. The most poignant question I have encountered is one that was put to a diocesan priest two months after the terrorists attacks on the World Trade Center, the Pentagon, and our civilian airplanes on September 11, 2001. Father John Dietzen, from the Diocese of Peoria, Illinois was quoted by the Catholic News Service as having taken the following question in his weekly column from a person in Maryland about the Afghan hijackers, *"...How does God deal with suicide bombers who believe they will go to "paradise" and be with Allah? How can they go to Hell if they do not believe in it? For that matter, how can anyone go to Hell who doesn't believe in it?"* For all intents and purposes, the questioner was wishing to know whether it is proper for anyone to either assume or hope that the souls of the individuals who commandeered our jetliners and guided them into their targets are now burning in the flames of Gehenna. Father Dietzen's response comes about as close to asserting the Truth as anyone I have ever heard broaching the subject of the fate of those who caused the U.S. so much suffering and grief. While his answer may be somewhat difficult for us to accept, there is no doubt that the Holy Spirit is speaking through him, *"...more than a few Americans, among them religious leaders, have publicly proclaimed that all the dead terrorists are burning in Hell, and those still alive will do so. Arrogance like this is unworthy of any thoughtful human being, let alone any Christian. Judgements like this about the condition and fate of other people's souls are wholly beyond our reach. The pretense of having sufficient knowledge and wisdom to make such judgements invades territory that belongs to God alone. God created all of us, including the terrorists, out of Love. And Jesus, as Saint Paul declares, died for each of us. It is, therefore, the worst sort of blasphemy to dare to tell God which of His children He will reject or to tell Jesus which of those for whom He died must be condemned. We must also confront our complete ignorance of how God's Grace and Truth may have transformed a person, not only during his or her life, but also in the last moments. We believe God performs incredible miracles of Mercy. Who knows which ones took place here? We don't know, of course, and we will never know in this life. But, it is with these instincts of faith and hope, aware that we all desperately need His Mercy, that the Church has us pray, just after the Consecration at the Holy Sacrifice of the Mass, that God will bring our deceased 'brothers and sisters, and all the departed,' all people in the world who have died, into the Light of His presence."*

Father Dietzen's response is neither cynical nor condescending to the slightest degree. We cannot self-appoint ourselves as jurists over our peers if we are blind to their motivations, the articles of their faith, or their visions and precepts. The inference in this entire matter is that Jesus Christ is Our Savior, Prophet, and King; and it is He who shall make the ultimate decision as to whether any soul is worthy of the Sacrifice He endured to redeem them. If we hold-out in resistance or defiance to the Truth of interpersonal forgiveness, we have no right to call ourselves Christians; even when it comes to the gruesome horror of the transgressions which were perpetrated against us by those foreign nationals in September 2001. We can call upon the preeminent authority, control, and tradition of our American democracy all we wish; but we cannot circumvent the rules of engagement that the Son of God placed before us from the summit of every mountaintop where He ever stood to speak, including the Hill of Mount Calvary where He was tortured, impaled, maimed, Crucified, and skewered. It may be rather difficult for us to accept; but vengeance is *His*, and not the rightful inheritance of any mortal man. If we attempt to catapult our intentions beyond what Jesus said by confirming that we are undertaking the effort of preventing further terrorism by prosecuting additional offensive wars, then we are no better than those who proclaim that brute force is more powerful than the ultimate influence of unconditional Love. For all the gloating we do here in America about freedom, learning, lore, and scholarship these days; can we not also be more spiritually articulate in expressing our disdain for the actions of others than by becoming the largest bully on the block, while exterminating massive numbers of innocent civilians in the process of trying to bring only a few-hundred criminals to justice? It is not unjustified for us to rethink this question based upon the teachings of Christ; for we are already capitulating to our own cravings for revenge if we do not accept the minimum standards of searching for peace in the midst of war as a means of regaining stability among the community of nations.

The fact remains, however, that we are still quite unwilling and rather hesitant to perceive the tragedies of life through a more spiritualized context; "...why does God allow such terrible things to happen," is the most popular question asked by those who care enough about peace and dignity to be concerned. It is precisely in this component of our social conscience that we can learn how to avoid such catastrophes in the future. The proper answer is that He lets them occur so as to allow us to establish new principles, make the correct changes, and redress the grievances which brought them about in the first place; toward the goal of never letting them happen again. Thereby, we are urged to make peace before war becomes a sustainable option; to heal our relationships with other peoples prior to taking a stand against them; and to proactively establish good will with our neighbors in advance to ward-off the possibility of first-strike offenses; be they rhetorical, inter-societal, punitive, or outright physically abusive. All of this is a procession that begins at the foundation of the decency in the human heart; which is the center of our faith and the catalyst of the Church. No single person or circle of peers can move in any direction but backward for the purpose of coming to terms with the Truth as it stands without engaging the virtues which are espoused by the Christian faithful, and that prove to the rest of the world that Christ is their Savior once they are deployed. This is one of the most prominent aspects of an address I have placed on the World Wide Web, www.ImmaculateMary.org, where I have displayed my first two books, entitled *Morning Star Over America* and *At the Water's Edge*. Through this venue, many people have submitted their comments, asked pertinent questions about the Church and the Catholic faith, or simply placed prayer petitions in writing for their personal intentions to be lifted to God. I once discovered that I, too, was faced with answering a terse interrogatory which was rather revealing to the tenor of our faith. A very concerned woman asked, *"...after Jesus' Ascension to Heaven—when the Disciples received gifts on Pentecost Sunday, some became teachers and doctors. We, too are followers of Jesus, so why do no others in our churches heal cancer, leukemia, heart attacks, or even order the stupid devil to leave poor little children alone in Jesus' Name? Where is the courage and faith of the Church? If you want, you can answer this question, if not—we don't have high expectations from our priests anyway. God Bless."*

Sadly enough, this person hit the nail right on the head regarding the fidelity of our trust that Jesus Christ will help us vocalize our intentions, ratify our actions toward the promotion of His Kingdom in our modern-day, and provide the miracles we require to prove to anyone in our midst that there is no greater prescience, power, or convalescence ever to be found anywhere in Creation than in Himself. But, with the Divine assistance and the intercession of the Blessed Virgin Mary, I was able to respond to her question in a most comprehensive way. We must always remember that our authority to conduct human affairs, be they private or public, is procured through our faith *in* the Church. There are many people who have busied themselves cross-examining the motivations of Jesus Christ as He continues to grow the maturity of the Magisterium, the Hierarchy, the Liturgies, and reaffirming His established Traditions by bringing His faithful people in alignment with His Will; not the other way around. There is no question that Roman Catholics and other Christians everywhere will be able to touch a dying child on the hand and immediately raise him from his deathbed at the precise moment when the very people who compose the Church stop doubting that it can be done. We must begin to realize that we are presently in a period of gestation, i.e., Jesus has vested us with every ascendency conceivable while we still reside in mortal flesh. He has placed the seed of perfection inside us which will sprout into all the miraculous power we will ever need in a million lifetimes. Moreover, by virtue of the graces that are still raining-down upon the Earth in reflection of the lives of those people whose legacies I discussed in Chapter 6 of this book, by the sacrifices of the suffering poor all around the globe, and through the supernatural intercession of the Immaculate Mother of God, we are given plentiful opportunities to wield the power that some among us still believe is missing. Do we remember how many times Jesus said, "...rise and go on, your faith has healed you?" What He seems to be saying to us today is, "...expect to wield no miracles for now; your doubts are holding you back!" Hence, the present is a pregnant moment in history for all of us; while God is waiting for His collective Church to overtake the world through a wielding of Holy Love that will conquer His opposition so quickly that anyone who stands against Him will assume that the entire universe somehow descended upon them and miraculously slapped the taste of obstinace out of their mouths.

    We are not asked to do this alone; for does not Our Lord also implore us to call upon the intercession of the Saints so as to bring every spiritual, mental, and physical healing we might ever seek from Him into being? We should always remember that the Church Triumphant in Heaven is composed of an immeasurably larger number of souls than the Faith Church on Earth. When we are seeking cures for cancer, leukemia, heart disease, and other afflictions and addictions, there is an entire Communion of Saints just waiting to be asked to go to God and beseech His Divine healing for us poor sinners who are still groveling on the soil atop the ground. The Blessed Mother once said that this is part of the "reciprocal" nature of the Mystical Body of Christ; that we are expected to turn to those who have already died and ask them to wield the intercessory powers they could have never owned before their mortal passing. In response to the question on my web site; if we are searching for means to mend our bodies and souls, our venue for achieving it is to look skyward and ask the Light of Paradise to expedite its swift resolution from beyond the graves of the faithful departed. What better way to prove to Jesus that we own a complete faithfulness in the invincible nature of His Paschal Resurrection? Indeed, the questioner should consider why the Holy Father in Vatican City anticipates at least two miracles from those who are beatified in order to establish the conditions necessary to canonize them as Saints? He knows, as does every citizen of Heaven, that this will bring us to focus our attention on the afterlife and realize that we are truly helpless without its inclusion in everything we do. Our Lord God Almighty is waiting for us to overturn our hearts and supplications to His Throne beyond the stars and recognize that His Son is the reason we have convened our faith in Him from the start. What good is there in professing our belief in a Prophet and King if we never ask Him to foresee our future or dispense His mighty blessings upon His people far below? Do we wish to see more evidence? Have we forgotten that there are prayer groups all over the world where infirm individuals are placed among those who are reciting the Sacred Mysteries of the Most Holy Rosary; and the instant they "lay their hands" on them while asking Jesus to restore them, the healing is begun. Let us also never forget that there are countless miraculous healings still ongoing at the various Marian Shrines around the globe; in Fatima, Lourdes, and Guadalupe, just to cite a few.

Miracles abound throughout the neighborhoods and hamlets in every quarter of the world, but too many people pass them off as mere coincidences or some physician's prescribed medication finally taking effect. I would respectfully ask that Regina, who is the woman that placed the question on my web site, to read the final *Essay* in my book, *At the Water's Edge*, which is dated February 10, 2001, and she will thereafter discover the true reason why Jesus Christ is having difficulty effecting the restoration of the nations in our day. The factual nature of the assertions I have made therein are quite revealing as to why the "supernature" of our own powers is not more prevalent to those who pine to see its presence before they die. It also cites the source of many other graces that are ours if only we will stop waiting for God to strike us on the brow with the handle of an ax before we finally begin to act through the mentioning of His Name in places where He has been chided and shunned for centuries before. When was the last time anyone such as Regina walked into a local tavern or department store and asked the patrons inside if they ever heard of the Most Holy Eucharist from the Sacred Altar of the

Roman Catholic Church? There is no greater healing to be found on the Earth than that which we are given in the Most Blessed Sacrament! For whatever reason, Christ's faithful people have chosen to take this Holy Communion for granted nowadays, not even mentioning it between Masses among themselves, let alone to someone who has never seen the inside of a Sanctuary or who thought the Holy Altar was a place where only a hymnal is laid. The very Crucifixion of Jesus Christ that has redeemed our mortal souls takes place before the ones who are so fortunate to attend; but we seem to just walk through the vestibule and out the front door with our minds trained upon what we are going to serve our guests for dinner at night. It seems as though it would be a hardship for anyone to mention that there are Bishops and other Ecclesiastical Fathers who have expelled demons from properties and articles, and exorcized the devil from possessed people by the scores in the history of the Church; and if this is not miraculous power and a signal grace from God that He has instilled the fire of Truth in His holy priests, then we had better worry whether the sun is going to rise tomorrow.

The last part of this discussion revolves around a manifestation which has existed since time immemorial. Have not many people thought about the fact that Jesus Christ has invited us to join Him on the Cross; to suffer for the sake of those whose souls would otherwise perish at the end of time; to mitigate the error of the millions who have cast their faith aside; to provide the ullage about which Saint Paul spoke that will crack the clinched fists of the defiant wide-open and remove the pigeon waste from their eyes so they can see what individual faith, personal nobility, community service, and sacrificial Love are all about? Human agony is no accident; and God knows from whence it is begotten. There is no sickness, cancer or disease in Paradise, no poverty, no punitive detention, and no needs of any other kind; because all souls who reside there are as perfect as before they were ever born. Why? Because they have again become the original essence of Divine obedience; saying only *yes* to God in all He requires, perceiving their peers with kind ingenuity, taking only what share they might need to survive, and leaving the door open to every avenue of holiness that ever existed in the history of humankind. Does our contemporary world sound much like this image of Heaven? The answer is obviously "no," and therein resides the reason why so much tension, grief, suffering, and restlessness remain over the entire face of the Earth. It exists, too, because humble people don the cloak of their religious vocations; holy men walk down the street wearing their Roman collars, while passers-by look at them like they are somehow freakishly out of place because they have not secluded themselves inside a monastery somewhere. When Regina left the comment on my web site that, "...we don't have high expectations from our priests anyway," she is admitting that her own heart has become calloused about their role and purpose in the conversion of humankind toward welcoming the Kingdom of God to the Earth. Many priests have not become indifferent by reasons of their own choosing; they are simply responding to the outright onslaught of audacity against them by other people who have become Protestantized, somehow deceived, and otherwise taught to diminish their own sacred envisionment of the Original Catholic and Apostolic Church by those who continue to refuse to muster the faith to remain true to all of the Seven Sacraments.

It is furthermore the commission of compassionate Christians to engage the debate about the so-called freedoms of those who claim to hold a legitimate right to exercise their deviant sexual orientation. Let there be no equivocation in the standing of the Church with regard to such abnormalities. Participating in lifestyles that are tolerant of the psychopathologies of homosexuality and lesbianism is an egregious offense against the Sacred Heart of Christ, is an illicit defilement that runs contrary to maintaining our corporal purity, is derogatory to the purpose of our intended gender, and is a violation of God's Holy Will as delineated through the Sacred Scriptures. In metaphoric terms, one might say that just because there may be a breach in the epidermis of our personal identity does not imply that we are not supposed to stop the bleeding. In other words, the psychological desires and uncontrollable urges of certain individuals may drive them into aberrant preferences; but they are responsible to ensure that they never act upon them or bring others to do so. To those who sponsor or march in public "gay pride" parades and display or foster such events to patronize people who are experimenting with their sexual identity, the Son of God would say that they have discriminated against *themselves* as human creatures by severing their souls from His primal obedience and, thereby, asserting their independence from the Holy Spirit and committing blasphemy against His Triune Dominion. Their initial instinct is to presume that humanity is rejecting them because we willfully choose to disavow their deliberate infractions of the Ordinances of God. Those who are afflicted by homoeroticism often try to justify their actions by integrating their sexual tendencies within their overall dharma. While this may be acceptable to the secular world, Jesus Christ does not see it in quite the same terms. He knows that certain individuals may not deliberately choose to entertain such thoughts and feelings, but He obviously also considers their transference into physical action an abomination of the highest domain. The difficulty in expressing His position clearly arises when

certain liberal social factions assert that those who support the poise of the
Church are somehow intolerant of other people, regardless of how flagrant
that particular error might be. The fact is, no one assesses the value of the
souls of those who are afflicted by unscrupulous temptations or rejects or
censures them in any way; we are simply stating the Truth about what the
Savior of the World has clearly proclaimed. We are supposed to admonish
one another for the purification and conversion of the Mystical Body of
Christ; which is a process known as dispensing the Spiritual Works of Mercy.
Chief among them is to teach our brethren that the human frame is a beatific
temple, especially regarding the expression of our personal sexuality.
Therefore, if someone is approached by a disciple of Jesus who extols the
tenets of the Holy Gospel for the purpose of amending their behavior, then
it is incumbent upon the latter to listen just as urgently as if he was audibly
hearing the voice of God.

Acts of sexual exploitation have led to many other perversions in
families and societies as a whole; not the least of which are massive numbers
of criminal offenses; the molestation of children, physical mutilation, rings of
prostitution, and even capital murder. Moreover, their victims who are
fortunate enough to survive are often emotionally scarred for life. Again, this
has nothing to do with determining the sacral standing of someone else's
spirit before the Throne of God, but is an appropriate means to redress their
conscience before they fall of their own accord into continuous mortal sin.
When someone is stricken by the passions and emotions of homosexuality, it
is wholly their charge to enlist the assistance of curative advisors and properly
trained clerics to help them convalesce. The world has been the foughten
field of many other battles, but none is as imperative for winning as this one.
The key is that homosexuals and lesbians should be treated with inclusive
Love, not a social demeanor which is afoul of the therapeutic consolation that
is so prevalent in a world already inundated with the Wisdom of Truth. Such
misguided souls should never be allowed to be smitten by feelings of
worthlessness or be shagged aside; because their self-esteem is already in a
precarious mode. It is true that the suicide rate among young people is higher
in the segment of the population who describe themselves as being "gay."
There may not be enough room in anyone's library to study the multifaceted
field of human sexuality; but no one can deny the Commandments of God
when it comes to defining who He has created us to be, because our
anatomical composition determines our innate orientation. Therefore, any
sexual act which does not naturally lead to the procreation of new life is in
direct contravention to the teachings of Christ; a provision which is clearly

defined in the *Catechism of the Catholic Church*. For those whose doubts have left them confused as to how to perceive their sexual identity, there is no substitute for complying with the Will of God as He has so profoundly expressed it through Jesus Christ, the Magnate of Purity in the Flesh.

Chapter Eleven
The Matriarch of All Creation

———————————

Contexted carefully within the proceeding eighteen pages, you will read about the very meaning of holy human obedience, the incarnate intersection of God and His worlds, the exemplary perfection of Motherhood, the initiation of the New Covenant of Jesus Christ and the fulfillment of the Mosaic Law of the Old, and the most divulging dialogue to ever take place between Heaven and Earth. The term *hyperdulia* is often used to describe the Roman Catholic veneration of the Blessed Virgin Mary as the most exalted of all creatures; but this adjective is insufficient to describe the adulation that this remarkably simple and virtuous Woman deserves from everyone who has ever been given the gift of life. Her Womb is the Fruitful Chamber from which the Savior of the World was born; and, thereafter, our very Eternal Salvation. Mary is more than the humble Maiden whose Edenic likeness we see in Nativity scenes during Christmastime, She is the perpetual Matriarch of all climates and seasons, the Patroness of our Absolution from God, and the Mediatrix of all Graces from the Kingdom of Paradise. Someday, the glorification of Her sacred role in our Redemption will not have to be placed in the eleventh chapter of anyone's book by reason that no secular practitioners would read it otherwise. The time will come when Her shining Face will be placed on the front of every newspaper on the globe, in living color on every television screen, above the altar in every church, on the dashboard of every automobile, before the bench in every courtroom; and inside every locket, pendant, and keepsake that was ever made or will be hewn long thereafter. Our Lady is the Perpetual Mother of every inch and scintilla of anything that is of God in all the universes combined, the seen and unseen; and every man, woman, child, and unborn fetus in the world. The moment the Angel Gabriel came to ask Her to be the Mother of Jesus Christ upon the Annunciation was the nearly-inexplicable venture of Our Divine Creator taking to the Flesh and living among His creatures. It is larger than the making of any nation, the liberation of any race, or the discovery and exploration of any spherical star. All human flagrance and indignity was annihilated by the supernatural resonance of Her *Fiat*, Her proclamation for God to, *Do unto Me as You Will,"* for this Woman was neither afraid nor confused; She knew exactly what was being sought from Her as though She had anticipated it in advance from the very moment She was Immaculately Conceived inside the Womb of Her own mother, Saint Anne. And, yet, Her compliance with the request of the Angel came almost too spontaneously for

Her to have pondered it in advance. She never had time to mull over the ramifications and repercussions of what it would mean to bear the Son of God in Her Womb; but She set-out at that very moment with Her Holy Countenance against the winds of an errant world; unfazed, undaunted, uninhibited, and unencumbered by any latent fears that might have caused a lesser woman to decline. She somehow knew that Her answer would mean the difference between the Salvation of every soul in the human race and their everlasting fate of never seeing Paradise again.

On December 8, 1854, Pope Pius IX proclaimed the dogma that the birth of the Mother of God was by reason of Her Immaculate Conception; and it has been celebrated as this Feast Day ever since. Pius did not create Her to be Immaculate like one might elevate a Cardinal, but was only responding to the Holy Spirit who affirmed that it was time for humanity to know that Mary was conceived, born, and lived-out Her immortal life on the Earth as a sinless Virgin; so much so that She has been seen preeminently back in the world on numerous occasions from Her high station as Queen of Heaven and Earth to respond in-kind to the acceptance of Her Motherhood by the Roman Catholic Church. She told the seers in Fatima, Portugal from May through October of 1917 that the world was in great need of change; that only by our prayers and sacrifices would we be able to live in peace throughout the rest of the 20th century and beyond. She warned that the conversion of humanity to Salvation in the Blood of Her Son was the only way to avoid international wars and concentric bloodbaths as the forces of evil continued to pummel the Earth. We did not listen; and the resulting effect was not only two World Wars just thirty years apart, but the continuing deterioration of the moral fabric of our global societies and the internal frameworks which made even decent people wonder if their entire lives had somehow gone mad. She predicted that the U.S.S.R. would continue to spread its error around the globe; and, indeed, this did come to pass. However, Mary did not leave us without redress against the elements by which we would long suffer and grieve the loss of our relatives, friends, and closest loved-ones. Under the intercessory guidance of the Blessed Virgin Mary, Pope John Paul II succeeded in assisting in the destruction of the Soviet regime, just as Mary promised would occur if humanity invoked Her aid. Although the forces of evil tried to stop his miraculous work when he was shot on May 13, 1981, the exact month and day of Her first appearance at Fatima, he lived to oversee the dissolution of the U.S.S.R., starting with the Kremlin, itself. Associated Press correspondent Mara Bellaby reported its anniversary quite correctly over the wire in December of 2001 from Moscow,

"...Bitterness. Nostalgia. Pride. With those contradictory emotions, Russia, Ukraine, and Belarus marked the 10ᵗʰ anniversary of the secret talks that sealed the collapse of the Soviet Union, wrenching apart the communist empire that helped define global politics for three-quarters of a century. From a hunting lodge in a Belarusian forest, former presidents Boris Yeltsin of Russia, Leonid Kravchuk of Ukraine, and Stanislav Shushkevich of Belarus announced to the world on December 8, 1991 that the U.S.S.R., 'as a subject of international and geopolitical reality, no longer exists.' Their bold new alliance effectively left former Soviet President Mikhail Gorbachev without a job—he resigned December 25, 1991—and ended Vladimir Lenin's political creation."

       This all began when the Mother of God miraculously appeared to three peasant children in Fatima, told them what was going to happen in Russia if humanity prayed sufficiently for its conversion, and left them with a Secret that would not be revealed for another 80 years. What was it? The attempted assassination of Pope John Paul II in 1981 was predicted by the Blessed Virgin in 1917; the same Pope whose commission was to oversee the elimination of the atheistic republics of the U.S.S.R.. She is the very Immaculate Conception whose dogma was proclaimed exactly 137 years to the day before these three socialists leaders met to dissolve their empire. Mary has always led humanity to the freedom, dignity, and Salvation we have found in Her Son, Jesus Christ. Therefore, it is only fitting that the dissolution of the U.S.S.R. would occur on the same day of His Birth, December 25ᵗʰ. It makes sense in hindsight because it has been too carefully orchestrated by God to be dismissed as coincidence by any mortal man. I wrote a poem about the Virgin Mary that I included in my first book, *Morning Star Over America*; and I have been asked by many who have contacted me to place it into another book. *The Final Colossus* is fashioned after *The New Colossus* which was written by Emma Lazarus and inscribed on the pedestal beneath the Statue of Liberty in New York Harbor. The story of how this came to be is quite unique to relate, so I will simply ask those who wish to know more about the events leading to the comparison of the highly visible Statue of Liberty and the universal Matriarch of All Creation to procure a copy of *Morning Star Over America*, turn to June 16, 1991, and it will all become very clear. Hereafter is the text of *The Final Colossus* as it was positioned in that volume in its original entirety.

The Final Colossus

Basking, bathing, brilliant! Outpouring the Wisdom of God!
The Visage of Heaven, flowing freely the tears of pristine Glory.
Clothed in unerring, inevitable Light. The Winds of change!
Eradicating, electrifying, compelling, beloved!
You teach the shedding of Earth amidst the corals of sin.
Go! Go into the world that knows no peace.
Greet, bless, call, embrace! Heal, sanctify, purify, caress!

You, the Virginal Shores of Paradisial Love.
Monogram and Monument to the Triune God.
The Trident, the Benevolent, the Salvific, the Bold.
You, the Sunlit Matron of God's Holy Ones,
lost in the portals of bewildering Death.
O' Perfect Glory, Mother of Life Renewed.
You, the Hands of Grace,
The Fair Maiden who birthed the pacific Pardon of fallen souls.

You, the Beatific Dawn of a Boundless Age.
Bring the solstice of Ecstatic Light to heirs and orphans.
To the Well of corpus hearts brooding in hopeless Dusk.
Seek ancient tundras and mystical parlors
where mortals huddle amidst battle and waste.
You, the flawless Blessing and newfound Trust of generations lost!

You, Matriarch and Queen of the lifeless Daughter in the Harbor.
Your Son is the Torch of Life to the children of Earth.
His Light unifies the blessed, the grated, the wretched,
the lost, the timid, the damned.

You! Summoned by the outstretched arms of Hope!
Stationed high above the stillness of invincible Freedom.

You celebrate the Destiny of man and beast, alike.
with Your Immaculate Crown of Stars,
to which the little Child in the Bay bows in deference,
her spiked chapeau heeled near her humbled feet.
She welcomes Your cultivating Touch to the unwitting masses,
the hopeless chest of inordinate pawns
awaiting their passage to the Celestial Port,
while the Streams of Paradise reflect your glistening Mantle.

Yes, You step into the world to claim the Unknown.
Clasping errant palms that flail in the dark,
pulling to beat their breasts in the vibrant New Groves
of the Land of God. You are the Parasol of Infinite Bliss.
Refined, Robust, impassioned Delight!
Where cities of angels moor to feast on placid temperaments.
Come this Day! Lift every age to Heaven's Door!

-William L. Roth, Jr
November 15, 1998
A gift from the Archangel Gabriel

Herein, I have rendered my loving devotion to the Woman Clothed with the Sun, so celebrated in the Book of Revelation. I have attempted to recite the almost unexpressible affection that humanity should have for Her, holding Her Immaculate Heart in the highest esteem before any other creature ever given life by God. I have seen and heard this Perfect Woman with my own eyes and ears; and I can tell you that She chooses Her words both meticulously and carefully because She knows that we are afraid of life, what it may bring, how we will be affected, and most importantly, how it will end. Mary is the truthful Mother of the Earth from whom the blossoming

Tree of Eternal Life has sprouted. She is the beauty who has finally forced the snarling canines of the mortal world to turn in disapproval of themselves and bite their own flesh, instead. Our Immaculate Mother wants us to know that only through our emulation of Jesus will we be capable of overcoming the perils of life and avoid the dangers of evil; and what She is really saying is that Satan hates us to the core and wants to singe our souls in the catastrophic flames inside the bowels of the fiery Abyss. Why? Because he loathes our Salvation to the *nth* degree and with every fiber of his wretched being. Can the cadavers of our dead consciences ever be useful for anything now? It is imperative that they must be revived altogether and resurrected as Truth and Love. However, for every condescending rung that Satan deplores our relationship with Jesus Christ, God's immeasurable Divinity embraces us overwhelmingly more. We are told upon our acceptance of the Cross that newer Rites of Grace will prevail, a systematic conversion of our hearts known as our redemptive *eutaxy*; or the well-arranged order of our spiritual purification. This is what Jesus and His Mother have come seeking from us now; and we shall never truly know the Almighty Father unless we submissively concur. Mary is the Advocate for all America before Jesus and the City of God; and all humanity on every corner of the globe is being overspread in the blinding firelight of Her compassion, instruction, advice, and intensely charitable urging. She is asking that we all shed our tumid pride . in favor of a more humble demeanor through the Light of Christ's Holy desires. She spreads the Good News of the Holy Gospel by enlisting all Christians in Her Army of supplicating patriots; those who stand before their enemies in the world and proclaim their battle cry of DOM!, *Deo Optimo Maximo*; to God, the Best, the Greatest!

One of the main precepts that the Holy Mother has been teaching us is that human life is supposed to be more than just a linear series of moments and coincidences which are somehow meant to be collecting in a vat somewhere beneath the tumblers of time. We are asked to step outside of our everyday lives with a different perspective; one which is facilitated by the extraordinary Love we gain through our new relationship with Christ. Our awareness must reside in the fact that the Son of God is not quite so timid as most of us seem to believe. Although He may have slipped quietly through the back corridor onto the globe upon His Virgin Birth at Christmas, He is knocking quite loudly on our portico doorways by now; and He will return in Glory to the thundering of Truth upon our souls with such ferocity that it will rock our haughty institutions completely off their foundations and turn the whole world upside down. Mary has made it quite clear to me that the

Holy Spirit desires to do more than just coax and advise humanity toward a more righteous course, but to also interrogate and rehabilitate our individual consciences as to why we have chosen to remain in the darkness of sin for so long. In reflection of the fact that we want more Light to come into the world to ease the pain and agony of our suffering and losses, we should be doing more to invite Jesus in. Thereafter, becoming re-entrenched in the physical world will run contrary to everything new and Divine that we should claim to profess. The disingenuous actions and irrelevant rhetoric of these modern times does nothing to prepare us for the imminent shock of encountering the Truth once again throughout the cross-section of every longitude; but only a concurrent evolution of our individual spiritual maturation into holiness and the conversion of *humankind entire* will suffice. The mediative role of the Blessed Virgin in this salvific process is precisely for the purpose of inducing us to remove our hands from our personal belongings and take-hold of the invisible aspects of immortal life instead. Mary is searching for people who will do more than just refrain from perpetuating rancorous malevolence; She expects us all to become interactive agents for change—to do better by those we have often taken for granted and repair our broken relationships within our families and societies through the unity of the Holy Spirit. Indeed, if She finds that there are such volunteers lacking in the world, She will set-out to recreate us into the decency that God requires by dispatching legions of Angels to teach us face-to-face; so that we will turn-away from ourselves and better perceive the lost dignity of other men; to their health and unification, and toward a broader sense of spiritual community for the entire species of humankind.

It is apparent that God is looking for more than just modest contingents of pious citizens to help Him spread His Word, but an entire coalition of massive forces of loving Christians who will fight against the influences of evil in the world. And, as though we have somehow squandered our happiness by exhausting all avenues of hope, we can look at the sun cresting beyond the hills of the western horizon and see a new Constellation in the distance, a series of Twelve Stars hovering as a Crown above the Virgin Mary's Veil; a dozen new reasons to remember that Christ Jesus has *never* forsaken us; and neither will He now or ever beyond the expiration of time. With this new strength hereafter, we have no alternative than to live with a refurbished vigor, a refashioned cause, and a heightened awareness to fight for God's honor with the intercession of His Mother directly overhead. Our Triumph over sin, death, and diablerie was confirmed by Jesus the instant He surrendered His Spirit to the Almighty Father on the Cross, while He looked skyward at those same Stars that would encircle His Mother once She was Assumed into Heaven to join Him upon a time preordained by God. These images are not some sort of unsubstantiated hyperboles put forth by a group of religious fanatics; they are the facts as they have been transferred by the Mother Church into our deposit of faith for the past 2000 years. They are not pipe-dreams or irrelevant postulates which are of no eternal inference in how the world is supposed to end, for the Mother of God has been, and always will be, the Woman through whom God has given us Our Savior and Lord. Mary is holding the very Christ Child in Her Arms today who was Slain on the Cross; and it is by venerating Her Immaculate Heart that we are taken closer to Him. They can see how pitifully we conduct ourselves in a world we cannot seem to understand. Although life appears to be a fortress surrounding us most of the time, it also tries to tear us down; and we are impotent to become a sovereign race on our own without their direct intervention from Heaven. Many of us see our existence as though human mortality is a prison, and the darkness in our lives is a shadow cast by the guard-towers onto the ground where we walk everyday. The fact remains, however, that we are not incarcerated at all, but flying freely through Creation like liberated eagles on the loose. I have learned in the past decade that, more than any human being in the universe, the Blessed Mother knows we are not meant to be isolated unto ourselves or segregated from one another. What we really hope to achieve in this life is not inconsequential to how time will ultimately expire; for God is listening to us like a spy in the bushes. Our walkways have been strewn with His Passionate indignity, and our Salvation is paved with His Redemptive Blood. Jesus Christ is a tangible participant in the way we live; and the power of His Sacrifice cannot pale through time or grow obsolete in the passing of the ages. In other words, His Blood still flows as sympathetically upon our souls as it did for the sinners in the very century when He laid-down His Life; it has never clotted, and no evil force can apply a tourniquet upon the Cross to keep the Crucifixion from immersing our souls in His absolution as well.

Therefore, we cannot try to live in a "touch-screen" reality here on Earth because we can feel our mortality through the expanse of our years; we know pain, sorrow, happiness, elation, and dejection because we are fully engaged with the events that lead to their generation. Although the soil of the globe is not a very polished surface to the touch, this does not imply that we must always be forced to grovel in it. Jesus Christ is still trying to lift us to a more splendid purpose through the Holy Gospel and His Beatific Mother whom He has sent in advance to proclaim it. When it seems as though our conscience is somehow atrophied from lack of use, or that our goodness has been gathering dust on our earthen shelves, or that our integrity has grown rusty inside the dungeon-like indifference of our lack of mutual Love, we are ushered into a higher level of consciousness through the Divine intercession of the Blessed Virgin Mary. The issues that She addresses may somewhat differ far and wide, but they are all for the same reasoning of taking us closer to understanding the advantages of enhancing our relationship with God. The main emphasis of Her miraculous messages is to secure the cessation of our human "motion," meaning that we should become less concerned with reaching for everything we can think of to grasp; to lessen the emphasis we place on our volitional affections, to address the conditions which tend to destroy our peace, and to accept the scrupulous Wisdom that is garnered through our closer relationship with Her. The nearest any language might come to describing this process is the original Latin term known as *sistere*, which means, "...to stand still," or to remain stationed. Her rationale behind such a proclamation is that it would be very difficult for any one of us to teach others about the peace of Christ if we are too busy to accept it ourselves. There is no means by which we can reprimand someone else for being overly possessive of material goods if we continue collecting them, too. Moreover, it would be quite hypocritical for us to ask our neighbors to pray for our spiritual conversion while we are sitting in the back of a theatre someplace watching a movie about violence, lust, and lies. Essentially, we must stop what we are doing, reassess our values and goals, and thereafter reconcile what we have done with the Christian mission to which our lives must be ingrained for the future. If there are any gaps in what we are doing and everything we profess to do as followers of Jesus, we are required to amend them through the seamless contrition we gain by accepting His Love. Any discrepancies that exist between our best intentions and our direct physical actions must be decreased by our continuing allegiance to the Cross. This is why the Holy Sacrifice of the Mass is the most powerful prayer; it takes us to the veritable Summit of Mount Calvary where we can embrace the Crucifixion as well as anyone who was watching in person on Good Friday. For those who might be searching for the promulgation of the role of Mary in the Salvation of humanity, Her Ecclesiastical Queenship is delineated quite profoundly in the *Catechism of the Roman Catholic Church,* the contemporary American translation, 1994, U. S. Catholic Conference, Inc.. It is entirely necessary and appropriate to explain the position of the Magisterium with regard to Her presence and purpose in our communion with Jesus Christ and our goal of being saved in the gift of His Sacrifice. Taken from *Part One, Section Two,*

Chapter Three, Article 9, Paragraph 6, pp 251-254):
"...The Virgin Mary is acknowledged and honored as being truly the Mother of God and of the Redeemer. She is clearly the Mother of the members of Christ since She has by Her charity joined in bringing about the birth of believers in the Church, who are members of its head. Mary, Mother of Christ, (is) Mother of the Church (Para. 6, 963). Mary's role in the Church is inseparable from Her union with Christ and flows directly from it. This union of the Mother with the Son in the work of Salvation is made manifest from the time of Christ's virginal conception up to His death; it is made manifest above all at the hour of His Passion. Thus, the Blessed Virgin advanced in Her pilgrimage of faith, and faithfully persevered in Her union with Her Son unto the Cross. There She stood, in keeping with the Divine Plan, enduring with Her only begotten Son, the intensity of His suffering, joining Herself with His Sacrifice in Her Mother's Heart, and lovingly consenting to the immolation of this Victim, born of Her: to be given, by the same Christ Jesus dying on the Cross, as a Mother to His disciple, with these words, 'Woman, behold your son.' (Para. 6, Part I, 964).

By Her complete adherence to the Father's Will, to His Son's Redemptive work, and to every prompting of the Holy Spirit, the Virgin Mary is the Church's model of faith and charity. Thus, She is a 'preeminent and wholly unique member of the Church,' indeed, She is the exemplary realization of the Church. Her role in relation to the Church and to all humanity goes still further. In a wholly singular way, She cooperated by Her obedience, faith, hope, and burning charity in the Savior's work of restoring supernatural life to souls. For this reason, She is a Mother to us in the Order of Grace. This Motherhood of Mary in the Order of Grace continues uninterruptedly from the consent which She loyally gave at the Annunciation and which She sustained without wavering beneath the Cross, until the eternal fulfillment of all the elect. Taken up to Heaven, She did not lay aside this saving Office, but by Her manifold intercession, continues to bring us the gifts of eternal Salvation. Therefore, the Blessed Virgin is invoked in the Church under the titles of Advocate, Helper, Benefactress, and Mediatrix. (Para. 6, Part I, 967-969).

The Church's devotion to the Blessed Virgin is intrinsic to Christian worship. The Church rightly honors the Blessed Virgin with special devotion. From the most ancient times, the Blessed Virgin has been honored with the title of 'Mother of God,' to whose protection the faithful fly in all their dangers and needs. This very special devotion differs essentially from the adoration which is given to the Incarnate Word and equally to the Father and the Holy Spirit, and greatly fosters this adoration. The liturgical Feasts dedicated to the Mother of God and Marian prayer, such as the Rosary, an 'epitome of the whole Gospel,' express this devotion to the Virgin Mary. (Para. 6, Part II, 971).

After speaking of the Church, her origin, mission, and destiny, we can find no better way to conclude than by looking to Mary. In Her, we contemplate what the Church already is in her mystery on her own 'pilgrimage of faith,' and what she will be in the Homeland at the end of her journey. There, in the Glory of the Most Holy and Undivided Trinity, in the communion of all the Saints, the Church is awaited by the One she venerates as Mother of her Lord and as her own Mother. In the meantime, the Mother of Jesus, in the Glory which She possesses in Body and Soul in Heaven, is the image and beginning of the Church as it is to be perfected in the world to come. Likewise, She shines forth on Earth, until the Day of the Lord shall cometh, a sign of certain hope and comfort to the pilgrim People of God." (Para. 6, Part III, 972).

With such a premiere mandate and set of credentials as these, there is no surprise in discovering that the Blessed Virgin Mary bears the commission and authority to rebuke and reprimand humanity for the errors we have wrought against all moral decency and the Kingdom of God, itself. She has been a lofty foot-soldier for the cause of Love around the globe; and our assignment for the future is to emulate Her lead. Which errors among those She is attempting to eradicate seem the most repugnant before the Throne of Her Son? Surely our sins against the sanctity of human life, the victimization of innocents, and our wilful violations against corporeal chastity rank as being the most egregious. However, if we approach the common pedestrian these days, he is likely to say that such problems are to be addressed only by professionals in the fields of law enforcement and psychological medicine. If we wait for them to change the world into a better place, not only will the cows come home, but so will every fatted calf walk through the gate before they are ever a thought in the mind of their Maker. Each member of the human race is responsible according to his capabilities to change the face of the Earth to be the likeness of Heaven. We often approach life, instead, while professing the finical habits of our own generalities and approximations; not caring enough to finally come to know one another that well. We place too much emphasis on our blindly practical procedures and social applications rather than inheriting the principles set into being by our more visionary friends. Such rules-of-thumb seem not to be so offensive to us anymore because our consciences have become anesthetized by our surly Western culture. We crane our necks upwardly in an effort to see the ornate cantilevers beneath the cornices of our elegant federal courthouses and other such architectural keepsakes at times, while mistakenly assuming that whatever decisions are rendered from underneath their coffers are always alright by God. What we often fail to recognize is that the hellbroth which is brewing from within our judicial system is the taste of death for millions of our citizens. For example, when the U. S. Supreme Court issued its infamous *Roe v. Wade* decision on January 22, 1973, effectively making infanticide legal in America today, all Creation took a giant leap backward, especially our free-world democracy, reverting almost completely back into its charlatan days. It was the single most arrogant, audacious, and Bohemian judgement of any ruling ever perpetrated by the High Court since its inception in the mid-18th century. Such a decision is wholly void of all judicial temperament and moral judgement; for these were not artists and writers of America renewed, but the prophesiers of a nation of impending horror, tragedy, destruction, agony, and regret. Thankfully, however, the decision was not unanimous, and some of their written opinions have been preserved for their modern successors to heed. In addition, beyond the legalese of the Supreme Court, does not the responsibility for protecting the life of all unborn children rightfully reside under the jurisdiction of the mothers who are carrying them, and the fathers by whom they were conceived?

The Blessed Virgin Mary has made it quite unequivocal through Her supernatural messages that it is obvious that *Roe v. Wade* must be overturned, and there is no question about that; but the women who nurture the unborn in their wombs must awaken to recognize the value of the priceless gift of life they have been afforded by God. This is why we must direct our national attention away from the expediency and selfishness of procuring an abortion; and the reason we must pray more intensely for a mutual understanding that the Almighty Father will provide for our children if we will only give them the opportunity to continue their lives. It is obvious that most pregnancies are terminated for financial conduciveness or simply because a mother does not wish to be burdened with raising her child. Furthermore, the excuse that a forcible impregnation or incest is sufficient justification to destroy an unborn child is totally without merit because the baby could care less who its biological parents are during this stage of his life. Such untenable extenuations hold absolutely no condonation in the Dominion of our Creator; and there is reason for us to believe that they never will. Pope John Paul II once sternly described America's fallacious system of choices as a

"...culture of death," from abortion, to capital punishment, to assisted suicide. Complying with his wishes might be a little hard to swallow for some of us nowadays, but his description of our country was precisely on the mark. He was referencing our refusal to love, our failing to acknowledge God's spiritual reasoning, and our blind infatuation with a false sense of liberty by which we believe we can do nearly anything we please and escape scot-free before the Eternal Wrath of our Heavenly Father. With all foresight accorded, His Immaculate Mother has better ideas for the nation over which She has been appointed as Patroness Saint. She has told me on any number of occasions that we place our wares on display before the rest of the world, boast of our abilities to tackle crippling diseases, launch dozens of pioneers into the depths of outer-space, scurry to the aid of our capitalist friends, spend trillions of dollars on buildings and roads, burn coal and oil like they are in infinite supply, and sit inside our hilltop mansions and sip wine from fine crystal glass; thereafter tossing them with a shatter into the glowing embers of our fireplaces to mimic the disgraceful way we discard those we detest; including the precious unborn, as though they are just as expendable as our obsolete artifacts that should have never been conceived.

Another issue of life and death might also seem beyond our control, but should we not further intervene to prevent the tragedy of suicide whenever we can? Desperate people killing themselves has been a great disfigurement to our national character for the past hundred years; and it is time we figured-out why this is so, and how we can prevent it from happening again. There is no doubt that its causative roots can be traced to our aura of permissiveness, too; that we expect far more from our children and unstable members of society than they can ever produce. We place so much emphasis upon interpersonal competition that they begin to wonder whether they will ever matriculate into our mainstream world or yield a share of the wealth for which many others are doing everything in their raw power to hoard. There are so-called "reality" television programs which hail the mutual extermination of those who cannot survive; rejecting the apparent "weakest link" of the group, saluting people who scoff at common sense, and slandering the lack of endurance of those who are not as fit as the majority whole. This is exactly the national pretext that Adolph Hitler espoused! We are being brainwashed in his own brand of evil, and are taking it lying down! Most Americans assess a high premium to the value of the intellect, while making it so difficult for the disadvantaged to succeed that they can barely sustain themselves on their own. Then, once we have purged the "undesirables" from within our midst and pigeon-holed them into obscurity, we label them as failures, hoping against hope that they will just somehow disappear. Those who cannot cope anymore are forced into oblivion; they recoil into their darkest rooms, defy their very own self-worth while expecting nothing from the social elite, and ponder what they can do to escape it once and for all. Self-destruction seems to be the consensus among most of them; at least to those who do not pursue a life of malicious recidivism for revenge, depending on drugs or alcohol for relief, effacing their own bodies for attention, concocting illusory fantasies to live; and avoiding any semblance of discipline, responsibility, order, and love. They are the poor souls who are lost because they have been discarded into the wild to fend for themselves; but they do not compose the entire group that is susceptible to the temptation to bring themselves harm. Let us not be deluded; suicide affects and transcends *all* social classes and every conceivable economic expanse. Many people who take their own lives could not deal with the abruptness of precipitous financial success; discovering that their peers pursued them only because of their wealth and name recognition. These are among those who hasten their own demise after tiring from the pretense of it all. Their achievements under the flashing neon lights and electronic strobes were alright for awhile, but their true souls were starving to death for the real meaning of life, the spiritual nourishment they required, and their hunger for compassion and a return to the simplicity of their childhood days. The entire fabric of our population has been stained by the blood of suicide, and the Blessed Virgin Mary maintains quite strongly that our prayers, good works, and direction of struggling people back to God will bring this scourge to an end.

As the *Roman Catechism* states, the recitation of the Holy Rosary is one means through which we can venerate the Blessed Mother as the Matriarch of All Creation; and God is overwhelmingly pleased when we pray it because it is our celebration of the Sacred Mysteries that He set into place to redeem us from condemnation. Rather than provide detailed instructions as to how it is prayed here in this text, perhaps it would be more practical to ask those who are interested to go to their local Marian Center, their parish priest, or local missionaries and convents to procure a rosary and the details of its recital from them. I would be remiss, however, if I did not include the Fifteen Sacred Mysteries in this section of my book to recount the Life of Jesus and Mary in remembrance of our faith. The applicable prayers for the Holy Rosary can be found in my concluding *Index* as a matter of course.

The Joyful Mysteries

First   The Annunciation of the Archangel Gabriel to Mary
Second   The Visitation of Mary to Her Cousin Elizabeth
Third   The Birth of Jesus in Bethlehem
Fourth   The Presentation of Jesus at the Temple
Fifth   The Finding of the Child Jesus in the Temple

The Sorrowful Mysteries

First   The Agony of Jesus in the Garden of Gethsemane
Second   The Scourging of Jesus at the Pillar
Third   The Crowing of Jesus with Thorns
Fourth   Jesus Carries the Cross to Mount Calvary
Fifth   The Crucifixion of Jesus on Mount Calvary

The Glorious Mysteries

First   The Resurrection of Jesus from the Sepulcher
Second   The Ascension of Jesus into Heaven
Third   The Descent of the Holy Spirit at Pentecost
Fourth   The Assumption of the Blessed Virgin Mary into Heaven
Fifth   The Crowning of Mary as Queen of Heaven and Earth

For all the benign gentleness that the Blessed Mother emanates before humanity in our time, I have a feeling that we have been offending Her Son for so long now that even *we* errantly assume that we will never be brought to final justice. However, through Her evocative expressions and outright proclamations, She would have us believe quite the opposite. While Our Lady teaches us that we should not be afraid of God, there is certainly reason for our anticipation to be chastised if we do not effect a change of course. The Holy Mother is plentifully congenial alright, but Her tenor of Eminence is proof enough that Heaven is going to start shooting back at our errancy in the very near future, led by the charge of this Immaculate Mother of God with such a profound allegiance to the Light of Paradise that She will make the conquest of France by Saint Joan of Arc look like a nanny slapping a child on the back of the hand. Through no vantage of my own procuring, I have been privileged to hear what our Divine Creator thinks about our modern world from His Mother; and running for our lives would almost seem at this point like the proper thing to do. There is no single adjective that can amplify or encapsulate Her beauty; nor can the most technologically advanced digital photography ever capture the depths of Her Grace. She is a teacher and ambassador for Christ Jesus who seeks every indulgence within Her capacity for the children She has come to instruct. She is our enabler before the Throne of God and our role-model of piety, humility, compassion, servitude, obedience, and trust. She prays on our behalf, and with us in person; imparting spiritual Wisdom to humankind in the Beatitudes and Virtues of Love. I have been a practitioner of quantitative methods by formal profession, as I mentioned before, having studied the fields of mathematics, physics, and computer science. I have had little difficulty in determining the structure of the material Earth, how one force can be distinguished from the next, and why they might mutually affect one another. I have since learned from the Virgin Mary that the Kingdom of God is entirely independent from my previous deductions; that miracles can arrive at any unexpected moment in time because they do not necessarily rely upon the functions by which we analyze the celestial motion of the Milky Way or the universe at large. There has never been any doubt that each of us is given a particular talent or aptitude through which we might earn a living or make a name for ourselves. What seems to be hidden from us, however, is that we are also enjoined to utilize these things for the purpose of advancing the causes of Heaven in tune with the requirements delineated in the Holy Bible. If anyone were to look-up the word "take" in the *Random House Dictionary*, he would see no-less than 102 meanings for its definition. It is a verb which implies what we, by our individually inherited human nature, seem to want to procure from nearly everything one might possibly conceive.

However, there is another term in this same reference book that more clearly describes what we are supposed to do with the very essence of our lives before God and humanity, alike. The verb is to "give," and it serves as our reminder from Heaven to offer everything at our disposal to make Christ's Kingship better known inside our own hearts and to every continental nation. By accepting the Truth of His Cross, our newer reason for living is to offer, vouchsafe, furnish, provide, supply, donate, contribute, confer, grant, and present anything and everything we can muster from the core of our very being to elevate humanity back to the dignity which will help them see the unblemished perfection of Jesus reflecting from our soul. This is what the Blessed Mother is teaching me, and is what God expects from every one of us.

I have come to know that the real champions on Earth do not appear dressed in partisan colors on a basketball court or on a baseball diamond to the roar of an approving crowd, but in the humble solitude of their anonymity as they pray by themselves in their secluded quarters, place their last few coins in the Church's collection basket, pick-up a stranger walking alongside the road in the rain; or even as innocent victims who are sequestered in jail cells around America and those who are confined to wheel-chairs for 50 years before they die. The best among us are the little children who crouch in corners with tears rolling down their cheeks, wondering why their mothers and fathers have left them; the people who leave food baskets on strangers' porches without a return address; and the unheralded heroes who stock the shelves at our marketplaces and mop the floors at night; all of whom we seem to take for granted once we make it to the top. Our Holy Mother is asking us to become the generous ones who will give our efforts and financial resources to feed the dying and heal the diseased half-way around the globe; those whose faces we shall never see before the moment when we might be so fortunate as to greet their souls in Paradise. There is no doubt that we reap what we sow; and the future is all-revealing and forever-telling about the goodness we can accomplish while never worrying whether our beneficiaries will ever know our real identity. Our Lady is asking for our prayers, peace, conversion, penance, and personal reconciliation in places like Medjugorje, (Yugoslavia) Banneux and Beauraing (Belgium), Zeitun (Egypt), Garabandal (Spain), Akita (Japan), Betania (Venezuela), Kibeho (Rwanda), Naju (Korea), the former Soviet Ukraine, and in dozens of miraculous sites across America. All of these cities are where Her supernatural apparitions and interlocutions have occurred during the 20th century; and many are still ongoing today.

The Mother of God is our indispensable liaison between our mortal spirits and the Sacred Heart of Jesus Christ; for She has already seen the Glory of His Eternal Resurrection and the billions of souls who have preceded us in death who have benefitted by immeasurable quanta through their acceptance of His Blood on the Cross as reparation for their sinful error. Her Mantle is a splendrous Pavilion under which we can huddle to receive Her Motherly caress while we watch Creation unfold according to God's foreordained Plan. The commission of Our Lady is to the conquering of human immorality, to foster peaceful accord where there is social instability, to teach humanity the true definition of Love, to lead us into lives of holiness, to implore us to never turn our backs on the suffering poor, and to repeatedly remind us that our contrition is the only way to ultimately achieve a happy life. Her personality, demeanor, intercessions, and blessings are all manifestations of Her greater purpose in leading us to Christ. I discovered this Truth quite poignantly and intensely while I was standing on a hill in the Village of Medjugorje in August 1989 when She miraculously appeared to the young seers there during the Vigil of Her Assumption into Heaven. I was one in a group of thousands who had collected ourselves in solemn procession up the steep side of the mountain, reciting the Passionate Stations of the Cross, waiting for what was to be my first supernatural encounter with the Divinity of God. I did not see Her with my eyes that night, but I knew beyond any sliver of doubt that She was in my midst; and the children of that tiny Yugoslavian hamlet were speaking to Her as well as I could see and hear any one of the multitudes beside whom I was kneeling. I had always believed in God, that Jesus Christ is the Savior of my mortal soul; and I have always attended Holy Mass on Sundays. Beyond that August evening, however, my entire religious life and physical existence have revolved around the Holy Spirit who is enlightening each one of us about the presence of the Messiah in the temporal world.

Part Four
The Convergence of Capitalism and Christianity

Chapter Twelve
The Separation of Church and State

The Presidents of the United States of America

President	Affiliation	Tenure of Office
1. George Washington	Federalist	1789-1797
2. John Adams	Federalist	1797-1801
3. Thomas Jefferson	Dem/Rep	1801-1809
4. James Madison	Dem/Rep	1809-1817
5. James Monroe	Dem/Rep	1817-1825
6. John Quincy Adams	Federalist	1825-1829
7. Andrew Jackson	Democrat	1829-1837
8. Martin Van Buren	Democrat	1837-1841
9. William H. Harrison	Whig	1841
10. John Tyler	Whig	1841-1845
11. James Knox Polk	Democrat	1845-1849
12. Zachary Taylor	Whig	1849-1850
13. Millard Fillmore	Whig	1850-1853
14. Franklin Pierce	Democrat	1853-1857
15. James Buchanan	Democrat	1857-1861
16. Abraham Lincoln	Republican	1861-1865
17. Andrew Johnson	Democrat	1865-1869
18. Ulysses S. Grant	Republican	1869-1877
19. Rutherford B. Hayes	Republican	1877-1881
20. James A. Garfield	Republican	1881
21. Chester A. Arthur	Republican	1881-1885
22. Grover Cleveland	Democrat	1885-1889
23. Benjamin Harrison	Republican	1889-1893
24. Grover Cleveland	Democrat	1893-1897
25. William McKinley	Republican	1897-1901
26. Theodore Roosevelt	Republican	1901-1909
27. William Howard Taft	Republican	1909-1913
28. Woodrow Wilson	Democrat	1913-1921

29.	Warren G. Harding	Republican	1921-1923
30.	Calvin Coolidge	Republican	1923-1929
31.	Herbert C. Hoover	Republican	1929-1933
32.	Franklin D. Roosevelt	Democrat	1933-1945
33.	Harry S Truman	Democrat	1945-1953
34.	Dwight D. Eisenhower	Republican	1953-1961
35.	John F. Kennedy	Democrat	1961-1963
36.	Lyndon B. Johnson	Democrat	1963-1969
37.	Richard M. Nixon	Republican	1969-1974
38.	Gerald R. Ford	Republican	1974-1977
39.	James E. Carter, Jr.	Democrat	1977-1981
40.	Ronald W. Reagan	Republican	1981-1989
41.	George H.W. Bush	Republican	1989-1993
42.	William J. Clinton	Democrat	1993-2001
43.	George W. Bush	Republican	2001-

Source: World Almanac

A Chronology of Papal Succession
The Supreme Pontiffs of the Holy Roman Catholic Church

Arpeggio	*Pope*	*A.D. Anno Domini*
001	Saint Peter	-67
002	Saint Linus	67-76
003	Saint Anacletus	76-88
004	Saint Clement	88-97
005	Saint Evaristus	97-105
006	Saint Alexander I	105-115
007	Saint Sixtus I	115-125
008	Saint Telesphorus	125-136
009	Saint Hyginus	136-140
010	Saint Pius I	140-155
011	Saint Anicetus	155-166
012	Saint Soter	166-175
013	Saint Eleutherius	175-189
014	Saint Victor I	189-199
015	Saint Zephyrinus	199-217
016	Saint Callistus I	217-222
017	Saint Urban I	222-230
018	Saint Pontian	230-235
019	Saint Anterus	235-236
020	Saint Fabian	236-250
021	Saint Cornelius	251-253
022	Saint Lucius I	253-254
023	Saint Stephen I	254-257
024	Saint Sixtus II	257-258
025	Saint Dionysius	259-268
026	Saint Felix I	269-274
027	Saint Eutychian	275-283
028	Saint Caius	283-296
029	Saint Marcellinus	296-304
030	Saint Marcellus I	308-309
031	Saint Eusebius	309-310
032	Saint Meltiades	311-314

033	Saint Sylvester I	314-335
034	Saint Marcus	336
035	Saint Julius I	337-352
036	Liberius	352-366
037	Saint Damasus I	366-384
038	Saint Siricius	384-399
039	Saint Anastasius I	399-401
040	Saint Innocent I	401-417
041	Saint Zozimus	417-418
042	Saint Boniface I	418-422
043	Saint Celestine I	422-432
044	Saint Sixtus III	432-440
045	Saint Leo I	440-461
046	Saint Hilary	461-468
047	Saint Simplicius	468-483
048	Saint Felix III (II)	483-492
049	Saint Gelasius I	492-496
050	Anastasius II	496-498
051	Saint Symmachus	498-514
052	Saint Hormisdas	514-523
053	Saint John I	523-526
054	Saint Felix IV (III)	526-530
055	Boniface II	530-532
056	John II	533-535
057	Saint Agapitus I	535-536
058	Saint Sylverius	536-537
059	Vigilius	537-555
060	Pelagius I	556-561
061	John III	561-574
062	Benedict I	575-579
063	Pelagius II	579-590
064	Saint Gregory I	590-604
065	Sabinianus	604-606
066	Boniface III	607
067	Saint Boniface IV	608-615
068	Saint Adeodatus I	615-618
069	Boniface V	619-625
070	Honorius I	625-638

071	Severinus	640
072	John IV	640-642
073	Theodore I	642-649
074	Saint Martin I	649-655
075	Saint Eugene I	655-657
076	Saint Vitalian	657-672
077	Adeodatus II	672-676
078	Donus	676-678
079	Saint Agatho	678-681
080	Saint Leo II	682-683
081	Saint Benedict II	684-685
082	John V	685-686
083	Conon	686-687
084	Saint Sergius I	687-701
085	John VI	701-705
086	John VII	705-707
087	Sisinnius	708
088	Constantine	708-715
089	Saint Gregory II	715-731
090	Saint Gregory III	731-741
091	Saint Zachary	741-752
092	Saint Stephen II	752
093	Stephen II (III)	752-757
094	Saint Paul I	757-767
095	Stephen III (IV)	768-772
096	Adrian I	772-795
097	Saint Leo III	795-816
098	Stephen IV (V)	816-817
099	Saint Paschal I	817-824
100	Eugene II	824-827
101	Valentine	827
102	Gregory IV	827-844
103	Sergius II	844-847
104	Saint Leo IV	847-855
105	Benedict III	855-858
106	Saint Nicholas I	858-867
107	Adrian II	867-872
108	John VIII	872-882

109	Marinus I	882-884
110	Saint Adrian III	884-885
111	Stephen V (VI)	885-891
112	Formosus	891-896
113	Boniface VI	896
114	Stephen VI (VII)	896-897
115	Romanus	897
116	Theodore II	897
117	John IX	898-900
118	Benedict IV	900-903
119	Leo V	903
120	Sergius III	904-911
121	Anastasius III	911-913
122	Landus	913-914
123	John X	914-928
124	Leo VI	928
125	Stephen VII (VIII)	928-931
126	John XI	931-935
127	Leo VII	936-939
128	Stephen VIII (IX)	939-942
129	Marinus II	942-946
130	Agapitus II	946-955
131	John XII	955-964
132	Leo VIII	963-965
133	Benedict V	965-966
134	John XIII	965-972
135	Benedict VI	973-974
136	Benedict VII	974-983
137	John XIV	983-984
138	John XV	985-996
139	Gregory V	996-999
140	Sylvester II	999-1003
141	John XVII	1003
142	John XVIII	1004-1009
143	Sergius IV	1009-1012
144	Benedict VIII	1012-1024
145	John XIX	1024-1032
146	Benedict IX	1032-1044

147	Sylvester III	1045
148	Benedict IX	1045
149	Gregory VI	1045-1046
150	Clement II	1046-1047
151	Benedict IX	1047-1048
152	Damasus II	1048
153	Saint Leo IX	1049-1054
154	Victor II	1055-1057
155	Stephen IX (X)	1057-1058
156	Nicholas II	1059-1061
157	Alexander II	1061-1073
158	Saint Gregory VII	1073-1085
159	Blessed Victor III	1086-1087
160	Blessed Urban II	1088-1099
161	Paschal II	1099-1118
162	Gelasius II	1118-1119
163	Callistus II	1119-1124
164	Honorius II	1124-1130
165	Innocent II	1130-1143
166	Celestine II	1143-1144
167	Lucius II	1144-1145
168	Blessed Eugene III	1145-1153
169	Anastasius IV	1153-1154
170	Adrian IV	1154-1159
171	Alexander III	1159-1181
172	Lucius III	1181-1185
173	Urban III	1185-1187
174	Gregory VIII	1187
175	Clement III	1187-1191
176	Celestine III	1191-1198
177	Innocent III	1198-1216
178	Honorius III	1216-1227
179	Gregory IX	1227-1241
180	Celestine IV	1241
181	Innocent IV	1243-1254
182	Alexander IV	1254-1261
183	Urban IV	1261-1264
184	Clement IV	1265-1268

185	Blessed Gregory X	1271-1276
186	Blessed Innocent V	1276
187	Adrian V	1276
188	John XXI	1276-1277
189	Nicholas III	1277-1280
190	Martin IV	1281-1285
191	Honorius IV	1285-1287
192	Nicholas IV	1288-1292
193	Saint Celestine V	1294
194	Boniface VIII	1294-1303
195	Blessed Benedict XI	1303-1304
196	Clement V	1305-1314
197	John XXII	1316-1334
198	Benedict XII	1334-1342
199	Clement VI	1342-1352
200	Innocent VI	1352-1362
201	Blessed Urban V	1362-1370
202	Gregory XI	1370-1378
203	Urban VI	1378-1389
204	Boniface IX	1389-1404
205	Innocent VII	1404-1406
206	Gregory XII	1406-1415
207	Martin V	1417-1431
208	Eugene IV	1431-1447
209	Nicholas V	1447-1455
210	Callistus III	1455-1458
211	Pius II	1458-1464
212	Paul II	1464-1471
213	Sixtus IV	1471-1484
214	Innocent VIII	1484-1492
215	Alexander VI	1492-1503
216	Pius III	1503
217	Julius II	1503-1513
218	Leo X	1513-1521
219	Adrian VI	1522-1523
220	Clement VII	1523-1534
221	Paul III	1534-1549
222	Julius III	1550-1555

223	Marcellus II	1555
224	Paul IV	1555-1559
225	Pius IV	1559-1565
226	Saint Pius V	1566-1572
227	Gregory XIII	1572-1585
228	Sixtus V	1585-1590
229	Urban VII	1590
230	Gregory XIV	1590-1591
231	Innocent IX	1591
232	Clement VIII	1592-1605
233	Leo XI	1605
234	Paul V	1605-1621
235	Gregory XV	1621-1623
236	Urban VIII	1623-1644
237	Innocent X	1644-1655
238	Alexander VII	1655-1667
239	Clement IX	1667-1669
240	Clement X	1670-1676
241	Blessed Innocent XI	1676-1689
242	Alexander VIII	1689-1691
243	Innocent XII	1691-1700
244	Clement XI	1700-1721
245	Innocent XIII	1721-1724
246	Benedict XIII	1724-1730
247	Clement XII	1730-1740
248	Benedict XIV	1740-1758
249	Clement XIII	1758-1769
250	Clement XIV	1769-1774
251	Pius VI	1775-1799
252	Pius VII	1800-1823
253	Leo XII	1823-1829
254	Pius VIII	1829-1830
255	Gregory XVI	1831-1846
256	Pius IX	1846-1878
257	Leo XIII	1878-1903
258	Saint Pius X	1903-1914
259	Benedict XV	1914-1922
260	Pius XI	1922-1939

261	Pius XII	1939-1958
262	John XXIII	1958-1963
263	Paul VI	1963-1978
264	John Paul I	1978
265	John Paul II	1978-

Source: *The Roman Liber Pontificalis*

This is the complete list of all the presidents and Popes; the names of over three-hundred of the most influential mortal human beings to ever set foot on the face of the Earth. Only one U.S. president was Roman Catholic by faith, John Fitzgerald Kennedy, who stated during the 1960 campaign that he was not the Catholic nominee for president, but the Democratic nominee who just happened to be Catholic. This was most certainly true; but without his allegiance to Pope John XXIII, his devotion to the Blessed Virgin Mary, and his willingness to pray the Holy Rosary on his knees for global unity before the Most Blessed Sacrament, the entire planet would have been literally blown into billions of tiny atmospheric pieces during the Russo-Cuban Missile Crisis of 1962. It is extremely unfortunate that more of his predecessors did not enlist the vision of Vatican State amidst our nation's most perilous tragedies. The office of the presidency is subordinate to every authentic transcendental power because there is too much political posturing that accompanies the role. Furthermore, it has only been in existence for 225 years, and we do not have it calibrated quite yet as to how we should discharge the duties of the Oval Office with more seemly discretion. One might imagine the thoughts of our 215th Pope, Alexander VI, in October 1492 when he heard that an Italian navigator in Spanish service named Christopher Columbus had embarked on an oceanic journey and discovered the New World, or what Pope Paul V was thinking when he learned subsequent to December 21, 1620 that the Pilgrims aboard the Mayflower had gone ashore for the very first time in what is now Plymouth, Massachusetts. It is true that the presidents of the United States have written many fateful chapters in the history of the world, but the popes of the Catholic Church, by virtue of their union through the Holy Spirit, have always known in advance how the storybook-life of our human experience would eventually end. The collective American electorate practically venerates those who have ascended into the White House, but God seems much more interested in the development of both hemispheres in toto than what happens only in our most industrious nation. The previous pages bear the names of those who have been elevated to the very pinnacle of what they did best; and it oftentimes seemed none-too-soon for the reasons they were chosen. With all due respect to our nation's former leaders, it is quite obvious that the Vicars of Christ have tipped the scales of human events more in the direction of Divine Love and moral reasoning than any public administrator might ever aspire to accomplish. While our presidents have governed a country which has launched manned orbiters into outer-space, the popes have been in direct communication with the very God who fashioned the Heavens above them. The leader of the free world might have pantomimed an occasional melody about social justice at times, but it was the Papal Encyclicals of his epoch that faithfully penned the score. Secular partisans speak from behind bland lecterns in Rose Garden ceremonies about the Light of righteousness flickering in far-off places; but the Pope in Rome is the prayerful soul who has reflected it best. It is true that the Vatican has declined to become too deeply involved in the political affairs of individual nations, except during the past half-century; but this does not infer that the Holy See does not have plenty to say about how some disenfranchised people are governed. We are reminded of the elderly Latin-American cleric who said, "...when I feed the poor, they call me a saint. But, when I ask why we *have* the poor, they call me a Communist."

There seems to be no credible evidence that the American Civil Liberties Union should ever be concerned that formal Christianity is about to overtake the government of the United States because most people who follow Jesus Christ have already disavowed about half of what our nation stands for. If only such radical organizations could sense the ideal intentions of Holy Love already blooming from the Apostolic Church, perhaps they would lay down their legal weaponry and join in the cause of prayer. Any commander-in-chief of the U.S. military should know that there is no greater influence than this in the universe. He might prosecute an effective international war pretty well, but only through the spiritual ingenuity espoused by the Successor to Saint Peter can he prevent his enemies from uprising again. Some presidents have signed bills into law providing for capital punishment for defendants who are condemned to death by the courts; but popes implore them to exercise mercy by commuting their sentences in the Name of the Lord. The occupants of 1600 Pennsylvania Avenue have sought the confession of many criminals toward the goal of making them pay for their crimes; but Supreme Pontiffs have dispensed the Sacrament of Confession so the guilty will be fully absolved. An author named Andre Gide once penned the phrase, "*...one does not discover new lands without consenting to lose sight of* *the shore."* This may be the philosophy of the secular world, but the Pope amplifies the universal Kingdom of God which allows us to conquer inequity all around the world while keeping our hearts firmly implanted in Jesus, the Rock. The office of the U.S. presidency has been the catalyst for calling many factions to mutual harmony, but only ordained priests under Papal authority hold the power to administer the Penitential Sacrament that reconciles humankind with their Almighty God. There are certain ironies that must never be overlooked inside this process, too. Effective leaders of democratic superpowers are successful only when their people prosper in the marketplace, sustain their broad-based infrastructures, and when their checking accounts are in the black; but the Bishop of Rome expounds the Commandment from Jesus Christ for us to relinquish our material assets, give what currency we have to the poor, and lead lives of more humble service. If he should ever finally succeed, the league of nations will be a more sanctified place for everyone to live. While presidents exploit the parameters of political realism, popes from generations past have attempted to lead the United States to a closer relationship with God, from the Philadelphian debates to our post-modern filibusters. Humanity should embrace the prayerful guidance from the Savior of the World as it is told through the infallible leadership of the Roman Pontiff; for this is where moral goodness resides. In acknowledging this apparency, America will more than willingly pursue the advice of the Roman Catholic Church for a closer understanding of the Truth.

Chapter Thirteen
Hastening Our Own Demise

———————————

We might be employing woefully unscrupulous judgement if we choose to become too isolated unto ourselves and appear to be not unlike many other international paranoiac-schizophrenics who are hiding in their subterranean quarters like those teenage children with suicidal tendencies or the adolescents who are crouching in desperation in the corners of their rooms. Are we so fearful that someone else may pilfer our freedoms that we are forced to stay within our continental borders and guard them all the time? This is the one and the same dysfunctional pathology which has ushered-in the demise of many democratic countries throughout history; and it is not beyond the realm of possibility of occurring in the United States as well. A great American scholar, author, and professor; Robert Reich, who served as the U.S. Secretary of Labor from 1993 to 1997; put it quite succinctly in a report he issued in early November 2001 regarding the inward turn of our nation's policies on foreign trade relations after the violent felling of the two World Trade Center towers. *"At first glance, the war on terrorism has generated a flowering of multilateralism. Western Europe and America haven't been closer since World War II. Suddenly, we're also close allies of Russia, China, Pakistan, and even places Americans hardly knew existed six weeks ago, such as Uzbekistan. With political alliance comes economic integration. There's even a move afoot to increase trade with Pakistan. The (Bush) administration is pushing Congress for authority to move trade treaties without amendment. Yet, most of this is symbolic. Terrorism is causing America and other advanced nations to step-back from globalization. This is reflected in the steep drops in global equities, higher interest rates on bonds of emerging markets, and higher insurance costs in doing business abroad; all because of the added risks of a world threatened by terrorism. Or, just look at the bottlenecks at our borders. Inspections of cargo inside trucks and tankers are dramatically slowing the flow of foreign parts and supplies, which is forcing American companies to stock more inventory and consider shifting some of their suppliers to the United States. Foreign travel is down, not only among tourists, but also corporate executives and staff. And, the costs of providing security for overseas staff are rising. You can bet on tighter controls over immigration to the United States. Legal immigrants accounted for more than a third of the growth of America's work force during the past decade. But, those days may be over. Many poorer nations are feeling the double punch of a slowing global economy and political unrest at home. They want rich nations to open their borders to exports of agricultural commodities, textiles, and steel. But, rich nations, including the United States, aren't in any mood. The Commerce Department's International Trade Commission recently found that America's steel industry has been seriously injured by foreign steelmakers, clearing the way for the White House to impose higher tariffs and quotas on foreign steel. The irony, of course, is that the best way to fight terrorism over the long term is to give young people in poorer nations reason to believe they can make it in the new global economy. A retreat from globalization is exactly what the terrorists want."* (Quoted in *Illinois Times* periodical, Springfield, Illinois, December 6, 2001).

Hereafter, we must begin to reach-out to foreign countries, despite the imminent danger, not only for the purpose of marketing our wares, but to stabilize the global economy, making the rest of humanity more self-reliant in the process. This revolves around three central prospects; our willingness to share our best technological secrets without fear of being invaded, the will of the U.S. citizenry to be uninhibited about the advancements of other sovereign republics, and effecting our psychological transformation from assuming that the supremacy of our nation will somehow always be intrinsically superior to everyone else. We wield a neoclassical stinginess which seems to be holding the rest of the world back from becoming independent by reason of their own abject poverty; but our perpetual guard has left us looking somewhat unstable among the ever-growing number of free democracies. As time continues to pass, the natural composition of the Earth's population will ultimately shift against us because there will be more so-called minorities who will rival or even surpass the census of American Caucasians. The English language will become a lesser venue for maintaining interpersonal communication, and our skyline-architectures will look less like our quaint little midwestern villages and towering square-cornered municipal broadways. Indeed, the prevalence of various opportunities for us to exercise our own peculiar sense of domestic dominance will be threatened by the sheer number of other groups evolving from different origins and walks of life. This is precisely the reason why we must not discriminate against or criminalize them by limiting their capacity to be self-actualized through entering our most elite educational institutions and other professional fields; for we need them to become the most productive of any in our history if freedom in America as we have known it since the great emancipations of 1865 and 1964 is to survive. Again, this requires more than just having a plan in place; we must be willing to act upon it now, at our earliest hour; and not wait for our children to inherit the burden of having an entire society of dependents heaped upon them in the next twenty or thirty years when we, who are responsible for them now, have either retired or been waked, mourned, and deposited cold in the grave.

This begs the question of the irrational motivations which continue to haunt us in the aftermath of having closed Ellis Island in New York Harbor on November 12, 1954, after processing more than 20 million immigrants since 1892. For those who are too young to remember it, Ellis Island is the 28-acre site which was considered the gateway to capitalism and true freedom for those leaving Europe and the other continents, trying to make it on their own in our "...land of the free, and home of the brave." It was named for Samuel Ellis, a rich New York merchant who had originally purchased it and gave it his name. Its possession was later transferred to New York State, and eventually to the control of the federal government in 1808. As many as 5,000 people a day were processed through the island from 1892 until it was closed. President Lyndon Johnson declared it a National Monument in 1965 and, after a $160 million renovation project was completed, it was reopened as a museum in 1990. It now boasts of the ethnic artifacts and oral histories of over four centuries of American immigrants, and is home to the American Immigrant Wall of Honor where the names of a half-million influential immigrants have been inscribed. Should we not at least consider that Ellis Island was, in its time, a precursor or parable to the United States as a whole for the ensuing 21st century? Will we not someday try to land our own national identity upon the beaches of the rest of the globe, a world that is changing so rapidly that we will be clamoring for them to allow us to remain at least a sliver inside the pie-chart of what the continental composition will look like compared to the size of our present-day influential Western culture? Our trains of thought are absolutely loath to go there at times, but such unavoidable changes in our national attitude and the assaults against our prideful posterity are bound to arrive very soon, if they are not already eroding the surface of our most endearing patriotic institutions. The architecture of the world is evolving so quickly that we can neither control nor contain it through any means-structuring of our own. Americans tend to forget that the best of humankind on the other continents is up-and-running while we are sound asleep in our beds at night; investing in the fluidity of our financial markets that are swiftly ticker-taping by the hour, planning their own investments, and multiplying the numbers of their children at an almost uncontrollable rate that is many times greater than our meager count of 285 million people have the capacity to generate.

Time itself will force the union of all peoples at the intersection of the present and the future; while we still seem to be unprepared to meet all these demographic and cultural changes, despite the fact that we have held almost total control over global politics and industrial advancement for the previous hundred years. Will we be known in the history books of the 22nd century as the empire that fell because we tried for too long to stand-out in isolation on our own? If we can conjure an image of the Statue of Liberty suddenly falling face-first into the waters of New York Harbor, this is what it will seem like to our great-grandchildren's progeny in those decades to come. Are we not unlike the haughty over-achievers who thought we could never be taken by storm or suffer the slow undoing and inexorable erosion of our own national security by stealing the "covers" of fortune and fame too rapidly for ourselves? It is not a national sense of unity which is running rampant in America today, but our errant assumption that we can remain anonymous to our fellow citizens and the rest of the world, alike, without the slightest inkling of what a true community is; while somehow still expecting to survive. This is the kind of self-righteous stuffiness that has made a mockery of our modern international relations, and is also partially the reason for the fall of the U.S.S.R.. They were so worried that the U. S. and China might someday attack them militarily that they kept their own people from enjoying the true fertility of the rest of the world; refusing to allow any religious tenets from influencing their decisions, and holding-out on their own through vague foreign policies consisting only of defensive armaments, concrete blocks, and barbed-wire. In case too few of us have placed our finger on the pulse of America today; footing the bill for a $100 billion missile defense system is a symptom of our own state of paranoia; refusing to participate in previously existing international peace accords and noncompliance with common sense environmental treaties *are* our concrete blocks; and closing our domestic borders to peace-loving peoples is our multi-thousand-mile strand of glistening razor-wire. Every time we forcibly detain a handcuffed prisoner in America today, we are saying, "...I am afraid of you." When we hear the clink of a prison door-jam closing behind our inmates, we are admitting, "...we do not need you anymore." This may be alright for their own protection and for society at large, but is this not also the approach we are taking toward the nations in Africa, to the Far East, Latin America, and even certain segments of our own population right here at home?

Would the indigenous native Americans who we remanded to segregated reservations during the 19th and early 20th centuries tell us that America is suffering from a congenital malady called "elitism," whose symptoms are lust for power, an imperialistic approach to the acquisition of real property, and a penchant for controlling the future of the world supermarkets? If we created Thirteen Colonies on the eastern seaboard on a continent which was already previously inhabited by a native race, why should the eastern hemisphere not believe that we might reverse course and assimilate their customs and policies, too? It may appear as though we are afraid of being overtaken by forces beyond our control because this is the impression we have evoked from the rest of the globe during the entire expanse of the years 1776 through 1992. If we are perceived as being inordinately concerned that we might perish in this ever-changing world, it is because of the reaction and retribution of our foreign neighbors who have been watching us try to make an industrious political mountain out of a native American molehill for the past two-hundred years. Outdoor amphitheaters in the age before electricity was first contained were positioned in clearings on the ground facing the western horizon so they could take advantage of the early-evening "flatlight" shining at an 180-degree angle across the stage floor. This was their window of opportunity for producing and presenting public events in their most clear, natural, and revealing format. Well, the 21st century has arrived; and the dusk of human existence on the Earth has finally come upon us; or so says the Gospel of Jesus Christ. Are we going to make the most of the Wisdom that God is pouring upon our great land to declare to the rest of the world that we are open to their most intense levels of scrutiny in determining whether we are truly the champion of human and civil rights, as many of our predecessors have claimed? We can remember that the first cash register was patented by James and John Ritty of Dayton, Ohio in November 1880; but we have strangely long-lost sight of the fate and value of the multiple-trillions of dollars we have wasted and the opportunities we have squandered to dignify the rest of humankind by our own domestic prosperity. America is at its best when we facilitate the inclusion of all peoples from every ethnicity and walk of life, rather than disavowing the greatness of the philanthropic legends from almost every foreign shore.

In God We Trust!

Just in case there are some readers who have trekked thus far in *When Legends Rise Again* and feel curious as to whether William Roth will ever end his tirade against the lack of morality, spiritual conscience, and civility in the United States of America, it may be pleasing for them to discover the fulcrum located here, in the middle of Chapter Thirteen, on page 214 of the body of its text. It should be quite obvious by now that America's explosion of industrial materialism has left our dying foreign neighbors impaled with the shrapnel from our neglect for far too long. And, it can hardly be any clearer that the older we middle-class Americans get, the more such things as our medical costs increase, while our ability to pay them sharply declines; for such is the effect of the diminishing returns in a free-market society. One might wonder whether it is plausible to determine the overall morality of a nation by its simple "ph factor" on a single important issue; and for the United States, that emission is our penchant for devaluing the life and death of our more helpless citizens. There is much more to say about the problems which exist in our great republic; and it is yet to be seen how we shall address them, pending the outcome of the future. Suffice it to say that I am not the first to be concerned about our fate before the judgement of God, even if the plentiful grace He has shined upon us has seemed insufficient at times for us to see beyond our own inequities well enough to come to grips with our commission for living-out His Truth. Yes, we are a country that is stuffed to the gills with noble men and women. Jesus Christ intended it that way; and He would never allow the most advanced democracy on the face of the globe to be the one in a hundred to somehow wander aimlessly from within His sight and cause Him to leave another ninety-nine just to track us down. By all means, He realizes that we are the defenders of an almost sacred freedom which had never been seen before the likes of Washington, Jefferson, and James Madison finally came along. America has been a bastion of hope for multiple-millions of meandering souls who could never realize their dreams on any other soil. We shall continue to prevail and succeed in this role because we have allowed our Divine Creator to form and shape us, to carry us in His Arms along the shores of greatness to that place we can only describe from within our hearts if it is very quiet outside. When we see the millions of celebrants standing amidst Times Square in the Big Apple every December 31st, anticipating the arrival of yet another new year, the whole world looks to us with a strange sensation of implied approval because they can visually see our expansive wishes for the coming of better seasons for all humankind;

not just Americans, not just the western hemisphere; but for all peoples in every land, foreign and domestic, colors abounding, hopes aloft, and spirits and psyches renewed.

It has been repeated in countless places throughout the decades that our American democratic experience will always be an unfinished creation because each new generation must come to plot their own definition of freedom on their own. Thanks to the trials we have endured to protect our homeland from all-out destruction, to the thousands of veterans whose lives are the very personification of heroism, to the mothers and fathers who have worked their fingers to the bare bones to keep their impressionable children aright; our superiority is the composition of our threaded blanket of responsible decency with which we would like to cover the entire globe. Our central objective has never been a matter of imperialism for the sake of calling the rest of the world our property to claim; but to enhance the opportunities for different races in regions which are oceans apart to choose for themselves how they wish to be governed. This is precisely what the two great World Wars were all about; and the conflicts in South Korea, Viet Nam, Bosnia, Kosova, Afghanistan, and all the rest of them, too. I have been told by the readers of some of the other books I have authored to "lighten up," to take it easy, inhale a deep breath of fresh air, and perhaps take a long pilgrimage to some of the more barbaric regions of the world, returning home thereafter with a renewed appreciation and invigorated sense of pride for the peaceful way we live here in America. My response is always that this would be a good idea; but the anarchy which exists in such places from which I would return will still be there. I have also heard that it is somewhat improper to lift-up the standard of living in other nations by trying to diminish ours here in the U.S.. In case an intelligent man might be incapable of seeing it, their plight is not a hopeless case; and we have the energy, resources, mobility, power, and courage to make a huge difference wherever we properly can. The decisions as to when and where are oftentimes the most difficult for us to ponder; for God understands with no uncertainty the responsibilities He has vested in us to turn outwardly toward the suffering world and not only to our native selves. It makes our hearts ache to see such suffering abroad because we realize what it means for a nation of people to be free. We have always hailed the principled purposes of sound organization, dignity for those who are hurting, the nurturing of our young, encouragement to the lost, and public assistance for the socially marginalized. Whether we have fully effected the proper courses and solutions in addressing these issues is a matter for another discussion. In the meantime, let there be no mistake about it. The record for sustaining human dignity and decency in the United States is second to none. We have never engaged in the systematic destruction of our civilian population; we treasure our vast environmental heartlands and mountains by setting them aside; we stand for the preservation of organic nature; and we govern ourselves pretty effectively through the common virtues of reason, intelligence, rationalism, sustained deduction, and logic.

No one in the world could claim that we have never tried to be the best in everything we do. Therefore, why would a man in his 40s such as myself, who has undying respect for the land of his birth, compose a polemic of critical themes such as those which are incorporated heretofore in this book? Because, above all things, I love my country and its people; our hopes for the future, the beauty of our valleys and streams, the compassion of our clergy, the skill of our doctors and nurses, the valor of our fallen countrymen, our mutual desires in solving the personal crises of people we don't even know, and standing as one society before the flying colors of Old Glory with our hands over our breasts in remembrance of the millions of souls who have inhabited this land with one end in sight: freedom, and our desire to preserve it. This is what Mel Gibson was screaming about when he acted the part of William Wallace in the motion picture *Braveheart*, just before an ax was felled by an executioner to sever his head from his shoulders. With a bellow from the depths of his disemboweled body and the stubbornness of a bull, he screamed, "...freeeeedom!!!" And, in this noble sacrifice, he set an entire Scottish nation free again to fight to their deaths to choose their own life's goals of their own accord, not to the command of some corrupted secular king. This, in itself, is the same interior drive which keeps most Americans wary against anyone who might wish to place our liberties at risk. Indeed, I hold to the prowess of all this courage, and more. However, we must not tire from seeing the journey of our great nation to its long-sought destiny of democratic perfection; if ever there was such a thing. Should our spirits ever be broken, it is because it hurts us to endure the waiting, trying to communicate effectively with our families and friends on a more civilized plane; and even addressing our enemies, as well. There is true power in this aspiration; this is what we are still searching for, and anything short of accomplishing it will never be enough. Beyond any doubt, the secret for solving many mysteries resides in our quest to keep rediscovering ourselves; to make and mold, to decipher and encrypt, and to loosen and to bind. Nothing shy of this is the reason why our patriotic citizens still clad themselves in leather vestments, sport multi-colored tattoos across their brows, drink cold Budweiser beer, and listen to Bob Seger & the Silver Bullet

Band while they ride their crackling Harley-Davidson motorcycles across the liberating frontier with their graying beards flying backwards in the wind. This is the source of our innate curiosity to explore such pristine places as the passages beyond the portals in our timid hearts; to inquire of our volcanoes why they become so angry every hundred years or so, and lay our prematurely-newborn babies in incubators to nurse them back to health like placing a tiny wooden splint on the wing of a crippled bird. This is a reflection of our almost godlike desires to preserve and protect anything as we will, or to suddenly condemn a convicted criminal to death with such a calculated vengeance that we might wish to ponder whether we are the victims of some clinical mental aberration or multiple-personalities disorder ourselves.

Why is it so difficult for us to define the excellence from which our most admirable behaviors have evolved? What makes us reflect the sequined nature of humanity-perfected in the morning, and then lead the lives of hellions by night? The answer is quite simple to detect—because we *can*; and this is our preferred definition of liberty—freedom from want, a place to call our own, endless reasons to begin anew, and the strength to effect social change. Our community spirit is often contorted by our wish to be unknowable sometimes, even to ourselves; and yet, we remain an integral part of the whole when there is a catastrophic human event to overcome or a continental reason to celebrate. Most Americans are rather reluctant to bow to the order of whims of any one particular person or aggressive sect who wishes to bridle our consciences; and this, for some readers, might become the seed of dissatisfaction with my books. Everyone with a sense of goodness in their veins believes that we should stand beside the weak and forsaken; and this is why our Hollywood movies and TV programs bring us to weep tears of joy when we see the underdog walk-away with the prize or Goliath finally paying his dues. Millions of Americans have listened to the great oratories of the imaginary President of the United States, Jeb Bartlett, on NBC's *West Wing* and gotten goose-bumps all over their body when Martin Sheen goes on a tare about social injustice, racial intolerance, and treating the poor with disdain. These are the origins and reflections of our American sense of cohesion; that we know the differences between right and wrong, good and bad, and darkness and light. We are apt to fight for a certain cause solely for the reason that it helps someone else, while casting the better lot of our own personal fortunes aside for awhile. Therefore, let me be clear. I am not some cranky antagonist with an ax to grind or politics to please; I bear no grudge against my fellow citizens; and I can take a punch to the gut for the cause of our freedom along with the best in our ranks. But, someone has *got* to speak-up about what is right in America by addressing the things that are wrong. My native soil is the nation I hold deeply in union with my very being; and I detest and deplore anyone who may attempt to convince me that we are not making the most of our time on Earth within the constraints of our human understanding. Education in the spiritual and corporal virtues is what this discussion is all about; not for the purpose of maligning a country whose principles are so well accorded with the Beatitudes of God. My purpose has never been to render an impolite or inaccurate judgement about the worth of our American soul; but we can do better by those around whom we live, and we must do so now if we insist upon referring to ourselves as being Christians. The previous twelve chapters of this manuscript have been replete with one example after the next, addressing areas where we need to refocus our more intensified efforts.

Why do those who accept and follow the Gospel of Jesus Christ refuse to concede to defeat in this raging battle for such goodness? As the great political strategist, James Carville, once put it, *"...because we have the facts on our side!"* If we allow the country we love so dearly to sink into any further moral decay, we will become our own worst enemies once we have seen the inevitable response of the Son of God. *Hastening Our Own Demise*, indeed! We cannot blame anyone but ourselves if we abandon every benison for which Christ was put to death on a Cross while we live in a republic in which we are free to worship Him as we please. We can sit at our desks and write our excuses in paperback diaries until we are blue in the face, but we will still be wasting our time if we remain in such obstinance about what the Holy Scriptures reveal. What we are looking for is most certainly not the product of someone's Tarot cards, the ridiculous "predictions" of compensated psychic hotline mediums, or even our embellished impressions of ourselves. Only the Truth as we know it to be through the Divine intercession of the Holy Spirit of Jesus Christ will set us on course to mending our ways, while providing for the common defense of every man, woman, and child alive; concurrently dispensing an equitable welfare, and sustaining our national esteem. Only through the beauty of our righteous desires will we ever be free to pursue our selfless expressions with any real hope of achieving them before we have grown too old to make them come true. America must become the leader in all spiritual righteousness if ever our reasons for building a society of order will be any more than a hash-mark in the passing annals of time. There is a piece of furniture that is native to France called a *prie-dieu*, which is used for kneeling during prayer, having a shelf above for a book. When they gave us the Statue of Liberty as a gift in June 1885, were they not also telling us that we are the seat of freedom to worship God as we *should*, not as though it is some kind of an option? When we said, "...give me your tired and your poor," were we not also charged with leading everyone who arrived at our shores to their dignity in Christ? Are we not the nation upon whose vast acreage millions of weary travelers still wish to fall to their knees, reach for the skies overhead, and invoke His Divine Wisdom to guide them to peace? We are not only the French carpentry for those who call this their home, but to every human soul who lives on the face of the globe. We own the freedom to consecrate this mission without having to surrender to the retribution of any Marxist-Leninist regimes, and we should start practicing it now!

This is why we were given the stars and stripes of idealism in America today. Let us ensure that our immortal legacy stands before the Heavens with the elegance of a thousand Secretariats galloping freely forever through the forests of the wild; or a musical score that will never expire; the glare of a tiger protecting her cubs; a child who can see beyond the breadth of his age; a scarlet letter being burned by the pure; and a forsaken orphan who has inherited the throne of a king. The soul of such legends as Carl Lewis, Sonny Liston, Tiger Woods, Michael Jordan, Pete Sampras, and Henry Aaron all pined to reach the summit of this pinnacle of elation; one for which many of them yearned and wondered inside from where their strength and perseverance was really derived. It came to them from the Glory of God, from their auspicious desires to make the best of their human domain, and through the freedom of this American nation that finally gave them a chance. Somewhere aloft, there is another Titanic that has been launched anew; one which is sailing on a starlit crest of dignity where there are no societal classes to segregate, no coal at the keel to heap into the boilers, and no more icebergs to dodge. This is the hope of our guarded American nation and the pearled legacy we must leave to her peoples, remembering that God shall exhume us as well from under our fathomed inequities if only we will let Him proceed. We must continue our mission to search the entire spectrum of moral Truth inside which all of these indelible events are poised. We may never reach the status of being "invincible" before the Son of Man returns, but our assignment will not be complete until we run with the swiftness of Michael Johnson's golden shoes past our own borders, into the expanse of the bubbling globe; to seek and find the lost of our species; to create new opportunities for suffering humanity, and to make God proud once again that we are His people who have chosen to succeed because His Son is the Champion in whose Name we compete.

I wrote the last few pages of this chapter on Christmas Eve 2001, and I could not help but think of all the harsh realities that were playing-out in the minds and hearts of so many hundreds-of-thousands of poor souls that night who had previously lost their loved-ones in the violence and tragedy which has become such a sad portion of our contemporary world; with all the terrorist bombings, airplane crashes, buildings destroyed, and entire neighborhoods veritably burned to the ground. As I thought about the Birth of Jesus and the peaceful accord meant especially for Christmas, I was also reminded of the multitudes of larger-than-life Americans we see everyday on the streets and in our workplaces; those who went-away to war and came home with their bodies deformed, limbs amputated, and spirits scarred. I wondered about all their dog tags laying on the shelves of their closets or in the bottom of the cedar chest now; and I know somehow deep inside that therein are inscribed the names of our contemporary Saints. The legacies of these truest American giants should be equally as emblazoned upon our grateful souls, as we pine for every name-tag around their necks to be transformed into a medal of honor on their lapels, with finely hewn letters hailing their identities: Raddemaker, Burton, Jones, Whitehurst, Turner, Belliard—and the list goes on and on. Our gratefulness should sprout far beyond our capacity to explain it; for America is free because, like the Christ-Child who bravely entered a world of such brutal corruption, these heroes fought for freedom and peace with no less love and devotion for the liberation of humankind.

Chapter Fourteen
Segregating the Rich from the Poor

———————————————

It would be interesting to discover from where humankind conceived the notion that the definition of "affluence" should be based solely upon the value of our material possessions and the purchasing-power of our currency. One would have thought that we should have learned not to place so much interest in such pseudo-assets after the Stock Market crashed in 1929. But, just like a good little capitalistic child, America got back on its hobby horse within the next few years thereafter and set the same volatile standard as its definition for success that it embraced before. I suppose people jumping headlong off our highest skyscrapers at the start of the Great Depression was insufficient reason for us to learn that there are more important things in life. Indeed, returning to such a false measure of fulfillment would evolve to be one of our greatest faux pas in the 20th century. There exists no defensible evidence to prove that there is any direct correlation between personal happiness and our mutual infatuation with the tangible aspects of the physical world. Once upon a time, we thought that asbestos was the greatest thing since sliced bread to contain the heat to keep us warm; and scientists were hailing the value of freon in our air conditioners as the best way to keep us cool in the summertime. We have since discovered, however, that the former causes lung cancer, and the latter leads to the depletion of the ozone layer in the Earth's atmosphere. So much for quick fixes. Is this not the predicate for a parable which should teach us that some of the very things we hold onto for comfort will eventually harm us, or even take the entire of humanity closer to death? The cold hard cash in our wallets and Savings & Loans will eventually do the same thing. Placing too much emphasis on personal wealth is somewhat like a man watching a motion picture and falling in love with the character being portrayed by the actress. He will never be able to secure a relationship with this imagined personality, and he is quite unlikely to ever meet the screen-star either. This is exactly the fallacious road that a blind lust for materialism takes us down. It brings us no closer to reality, no nearer to God, and even farther away from the Truth. A close friend once told me about a comrade of his who came to his house when his mother died in 1984. It was late August, and the visitor was working in the fields, harvesting the corn crop, when he heard the news. My friend was quite touched when his compassionate caller arrived in his old farm clothes; never-minding the preposterous way that others came in suit and tie, forgetting about the formal protocol of such a morbid occasion, and just walking through the doorway with a ripped undershirt and faded blue jeans on his lanky frame. This was one of the most profoundly honest displays of compassion that could have ever been dispensed. The young farmer, whose name I think was Larry, had only one mission in mind that night; getting quickly to the side of his grieving friend.

There will be a time in the future, even if it is when most of us lay upon our deathbeds, when every aspect of human existence will become this crystal clear. When certain people have said that they were so frightened at times that they could envision the entire span of their life passing before their eyes, they were not just imagining it; but God had spared them in the subsequent moments for reasons known only to Him. The collection of our years is composed of an absolutely innumerable amount of little "specks," most all of which are either too small for us to see with our naked eyes, or that pass-by too quickly for us to notice them. One of God's more urgent intentions is to slow us down so we can see these unique particles of our mortal existence more clearly; to "...stop and smell the roses," as some songwriters have penned it. Every day we live is a "still photograph" in the swiftly-reeling years of our passing mortality. We remember not when we began to focus upon them in our infancy; and God only knows when we shall finally see our last. The most important point, however, is whether we remember what we endured; if we learned anything from the experience, or would we change any part of it if we could go backward in time? Did we play a role in making the course of human history a more peaceful progression? When we speak about the virtues of trust and interest, participation and evolution, and action and design; are we referring to our somewhat limited capacity to bring the world to closure at the velocity of God, or in a much more hastened pace which better fits our needs? There are certain sights, lingering echoes, and other environmental influences which give us a sense of security when we are older; like the sound of a chicken frying in a pan, or seeing a laborer washing a window somewhere. For others, that "almost home" sensation might be hearing the crack of a baseball flying off a bat in an open field in their neighborhood park. We know that we gain a perception of reminiscence from these things because they are the reflections of our past; inducing almost sacred images to tweak our more nostalgic side, taking us back to our roots. While this may seem to be all well and good for sustaining our sense of continuity, what must it be like for those whose childhood was completely void of any such Americana; the little ones who were subjected only to the constancy of neglect, repeated physical abuse, exposure to the outside elements, and a total lack of compassion from the people who were supposed to love them? In this context, *we* are the rich, and they are the poor; even if some of them have come of age in our western civilization and are now living in a seaside mansion in the city of Malibu.

There is an entire chasm dividing our peace-of-mind from the nightmares of our younger days; one that money cannot buy. Nothing short of the Holy Eucharist on our tongues can erase the memories which keep our mind-waves swirling around in the past; no plush townhouses, extravagant automobiles, or even dining in the most fancy restaurants will expunge them from our train of thoughts. In many unique ways, the inequities of our emotional state are as impressed inside our intellect as how we apportion our material goods. While most of us were raised to the sweet sound of French horn melodies in our ears, others heard only screams of agony, snakes hissing at their feet, missiles firing overhead, and their stomachs growling from lingering hunger pains. They were impoverished *beyond* their physical surroundings; likewise starved of affection, robbed of their innocence, stripped of dignity, and enchained by hatred. When middle-class people refer to the way we live as being our simple "ambience," they perceive our lives as the closest thing to Paradise they have ever seen. When a child is segregated from the ramparts of decency, cast to the wolves without justification, tossed over the cliffs of psychological aggravation, and gnarled by the outright evil of predatory fiends, what can be said about the fortunes he has amassed before the Cross of the Savior of the human race? There are a lot of Americans who continue to live in complete agony because of their foregone experiences; somehow believing the misconception that they can conceal their pain inside the distractions of epicurean indulgence, monetary abundance, and sparkling jewels. Most of them might be the first to tell us that they are leading a life of total fabrication because their entire existence is the essence of a lie. Such a pretense of peace cannot live for very long because the human heart will eventually expose what is hidden deep inside the soul. The question remains on the table as to whether we, as a mobilized nation of compassionate Americans, have done enough to address what we know to be true about the inner-feelings of our citizens. While there is no doubt that it costs a great deal of money to tend to the needs of everyone, it is rather obvious that the indigent among us are the least to seek proper professional care. I have observed many of them come and go through the years I have attended Holy Mass at the Cathedral of the Immaculate Conception in Springfield, Illinois everyday; and the attention we should show them is somehow missing in the swiftness of our lives. So much of this can be amended because we do, in fact, live in a Christian-oriented democracy. There are psychiatric institutions all across the U.S. where manic-depressive patients, the mentally deranged, and the clinically retarded are treated with concern, respect, dignity and love.

The long-standing question continues to remain as to whether this approach of segregating them from the rest of society is the proper course to take. Have any people come to believe that they are somehow intellectually unstable because the rest of us have told them so? Are they living-out a false prophecy when the rest of society callously claims they should be secluded in the confines of their homes? This is not even slightly the laughing matter that the likes of H. Ross Perot tried to make it when he joked about having an insane relative living in the attic of his Texas mansion. These poor people are in serious trouble, and there are many actions we can take to make their lives more compatible with ours. We have forded great lengths in improving their chances of being healed, both on a national and state level, in the past fifty years. I had the opportunity to visit the Jacksonville Developmental Center in Illinois to see the way these people are housed in dormitory-like structures and taught to sculpt a type of a laboratorical existence for themselves. Their pitiful nature is a sight to behold; not that they are mistreated or wrongfully castigated by any means, but in the heart-wrenching way they sit idly in their chairs and on the benches outside their rooms and rock back and forth with their hands between their knees like many primates do. After having returned to my own residence since then, I have often pondered the passage in the Bible where Jesus commands us all to storehouse our riches in Heaven. Truly, indeed, these mentally-challenged people must already have a massive stockpile of wealth waiting for them once they pass-away into the Glory of His Light. While I am certainly no Church theologian, I cannot help but believe that such innocuous creatures are surely not held accountable for their sins because they have not the capacity to maintain the integrity of their social conscience that the rest of us are required to guard; and they are the least responsible for the deceit and greed which have made an unmitigated dogfight out of the more "civilized" world. They reside beyond the mainstream of our systems of public education; they are deprived of the opportunity to exchange our everyday wares, and are taught only what is sufficient for them to know how to feed and dress themselves, tend to their personal hygiene, and perform some type of perfunctory task to pass the time of day. Most of the mental patients I have seen will never become so advanced as to ever be able to be released from their institutional environments. They take medicine to calm their nerves, stop their illusory fears, and keep them from having convulsions at the cafeteria tables. Some of them lose control of their bodily functions while watching game-shows on the commissary television set, and others try to burst through locked doors and kick the panels off the passages leading into their nurses' private lounge. And, what is society's reaction to this while their doctors are forced to alter their medical regiment to counteract the side-effects of the ones they are on, until their trembling bodies grow immune to them, too; and the whole process must begin anew? In the meantime, thousands of people drive past these places in caravans of BMWs everyday and never proffer a parting glance, let alone stop to visit them once in awhile.

It is probably quite obvious that everyone in America has seen the television commercials advertising the body-enhancing program consisting of electrical wires and nodes which are used to stimulate the muscular system to get their physiques into shape. This process, medically known as "faradism," has been utilized for many decades by professionals in the business, and its application was performed on mentally retarded and physically handicapped people when it was originally introduced. There has even been the extreme use of such electrical current for pathological purposes called "electro-shock" therapy, where discontinuous alternating current is actually allowed to enter the brain through the use of a conductant placed on the temples, near the ears. This usually sends the patient into an induced convulsion for a brief period of time, but the benefits have been widely acclaimed for the elimination of the most serious symptoms of manic-depression, reducing the occurrence of grand-mal seizures, and even eradicating periodic tendencies toward self-masochism and thoughts of suicide. Again, I have not studied a great deal about the latent effects of such harsh medical procedures or the long-term prognosis of the participating subjects, but the entire matter has brought me to think about how fortunate are the rest of us who simply wake in the morning to the sound of our alarm clocks, dress ourselves for work everyday, and go about tending to our lives and families as though our brothers and sisters inside these places do not even exist. But, is this the true reality which is effecting change in the realm of human immortality that we cannot see with our eyes? *Are these poor individuals in mental institutions the burnishing fabric of a perfected humanity with which Jesus is also polishing our souls?* Perhaps we are the ones to be pitied because we are so out of touch with the Truth of the Cross, while those who stand barefooted inside their stark barracks on cold tile floors with steel bars on the windows look-out at a secular world which Our Lord and Savior will eventually rebuke in time or even reject as being unworthy of His Divine Mercy altogether. I am not suggesting that this is what we deserve, but the matter is certainly a prime topic for further discussion. Perhaps the rest of us are not as well-off as we might have originally assumed; maybe most of the people in our psychiatric wards are the geniuses with whom God has endowed the capacity to judge what we have done for the oppressed and forsaken with the health that we are taking for granted. Only He knows where these poor people would be if there were not caring workers like those developmental counselors, QMRPs, and other advocates who tend to the needs of the sick; monitor their progress, fill-out the reports, and serve as ombudsmen for their families and friends.

Has the thought ever occurred to most of the children whose parents are suffering from Alzheimer's disease that such symptoms of senility have been in existence since man first started the process of aging? This terrible affliction is a combination of the hardening of the cranium arteries and a dysfunctional gene. It is as though we can approach our parents to discuss the particulars of a given day in the morning, and within a matter of the passing of the lunch hour, they can neither recognize who we are nor understand a syllable we are saying. Here, too, our thoughts and emotions run completely beyond control because we cannot decide what in the world is going on; so we simply turn our faces to the sky and ask God "why." We pound our fists into the cushions of the waiting-room chairs at our local hospices and require to know from Him what our parents ever did wrong. The truth of all this resides in the fact that our loved-ones are passing ever-so slowly closer to the Dominion of Heaven. Their dignity is not lost because they have been asked to join the Redeemer of the World on the Cross. From our dimmed perspective, however, it seems as though they are as helpless as toddlers in the backseats of our cars. But, to God, they have become the Saints and makers of a new age of change. We do not know what they are thinking because most of them are unable to converse with us anymore. They seem not to be writhing in pain or suffering any type of notable migraine distress. It would be ridiculous for us to believe that their consciousness has been relocated to some type of animated suspension, or that the psyche of a person can be suddenly nowhere in Creation at all. In truth, the farther they seem to slip away from us is directly related to their closer proximity to Paradise. They have joined the manifest of those who are sailing atop the tidal waves of the same Ocean of Mercy in which Jesus is immersing the entire circumference of the globe. Therein is their good fortune and their willing participation in the conversion of humankind to Love. We can no longer express any doubt that we live in poverty when we set-out to the endless pursuit of material wealth; for all of our riches are positioned beyond the brink of our death. If we ponder this with a firm sense of logic to our thoughts, we will be convinced that it is the affluent who are starving for the knowledge of Truth; they are the ones who are segregated from the spiritually rich in the eyes of our Almighty Father; but the suffering, the poor, infirm, and neglected are they who shall inherit their crowns. While our daily expenditure of the material Earth makes us look like perpetual "users" in the eyes of God's good graces, those who have little to their names are the ones who are actually paying the fees. When our doubts in His Love cast a cloud of darkness over the world, the Light of their union with the Crucifixion helps us to see beyond our errors. It sounds pretty much like we who hold control over the trappings of the globe are the ones who are truly deprived, walking-down a wayward path, living like paupers in a Kingdom of higher dimensions; while those who are undergoing their own personal trials and tribulations are the children of God who shall be first in the contemporary succession of Saints. When evil tries to douse the reflection of Heaven from within our midst, those who are agonizing their last will always keep it shining. So, if it seems like our poorer outcasts do not fit in our present company, we can almost bet our last dime that they are the life of the party in the spiritual world of holiness we cannot yet see. Such is the reciprocal justice of the Lamb of God; that He is also our Shepherd who is concealed so inconspicuously in the identity of those whom we might least expect.

The sooner we Americans understand that there is no such thing as an "expendable" person anywhere on the face of the globe; whether they wish us virtue or harm, no matter what their color or creed, and notwithstanding their cultural anomalies; the more we will be blessed with the banner processions from God which will elevate us to the highly revered plateau of unconditional absolution. We realize, of course, that we cannot mutate a goat into a sheep; wheat will not deteriorate into chaff, and flowers will always be more evocative to our emotions than weeds; and so it is that the march of human destiny shall never be Divine unless we embrace *all* humanity as our very own. This is precisely what makes our duty to provide for their inclusion in the finer things of life unavoidable; all to their nourishment; affording them decent, safe, and sanitary housing; and providing equal protection under the law and access to nondiscriminatory opportunities which are explicitly mandated by Christ's Proverbial definitions of good, just, and right. There is nothing wrong with reciting His words in their proper context and perspective when reprimanding our brothers and sisters because this is God's tireless wish for us to herald the presanctified actions of His Sacrificed Son for the spiritual conversion of the ulterior world. When we deploy our efforts toward the goal of improving the lives of those who suffer, we are speaking His Word loudly and clearly. Our purposes are not unethical when we teach our children to learn from their own experiences about how to be self-sufficient and independent; but it is improper to urge them to become inordinately wealthy in a larger society where there continues to exist unfair standards for achieving the end which will make everyone a portion of the whole. It is perfectly alright to be "set apart" if it means being identified as the most charitable, consoling, peaceful, and holy in a particular circle of peers. Indeed, it may even be acceptable to pursue the comforts of penthouses and ocean-side condominiums if every other person on the Earth has equal access to them as well. We might remember when we may have been caught chewing bubble-gum in English class, and the most popular acclamation from our teacher was, *"...I hope you brought enough for everybody!"* As simplistic as it may seem, this is exactly what Jesus Christ is saying to us now. There is no transgression in building a million-dollar home if we know for sure that there will never again be anyone else sleeping out in the cold. It should be painfully obvious that the subtle implications of this prospect are fairly unequivocal. When we stand before Jesus in final judgement someday and beg Him to select our soul for the heights of Heaven and not the fires of the Abyss, it would not be unlike Him to ask us the rhetorical question as to whether *we* made our choices on behalf of others with the same measure by which we are asking to be sustained. Everyone knows that the decisions we make in this life are, for the most part, a product of our own free will. Later, however, when all is said and done, and the cards are all revealed, will we own a record that will expose us as being the indignant women and gentlemen who led condescending lives? Did we segregate our allegiance according to our impressions of who might do us the most good down the road, or those from whom we knew we would someday profit by our loyalty? It seems like a greater advantage to fill our own warehouses with rainy-day commodities now than to risk the possibility of running shy of necessary goods later by filling-up a stranger's cupboard on a bright, sunshiny afternoon.

We may be too afraid that some type of paralysis could set in if we spend too much time responding to the summons of our neighbors while preparing our own nests for the monsoon showers that are about to fall. It is too easy for us to dispatch them to the state government for a little slice of pogey, when the responsibility for their welfare rests squarely upon the expendability of our private estates. There is a small gleam of hope in every possibility; and this is what our prayers are for. Rarely, if ever, has anyone given to the cause of Christianity who was not repaid a hundredfold by some unexpected boon. After all, we shall never outdo God in generosity. If only we could wrench our emotions completely past their vertical plumb and begin to spiritualize our every thought, intention, and action; God will take the helm of our mortal existence and transform it into a parable of His Reign. We have undoubtedly heard the *Star Trek* Vulcan offer his valedictory *"...live long and prosper,"* wish with the fingers on his right hand displaying a modified version of the "V" for victory sign; but most of us who saw it thought it was more of a novel than a blessing. Who among us is to say that Leonard Nimoy's caricature of a man from another planet might have borne a little bit of Truth along the way? I am not inclined to believe that even men who are pretending to be people of good will on a stage can simply make it up. There has got to be some sincerity in the heart of an actor to convince us that what he is saying is in communion with the Truth. Please do not be offended by what I have said before; there is probably no doubt that Jesus Christ has seen *Star Trek: The Next Generation* and shed as many tears as the rest of us while the final plot unfolds, the evil forces are subdued, and our heroes are magically beamed back aboard the Enterprise just in time to miss an explosion that would have otherwise ensured their certain death. We do not dare scoff at this presumption, because God sees and hears our good intentions for the prevailing of unfettered righteousness through every venue of the world—whether it be a broadcast before millions of television viewers of a triumph that comes alive through an orchestrated crescendo, or the real peace which seems to happen only a sliver at a time.

The important question is why must we resort to "staged" situations which supposedly occur in outer-space to achieve the celestial excellence that God requires right here on Earth? Why can we not slap the upper-left corner of our lapels and speak to our friends over an imaginary "communicator" like they do on TV? The answer is quite simply because human life is a reality, not some fantasy on a theatrical set. It is natural for us to reach for our dreams, but we are also asked to employ the instincts of our moral consciousness to heal the world we see. When we succeed in conquering the voyeurism which tries to rob us of our purity, and rid our actions of every obsessive compulsion, we will know that not a screenwriter on the planet could ever script a moving picture with a more heroic climax than what we have wrought through the factual codicils of our lives. Once we have committed ourselves to the solemn oath that we will hold true to the profession of our Christian faith, we will overturn every leaf, root-out all evil, investigate every nook and cranny, and crawl to any measurable length to neutralize the disparity of humankind under the relevance of the Holy Cross. The voracity of our desire for exploring the unknown keeps us quite busy seeking new adventures on which to embark, conjuring unorthodox ways to strike a sample from the previously untouched, and speculating about what our acquisitions really mean. Our higher intuition tells us that our mortal composition is almost incomplete if we refuse to pursue the calling of the conscionable intellect. Hence, *"...as it was and ever shall be,"* is quite alright as long as we make provisions to hoist the weakest members of humankind soundly upon our backs and deliver them to a station where they will be wholly persuaded to join us in accepting Jesus Christ as their Eternal Redeemer, too. There is no greater implication for our moral potency; or so say the ancient Greeks about the definition of happiness: *"The full use of your powers along lines of excellence."* How could we cause our Creator to be any more jubilant than to know that we have invoked and actualized every scintilla of gray-matter in our brains to deliver the world back to the genius who first gave us birth? No etcetera could be more grand; no excursion would be of a more notable course; and not another destiny would be as suitable for the repatriation of humanity to the citizens of the New Jerusalem.

It is obvious that the immensity of landing on the lunar surface in 1969 was one of the more unparalleled achievements we could have ever claimed. But, let us hypothetically digress for a moment. What would have happened if someone from another time in universal history had stepped from behind a giant rock while our astronauts were there and said that he had lived on the Earth during the latter Quaternary Period; perhaps a wrinkled old gentlemen with long gray hair and wincing eyes? He might have proclaimed that he had taken part in an earlier experiment to transfer antimatter into space through the element of time; and he was the only one to survive because he had made his way into the center of the moon where there was oxygen aplenty and sufficient food to keep him alive henceforth for another 400 years. What, then, would we do if he suddenly announced that his name was *Moses*, whose grave we never found; and that he had been involved with delivering messages to humanity from God which he had received on the summit of a mountain range? Would we still be beating our breasts as proudly as before? Might we be as gloating that we are a people set apart because of the modernization of our advanced technologies; or would we finally believe anew that our physical transformation was at a pace already predetermined by the Wisdom of our Maker? This obviously never happened, and likely never will; but it is another parable to teach us that we are not the cynosure of all immortal vision; and neither are we meant to be anything greater for the present than our brothers' keeper on the platform of the Earth where we gather as one at our Almighty Father's feet, preserved through every convenience to serve at His command. If we can travel safely to another sphere which boasts of a gravity completely separate from our own, and defy them both by overcoming the weight of our massive bearing, endure the infernos of friction while re-entering our lower atmosphere, and touch-down safely without flying into pieces; then how can we walk-down the streets of Chicago, New York, Dallas, and San Francisco on a planet which can be hidden behind our thumb from the Sea of Tranquility without recognizing the face of every single human being we might happen to pass? How can it be true that we have become so subdivided, so disinterested, lacking in communal spirit, and so reticent to call ourselves to humble silence and listen to the guidance of the Holy Spirit in our hearts who has made us in the very image and likeness of our God?

If it is the value of our personal wealth which is all that ultimately keeps us segregated right up to the end of time, we can be relatively assured that Jesus will break every single piggy bank on the face of the globe and retrieve our riches for Himself before our lives are through. We own the technological assets in America to display the Cross of Mount Calvary on every television screen in both earthen hemispheres, but most of us would rather watch people punch the tar out of each other in a square boxing ring, wrestle alligators to the ground and yank reptiles out of trees, cook oriental food, and play football in a blinding blizzard. If the Creator of Heaven and Earth ever decided to abandon the logic that even Mr. Spock may not have quite fully understood and allowed the imaginary Roman Vulcan "god" of fire to have his way, there would not be enough left of the world once he was finished to sift through the ashes to determine whether we ever had the opportunity to write one another condolence letters of farewell. This is the summation of our inherent tendency to remain anonymous to the rest of society; we turn only unto ourselves for judgements that we have not the proper scruples to accurately render; we sever our relationships with our friends over some of the most minuscule offenses, we acquiesce only after we have been shamed into conceding; and we are often the last to pick-up the telephone and tell someone that we apologize. There are much more intense divisions in the world than those we see everyday in the newspaper; rocks being thrown and suicide bombs exploding on the West Bank in Israel, Christians being detained in foreign lands for reading the Gospel on the public square, dockets at our courthouses overflowing with backdoor neighbors suing each other over the location of the fences along their property lines, estranged husbands taking their children across state borders to get them away from their wives, and corporations purchasing our mom-and-pop corner cafes for exorbitant prices so they can sneak their huge shopping malls onto the vacant lots beside our local Church parsonages. Were we to ever enlist as much effort in coming together as we do ripping ourselves apart, it would be difficult to find a seat when everyone goes in prayerful thanksgiving to their temples, mosques, and towering Catholic cathedrals. And, unity for the sake of "diversity" is not what God is seeking, either; but one humanity under the Truth of Love; and also purity, respect, adherence to the Commandments, and full agreement with, *"...Love one another, as I have loved you."* The power in our compliance with this mandate is the secret to the success of our human experience as defined by the Angelic Hosts, the Communion of Saints, and especially by God, Himself. Segregation? Someday, there will be reason for succeeding generations to believe that there never was such a thing!

Chapter Fifteen
When the Bough Finally Breaks

———————————

I have always believed that human thoughts are mere factual spasms, and that our dreams are only irrational ones. So, what is the price for thinking? Its absence is a rather slippery-slope; so better for us to employ it now than to risk gambling-away our growth and change toward spiritual maturity; to effect an action or prohibit one; to force a new design, or destroy a more vile intention. Our resultant renderings are the hewing of a fresh Creation; or allowing it to remain untouched unto itself; all to the polishing of the glassy shadows behind our refinement; the stature in which we stand aright, or the better fare which is ours for seeking. Therefore, the mind has always been an intrinsic partner in our mortal life, forcing an existence of intelligence over every matter of the intuition; tending to the details which are far too savvy for our confusion to discombobulate, and satisfied in knowing that its job is never done. Should we complete the world without a fair slice of such ingenuity, we would be remiss in giving God a chance to discover us for what we mean to Truth; too shallow to crest the labors of our friends; too discreet to ever discern the motivations of our foes, and not even slightly capped with an umbered dignity beyond the brashness of our souls. When our record of goodness looks more like a rapsheet in disguise, or when our accomplishments are too vague to be observed with even the slightest whit of Divinity, this is when we try to conceal our darkness by showing-up before the Throne of Christ in boldface fabrication and almost incognito to the Saints. When culprits and villains try to conscript us into their lustful ranks, we often not-so-respectfully accept their overtures; refusing to select the wiser call with an ace of spades in hand, discarding our opportunities to hail our righteousness above the artful crafts of leather, lace, and highly distilled *spiritus*. There must assuredly be a fine-line separating true Wisdom and random correctness; and only a hair dividing moral Truth and accidental excellence. But, we are the witty ones who like to spend our time remarking the distinctions between the two; for we are far too preoccupied with discerning the reason for the Plan than offering our participation in it; especially when it comes to the abounding sentiments put-forth by the King of Nobleness whose Words deflect our babbling. Perhaps we have placed our feathered writing pens and opaque parchment papers much too close to the candlelight flames and have accidently set our souls afire; or maybe the essential bounty of our mutual indebtedness makes us all species of a kind; and let no one ever assume that any unknown spontaneous combustion can rid us of our callousness or cast our ills aside. Only Jesus Christ can remove the broad-bands from our eyes, pull the hyaline swords of jealousy from the pittance in our gagging gullets, excise the shackles from our walking shoes, restore our lost virginity, suture the breach in our skewered innocence, and fall the giant redwoods of our arrogance from the rainbow-pupils in our eyes.

We wield a manifold assortment of illegitimacies in our inventory which cannot self-destruct; and we own no power from within to strip the world of ignorance or dress its skinny manakin in a shiny pearl barrette and ballroom dinner gown. Now and today, while we are yet mortally alive in the flesh, and active, too; this is our moment to pursue His Love before we die too soon and our descendants wail over our tombs with dirges about what might have been. The well of time is nearly dry; the day is almost spent; our windows will not remain ajar forever; and we hold in our presence the irons and elements quite within our reach to personify the Earth as an address to which the Savior of the World will wish to call and proudly claim as His own again. We oftentimes tire much too easily; our attention grows premature by mistake; and our awareness withers, too. However, now is not the time for us to slacken or take a break to tally what we've earned because more important days are here; the camel's back can bear no more; the cup is overflowing beyond its brim; and the bough of our mortality is fully burdened past the hilt and creaking loudly beneath the strain. Should it break inside our age in time, *we* shall be the indicted ones left holding the receptacle of conceit; too vain and shocked to realize that the obesity of our errors has been the bother all along. I have often thought of the wedding vows that we have taken with Mary's Son of Man, and whether our allegiance to our engagement is worthy of the Banns for which He gave His Life while agonizing on the Cross. If we can sustain the unsurpassed intensity of Love for Him that our earthling brides and grooms promise under oath, then how could God ever do anything but succeed in unifying us inside His United Kingdom once again? The loyalty between our husbands and wives on the day they consecrate their nuptials is defined quite appropriately as being not unlike the preservation of our endearing future with the Messiah who hails from Paradise. It is as though the institution of holy matrimony is a secret passageway or corridor where man and wife retreat to escape the brute forces of malevolence, to remind themselves that they are a singular entity in the same mysterious way that all humanity composes the Mystical Body of Christ. Our betrothal to the Lamb of God is no-less a Sacrament; for it is in our faith in Him that we hold-fast to the Triune Deity whose procreative fidelity gave us life in the age of Genesis. We will live in this connubial bliss as long as we maintain our purity; forever past Eternity; and through the darkest hours in between. There is no doubt that we cannot falter or engage a bribe when asking one another for an exchange of personal absolution; for if the seller were to accept any advancement for this honesty, he would become the fraudulence that denies God's Kingdom; to wit: committing a blasphemy which would *never* spare his soul! We should accept each other's vindication with the gifted presence of our wedding day; and this must ring as loudly with Eternal Truth as when we hear the call of God.

This is our moment of a new cohesion and a trust which cannot fade with doubt or incontinence, for the evening is now at hand; our caps and gowns are waiting to be donned quite properly as the Pomp and Circumstance medley is sung by the Cherubim and Seraphim in the hallways of our legacies; we who will soon be graduated to the higher mansions of God where our memories shall never fade. Who could fail to recall the masterpiece, *Musicks Empire* from *Trypitch*, by Andrew Marvell (1621-1678) and Lloyd Pfautsch, whose work was commissioned by the State College of Arkansas for the dedication of its new Fine Arts Center on February 25, 1968? This is precisely how Jesus is singing to our souls as our courtship in His dignity continues day-by-day. Indeed, is not the sonata we hear at the center of our hearts our dutiful Consecration to the Sacred Heart of Christ with all His Honor Guard in tow? If those who are reading this chapter will pardon my impoverished attempt at an amateurish form of poetics, I shall precede the Arkansan memoire with a few proclamations of my own. *"The songs which play in our heads are our outward signs that the grace of God is hereby reigning within the atriums of our hopes; to send our dreams to bed and make them ring-in Truth for once; to elevate our spirits high above the vision we cannot quite see; to allow us to savor an early Victory! The rhymes and reasons for His Love may still be unbeknownst to us; but let us leave it at this for now; accepting a perfection we do not wholly comprehend, walking in blindness to the soreness of our sight; and indulging God through the endurance of our plight! These are my prosaic words for our rededication to the Land of the Living that is so espoused by those of larger faith; by the sick and dying who are suffering in our place!"*

Musicks Empire

First was the World as one great Cymbal made,
Where Jarring Winds to infant Nature Plaid.
All Musick was a solitary sound,
To hollow rocks and murmuring Fountains bound.
Jubal first made the wilder notes agree;
And Jubal tuned the Musicks Jubilee:
He called the Echoes from their sullen Cell,
And built the Organs City where they dwell.
Each sought a consort in that lovely place;
And Virgin Trebles wed the manly Base.
From whence the Progeny of numbers new
Into harmonious Colonies withdrew.
Some to the Lute, some to the Viol went.
And others chose the Coronet, eloquent.
These practicing the Wind, and those the Wire,
To sing men's Triumphs, or in Heaven's choir.
Then Musick, the Mosaique of the Air,
Did of all these a solemn noise prepare:
With which She gained the Empire of the Ear,
Including all between the Earth and Sphear.
Victorious sounds! Yet, here your homage do—
Unto a gentler Conqueror than you;
Who, though He flies the Musick of His praise,
Would with you Heavens Hallelujahs raise!

-Andrew Marvell & Lloyd Pfautsch

We might have become a smidgeon too eccentric for our own good in our search for Divine Grace, but we certainly cannot be too robust in the heartiness of our faith; and it is absolutely impossible to be too much in Love. If our deference always coincides with supplanting our will with God's, we shall not stray from the Pinion of His Right Hand or wander too far beyond His sight. This brings us to the matter of whether we really *trust* in Him to keep us on the straight and narrow course. We may remember during the end of the Cold War in the late 1980s when our nation was engaged in mutual disarmament treaties with the U.S.S.R. so as to prevent the possibility and necessity of a nuclear conflict. U.S. President Ronald Reagan spoke one of the most contradicting statements to ever leave the lips of a Commander-in-Chief; "...trust, but verify," is what he said about our mutual assurances regarding the Russians upholding their part of the bargain by reducing the number of their warheads. He meant that we should accept that our foreign neighbor was, in fact, deprogramming its missiles right along with the U.S.A., but that it would be necessary for us to dispatch our own representatives to the Kremlin in order to personally inspect their work, just to be sure. Trust, but verify? This is a nonsensical oxymoron of the highest degree, if ever there was one! There is no difference in someone else saying, "...I will have faith in God once I have seen Him with my own eyes." There is no such phenomenon as having faith in something you have already perceived, or trusting another party whose actions you are required to certify. Unfortunately, Mr. Reagan's fallacious mind-set was no proof at all that our nuclear disarmament treaties were worth the paper on which they were forged and sealed. His attempt to delude other republics into believing that our trust was sincere became somewhat of a joke to those whose profession is to instruct humanity in the virtues of reliance and surety. It was never a matter of whether we should have, in fact, traveled to Russia to make sure they were reducing their arsenals; but we should never have said at the outset that we "trusted" them. Such doublespeak is the reason why so many ordinary Americans have become callous and angered by our own domestic political structure. In a like manner, therefore, can we not hear the scornful gasps from the heights of Paradise when we who live on the Earth pledge our allegiance to God with every sliver of our hearts, souls, and minds; while otherwise behaving toward one another as though He does not even exist? We should remember that we are still living in very dark and dangerous times; much like it has been during the entire course of American history; and there is no doubt that our most sacred institutions are in peril and about to fall before the higher purposes of Love. The faithful will be forced to prosecute the wretched in order to sustain the peace; the most cherished walls of our capitalistic establishments will come tumbling to the ground; our interstate infrastructures will collapse; multinational networks will dissolve; our ease of mobility will be impeded; most every form of airborne communication will be interrupted; neighborhoods will perish in the fiery aftermath of our having impassioned the Wrath of Christ's Final Judgement; and we will stand naked in the galaxy with no scapegoats to blame, not a single hostage to take, and no tenable excuses within reach to explain why we finally let Him down.

There are scores of grievous enemies to our spiritual virtuosity that seem to hound us almost everyday; not the least of which are our reluctance, fear, animosity, force of habit, disdain, apathy, rejection, distraction, impurity, and pride. And, to top it all off; each and every one of these is exacerbated by the worst culprit of all: temptation. These are the decadent forces which perplex our better judgement in choosing Christ's goodness over the improprieties of the secular world. The Church teaches us through the Holy Scriptures that prayer from the heart affords us the means to see more clearly and engage the wiser course. Taken from the Epistle of Saint Paul to the Philippians (3:8), we are exhorted to fully embrace the surpassing knowledge of our Divine Lord, *"...God, Himself, can testify how much I long for each of you with the affection of Jesus Christ!"* Herein, Paul is asserting that only in Our Savior are we truly capable of uniting as one people under God for the purpose of eliminating the barriers that still divide us. We are called to do this through our daily reading of the Bible Chapters in communion with our prayers and remember that an open dialogue between God in Heaven and His faithful people should always be maintained through the intercession of the Holy Spirit. *"We speak to Him when we pray; and we listen to Him when we read the Divine Oracles,"* so says Paul in his letters. This is the implicit foundation for our Christian hope and the mainstay of our Christian witness. In continuing to address the Romans (15:13), Saint Paul further exhorts, *"...so may God, the source of all hope, fill you will all joy and peace in believing so that, through the power of the Holy Spirit, you may have hope in abundance."* Hence, our faith is somewhat hollow if we do not hope from deep within our hearts that the Kingdom of God is ringing forever true and that we shall see it someday without the slightest inhibition or physical encumbrance to hinder our way. The Mother Church assures us that our Love for God and for one another is at the origin of our prayers; and the Roman Catechism has gone so far as to include the Prayer of Saint John Vianney in its body as an example; in the words of the *Cure of Ars*, *"...I love you, O my God, and my only desire is to love you until the last breath of my life. I love you, O my infinitely lovable God, and I would rather die loving you than live without loving you. I love you, Lord, and the only grace I ask is to love you eternally...My God, if my tongue cannot say in every moment that I love you, I want my heart to repeat it to you as often as I draw breath."* (Part Four, Section One, Chapter Two, Article One, Number 2658).

What is revealed in this literati perfectly reflects the humble submission by which we must perceive the mortal world and our lives within it through the purview of our likeness of Jesus Christ, Who is all Love; and from the vision by which Heaven is already looking down. It is therein that we fully understand that our earthly reality is now at full tilt by reason of the bourgeois stagnation and philistine indignation of our outright indifference toward God. Humanity has become so battered, fractured, burdened, broken, ruptured, and torn by the diversions of our own making that our civilization is now on the brink of swift expulsion; and most people we meet in our common areas and marketplaces seem zealously proud that this has been allowed to occur. Instead of living-out the promises of hope with which we should pray for strength and guidance, our faithlessness has reduced the world into an almost peasantlike existence and opened the passageway through which every conceivable type of boorish, rude, and sordid misdemeanor and felonious act has been allowed to enter and steal the focus of our purposes away from Heaven. This is also why the Catechism leads us forward to what is known as "popular piety;" exhorting that our catechesis should fully acknowledge all forms of holy meditations, charismatic cenacles, and suitable devotions to keep our piety in check. It is completely permissible for Christians of all walks of life to honor the Reigns of Jesus Christ and His Immaculate Mother through the venues of venerating blessed relics, traveling on religious pilgrimages, attending conferences and retreats, offering Holy Hours in our sanctuaries, retracing the Stations of the Cross (see *Index*), reciting the Mysteries of the Rosary, and wearing sanctified medals and the Brown Scapular around our necks. Whatever it takes to bring us closer to our union in the Sacred Heart of Christ will ease the burden of our disquietude and pull the mortal Earth back from the precipice of splitting half-way to the core. Only by our invocation of the Paraclete of the Son of God can we succeed in bringing this resolution to pass. *"And, the one Name that contains everything is the one He received in His Incarnation: JESUS! This Divine acclamation may not be spoken by human lips, but by assuming our humanity, the Word of God hands it over to us as we invoke it: JESUS! It is affirmed by the Roman Catholic Church that the Name "Jesus" contains all; God and man, and the whole economy of Creation and Salvation. To pray JESUS is to beseech Him and call Him within us. His Name is the only one containing the Divine presence it signifies; Jesus is the Messianic Risen One; and whoever invokes the Name of Jesus is welcoming the Son of God who loves him, and who wilfully gave Himself up for him.* (*Romans* 10:13, *Acts* 2:21, 3:15-16, and *Galatians* 2:20). *It is true that no one can say 'Jesus is Lord' except by the power of the Holy Spirit.* (1 *Corinthians* 12:3) *Every time we pray to Jesus, it is the Holy Spirit who draws us on the way of prayer by His prevenient Grace. Since He teaches us to pray by recalling Christ, how could we not pray to the Spirit, too? This is why the Church summons us to call upon the Holy Paraclete everyday;"* as does the Supreme Pontiff who is situated at the Holy See in Rome. Indeed, Saint Gregory of

Nazianzus wrote, *"...if the Spirit should not be worshiped, how can He divinize me through the Sacrament of Baptism? If He should be worshiped, should He not also be the object of Adoration?"* (The *Catechism; The Way of Prayer*, Article Two, Number 2666, 2670).

Herein, we are discovering what God the Father wishes us to accomplish toward eradicating the suffering and phantom labor-pains of a world which is so filled with the afterbirth of our committing countless cruel transgression against His dignity. Now, we are walking in a new millennium during a time when the horrors of all Hell are breaking loose because we have failed to guard the grate covering the pit into which the evil of Satan was cast by Jesus from the Cross. It is truly repugnant that any one of us would stoop to associate with those who hate us, despite the Passion that has brought their haughty arrogance crashing to the ground. Our obstinance in the face of these revolting developments is outright vexatious to the followers of Christendom who hail and accept the reasons why Jesus was Crucified and was raised from the dead. Why should the Tree of Life in whose bough we now rest not turn to God and ask Him to sever us from its mainline trunk so the gangrene with which we have infected it will not be allowed to spread to other universes and jeopardize the highly pristine nature of their eternal existence, too? How can we suspect that we are *"...not long for this life,"* when God looks down upon His footstool and sees it still crawling with vermin from the netherworld? Even though He is the God of all Creation, do we not reckon that He is capable of discerning those who spread their errors from among the souls whose rapture is guaranteed? Henceforth, when the future arrives much too soon for many, let us not be overly confident that the earthquakes we presume to feel have not been transposed into the bough of Creation which has finally broken; and we feel the pinch of Newton's gravity plummeting our spirits in rapid succession like apples descending from their berths.

Divine human Love, therefore, is what Our Heavenly Father mandates in order to avert such a catastrophe, a sinless affection which cannot be acquired anywhere else in the world but through the workings of the Holy Spirit; our all-out thrust to make our thoughts and actions synonymous with His charitable Truth and the equation of our motivations with His peculiar fascination to remake the universe into the likeness of His Kingdom; and to rid our lives of all superfluous consternation that has nothing to do with His Will. For lack of a better term; *tenderness* seems to be the best way to describe how we should approach one another; sharing our common achievements, expunging our particular faults; refurbishing the edges around our withering hearts and interpersonal relationships; and looking to the future with the anticipation that Jesus Christ is always guiding us there. Love! How can anything of such sympathetic magnitude be so misconstrued by modern man? Do we not agree that our tendance to the sick is a sweet fruit of it; or that the preserves from our gardens which we offer in utter admiration for those to whom we are not even related is another way to display what we cannot define with our words? There is no doubt that such actions are expressions of the goal of God for His people; and for this, the bough of life is still waving in the breeze with a little more consolation in its spine. The matter is not so much that we produce darkness in the mortal world because such lacking is an integral part from whence we were cast asunder when Adam and Eve took their fall. If we do nothing in the darkness than spend our time pursuing it, we will never become the generative stars of our new age of spiritual beatification, so profoundly sought in us by Jesus through His Church. We are much too impotent to ever effect a hoax, fraud, or deception over His Wisdom because His genius is the Seat from where all sacred knowledge flows. As Saint Paul has so aptly stated; we *are* Christ when we put Him on our souls much like the vestments that our Monseigneur's wear while offering daily Mass. Imagine what (the late) Bishop Fulton Sheen would say through the quickness of his wit and sharp nature of his humor about the cataclysmic events that are ongoing in the United States today? He once told the story about boarding an airplane and remarking to a fellow passenger what a beautiful woman was sitting in another seat nearby. As soon as these details left his lips, he said, "...it is alright to look at the menu, even though I have no intention of placing an order," referring to the fact that priests do not marry and take an oath of abstinence from parabiotic relations. While this brought most of us to chuckle, he might have inadvertently been telling us through the intervention of the Holy Spirit that we are not supposed to stop being human just because we have dedicated ourselves to the endless pursuit of the perfection of Christ. Our loving purpose is to become the best we know how in imitating the compassionate purity of the Son of God; and we should never resort to some type of self-destruction if we cannot achieve it overnight. We are perfected in the process of attempting to become sinless in the likeness of Our Lord.

　　　Dare we cry-out to Him and say that we fear our labors to be too poor and unattended to satisfy the ordinances of His Grace? If there is one thing for sure that humankind should comprehend; we must not surrender our efforts to become the reflection of Jesus' Love in America or anywhere else on the face of the globe just because we do not fully know what it means.

Humanity is not in the business of keeping score; and neither is God for that matter; with regard to how much we refund to Him when we have only little to our name. Our entire proficiency in being Christians is to give to Heaven by offering our suffering brothers our every asset to the alleviation of their pain, and we will have already secured our Victory in piousness and Redemption before our lives are through. This is the meaning of exempting ourselves from the sentence which has heretofore been meted-out by Christ to those who reject His Gospel message with malice aforethought. Not behind any mountain or inside the belly of any canyon can we hide our actions and intentions from Him; and we should be humbly sufficed to know that He cares enough about us to observe our servitude with such scrutiny. When we are pleased in our self-realization that the Sacred Scriptures are being fulfilled in us, then the evening will arrive with a solemn crisp to its harbor lights and not with a repulsive shamefulness to slap us in the face. *"Now we see indistinctly as in a mirror,"* says the Holy Word to us. And, what of this image that is shining back into our face? We remember from our childhood hearing about the literary phenomenon called a "palindrome," in which a word or sentence reads the same backward as it does forward; such as the first name *Otto*; or the complimentary introduction, *"...Madam, I'm Adam,"* and *"Poor Dan is in a droop."* It might seem like we are too much involved with this kind of a paradox sometimes when referring to many things, but it is often how we feel if we attempt to look for God in other places before we investigate whether He is fully present in ourselves. We seem to be simply repeating the same expressions over and again, both forward and backward, and errantly appear to be getting no closer to Him. This seeming contradiction arises when we seek the Lord only in the "tangible," as though His Spirit should always be an incarnated object within the reach of our hands and the focus of our human eyes. While there is no doubt that He blesses our homes, articles, and churches through the silence of His Divine presence that is speaking quite loudly through the words of His priests and disciples, it is toward the origin of these benisons that we are urged to look. This is why we see ourselves when we peer into the looking-glass while searching for evidence of our Creator on the Earth. He lives within our hearts, a physicality we can see only when we serve humankind with every fiber of Christian conviction that can be mustered from a people who are so given to Love.

We are presently living under the supremacy, domain, constancy, and Kingship of the Ruler of the Ages whose dominion is without end; exhuming our dignity from beneath the yokel pestilence that we have become to almost everything previously known prior to His Virgin Incarnation. Our thirst for

Redemption is not the manifesto of some elusive cult which has only now become estranged from the American mainstream; but an allegiance to a New Republic of excellence known to no other world; at least those we know about that cannot escape the garishness of the beaming sun; which, itself, seems to be boasting quite proudly in its finest hour. When we ponder such metaphors as planets situated like robin's nests at the intersection of sprawling branches on a sycamore tree; this we cannot do without enlisting the poetic beauty of God's Triumph running almost spellbound through the main streets inside the conscience of our souls. If we should, indeed, be terrified that the celestial stars may rock themselves to sleep while encamping in our midst; or that they might somehow miss something awesome from humankind; perhaps our occasional rocketry will keep them alert for our ensuing overtures of the airs. When shall we propose to them that their exemplary silence is a matter of grave curiosity for us; what could ever be their purpose than to serve only as distant reminders that there are other mountains in the universe for humankind to climb? *"Why not conquer your own summits before lurking upon our spheres?"* This would not be an inappropriate interrogatory for even the Angels to put before those who inhabit the Earth while referencing their auric haloes and seeing us try to mock the inquisitiveness of God; asking why we have never succumbed to the fear of our impending death before entering the foyer of Eternal Absolution and viewing Creation from the other side of success. The derivation of our faith is a product of the one and the same Love in which we choose to believe. There can be no refutation to what we do and say, as long as their entirety is wrapped by the Sacred Hands which have fashioned all the stars and hung the moon in the void of space. The first Apostles rhetorically queried from Christ as to where else they could go for a final vindication from their sins? We are that same living inquisition in the mortal world today.

Our pasty yearnings and starvation for the Truth can only be satisfied by this same Messiah; presently here and forever He shall be; our future and our brigade, our full-blown and laid-out Innocence beyond the baptisms of our youth; the brazier in which our hopes are kept aflame, the assimilation of our goodness within His supreme galore, the gallery to our sleeping rooms, the veranda of our opulence, the isinglass of our divinity, the metropolitan of our parishes, the foreword of our bon vivant, the lovage in our window-box, the ordination of God's monarchy, the axiom of our citadels, the protection of the innocents, the consul of our pardoning, the stricture of the insolent, and the ringdove of the New Covenant. *Now we know that the wild nights we suffered have only been the running of the mills inside our pondering of the yonder*

Dawn; for without our having resurfaced from the depths of the despair we were given from poor Adam's last gasp, we should surely have never been envisioned by the blessed or seen beyond the parapets of the castles in the skies.   Desist not!—dearest Jesus in your search for dying men; for we can still be heard beneath the firebrands of the fiendish cohorts from the Deep who would rather take us back again! Remember the Tree which Thou didst deny our liberties; in which you placed us heretofore to rot in the seasoned fall from there! We have learned our lesson with an uninterrupted glee; with no respite or oasis in between; we have suffered long and hard to please Thee in return for the Prophecy which has regained our Paradise once more! Death has breathed its last!—and we shall be the fruitful reminders that Christ has been triumphant in its wake!

- William L. Roth, Jr

Chapter Sixteen
All Under One Cross

There must be no doubt that Satan has ofttimes wrenched his crooked neck while looking upon the Son of Man being Crucified on the Cross at the summit of Mount Calvary, then jeered rabidly about us; and thereafter quickly glared back toward the Face of God, asking Him why a brash humanity should be the profiteer of such a Divine Catastrophe. The evil sorcerers to which we are regularly subjected have probably imagined that they are doing pretty well in distracting us with every temptation we could possibly imagine; and they would have us believe that the Death of Christ is no more than another capital sentence being carried-out through the offices of the executioners of His day. The legions of hatred that Satan unleashed against us before that Good Friday when Jesus finally conquered him were of forces seemingly yet untold; but he was still beaten; and his evil can now never retrace a single step of his horrible legacy with any prospect of succeeding; not through another Pontius Pilate, a soldier of misfortune, a hardened-steel spike, a faithless sword-bearer, or any unfounded criminality. When Simon was ordained as Pope Peter by the Son of God, he knew that his triad of misgivings against Jesus were forgiven, as well as the sins of all humanity; and that his new commission was to guide the Christian Church as its founding *Pontifex Maximus*, the Supreme Pontiff through whose successors the Keys to Paradise have since been carried for 2000 years thereafter. We have learned, herein, that our entranceway to Paradise is not a free-for-all which can be attained by the simple occasion of our deaths; but that we are required to *do* something in order to be saved. What this must be is a matter of our own accord, and is exactly why I have written this book. It seems as though the Holy Spirit is leading us back to the bank of a river in our search for new meaning in life; and this is where our acceptance of His Love takes us to our knees where we see more clearly what Jesus had previously written in the sand with His finger, so ably referenced in the Sacred Scriptures. Now we can sense that an excerpt from His inscription must read, *"...Go ye, therefore, onward to the Morning and drink of Me!"* He has laid low our pride from beyond that day, calling us to humble ourselves in sight of His Light; just like little children squatting on their haunches while pushing their model cars across the ground in perfect genuflection of His Will. It is from there that our souls look upward and perceive this giant-of-a-man from the depths of our hearts upon whom we focus with the clarity of holy Love and envision that He continues to stroll past our portico every day, stopping to knock each time, and finding no one at home, goes on His way until tomorrow dawns again and He can revisit the hindsight of our aging hearts. We are capable of seeing the slow motion of His gait, so elongated in its length that His foresteps seem to go beyond the focus of our eyes when He takes another stride. His towering legs appear to end where the clouds meet His waist; and His view of the Heavens must be a sight to behold as He surely reaches-out once in awhile to tickle the sparkling visage of the storied Morning Star.

We search for new ways to communicate our beatific visions by which we also journey across the breadth of time and space; wondering how to illuminate our Love for the lost of humankind, wishing to be both descriptive and specific; and yet, hoping that the product of our meditations never appear to be a wild scattershot collection of completely discordant events. There is no substitute for understanding that our goal must be an unparalleled unification in the Savior of our souls; unlike any other we have ever known on the Earth before our time, or inside our span of life; or that our successors will ever come to know. It is true that the Holy Cross was never splintered into pieces until after it was deployed for the bearing of our Salvation in the Body of Jesus Christ; and this is also our charge to this day. The world is still being crucified by the things which divide us; and we must never become fractured by so much as a hair until Christ returns to pare us again into our separate destinations by the Divine criterion of His Own judicious means. It seems as though we are subjected to uncontrollable ravages rivaling that of the worst fires, winds, and rainstorms in our effort to unite the globe sometimes. Most of our enemies tend to circulate outright lies against our best intentions; others look inward unto themselves as a way of censuring those who live in their midst; and many sects resort to physical abuse and warfare to display their inner-disdain. The latter is the irrational source behind the attacks of terror upon the United States in September 2001. If anyone on the face of the Earth has not heard by now that America and all freedom-loving democracies in her likeness have come under frontal assault these days, they must be living like a hermit in the topmost branch of a tree at the summit of the Chilean Andes somewhere. The people of the United States were forced to grapple with a tragedy which was never theretofore seen on the mainland continent of the Land of the Free. Who could have imagined that anyone would be so influenced by the forces of evil as to commandeer four state-of-the-art jetliners with dozens of unwitting passengers aboard and fly three of them with wanton disrepute into skyscrapers filled with workers as busy as bees-in-a-hive on any ordinary day? If not for the valorous courage of our brave citizens who were riding aboard the fourth airplane, God only knows what else might have been destroyed. Even so, there were some 3,000 innocent people who died in the World Trade Center, all the passengers on the planes, and scores more who were working at the U. S. Pentagon. Policemen and firefighters lost their lives by the hundreds, most of whom had gone inside the Trade Center while the towers were still boiling with flames to rescue those who could not make their way to an exit for themselves.

The likes of such a hellish act was dressed-down quite profoundly by U.S. President George W. Bush during an address to the nation from the Well of the House of Representatives on Capitol Hill. I shall never forget his speech that evening because it was delivered by satellite television to the entire world on September 20, 2001; the date of the occasion of my 40th birthday. Standing at the podium with a great sense of urgency on his brow, this President, who had taken the Oath of Office as America's chief executive only eight months before, was forced to somehow help our citizens cope with the legions of evil that we had previously ignored for far too long; but now we were staring its wicked face straight in the eye. To paraphrase the words of Abraham Lincoln: all the world will long remember and never forget what this 43rd U.S. President told his country in the wake of such grievous acts; *"…The terrorist's directive commands them to kill Christians and Jews, to kill all Americans and make no distinctions among military and civilians, including women and children…We have seen their kind before. They're the heirs of all the murderous ideologies of the 20th century. By sacrificing human life to serve their radical visions, by abandoning every value except the will to power, they follow in the path of Fascism, Nazism, and totalitarianism. And, they will follow that path all the way to where it ends in history's unmarked grave of discarded lies…Some speak of an age of terror. I know there are struggles ahead and dangers to face. But, this country will define our times, not be defined by them…Great harm has been done to us. We have suffered great loss. And, in our grief and anger, we have found our mission and our moment. Freedom and fear are at war. The advance of human freedom, the great achievement of our time, and the great hope of every time, now depends on us. Our nation, this generation, will lift the dark threat of violence from our people and our future. We will rally the world to this cause by our efforts, by our courage. We will not tire, we will not falter, and we will not fail."* (Excerpted from *The Congressional Record.*)

Is this not the essence of the same speech that the lone Apostle, Saint John, delivered to the faithful flock of seers on the day Jesus Christ was slain on the Cross on Good Friday? After Our Lord handed-over His Spirit to God, and the Deposition of His Sacred Body was commenced; the first location His Remains were laid was in the Bosom of the kind Maiden who had borne Him into the Flesh, our very own Immaculate Mother of Sorrows. Did not Saint John then turn to a grieving court of faithful Christians who were, themselves, mourning in quite gruesome despondence and inquire how a Man-God of such Divine Love and stature could be Crucified by an evil-filled *coup de main* of criminal marauders? How could it be true that it would befall a single mortal man, the Apostle whom Jesus loved, to address the whole of His disciples who had not fled and say that their grief was surely not in vain, and that they would set-out to exact vengeance upon those who were responsible for such a malicious act of murder? Surely our prior enlistment in conquering the forces of evil which make some men resort to violence instead of peaceful negotiation may have rendered President Bush's words unnecessary in our age. If we would have better lent to the urgency of our own intentions by professing our Christian virtues with greater intensity in places where rogue factions have been allowed to prosper today, is it not true that they might have taken the solemn oath of the Prince of Peace instead? There can be no refuting the fact that America's own defiance against the fruitful tenets of Christianity, led by our more faithless citizens such as the ACLU who have done everything in their power to strip our nation's government of religion, is to blame for our having turned to profit and materiel over international peace and sovereignty. Every time we see infidels, atheists, and agnostics on the street; we are looking into the faces of the *real* culprits who are responsible for every form of violence in America and the forceful attacks of aggression against her from the firepower of our foreign neighbors. If Saint John were to have miraculously appeared in the Well of the House that day when President Bush gave his consoling speech, he would have delivered a message to us from Jesus Christ consisting of no-less than this: *"...If I close Heaven so that there is no rain, if I command the locust to devour the land, if I send pestilence among My people; and if My people, upon whom My Name has been pronounced, humble themselves and pray, and seek My presence and turn from their evil ways; I will hear them from Heaven and pardon their sins, and revive their land."* (II Chron. 7:13-14)

In light of such a Divine Proclamation, it would undoubtedly behoove us to listen more intently to the many cries for help from those who surround us everyday. When a priest or missionary says that he has come before us to seek prayerful and material assistance for the poor; that he has seen people who are living in such poverty that they barely have two coins to rub together, we can properly assume that they are only pennies, and not silver dollars. If we discover that their health is failing, there is no question that the diagnosis is probably AIDS or rubeola, and not a common cold. Those who are living in the streets where the sun of prosperity never shines on them are more than likely walking in the mud, and not down the center of Hollywood Boulevard. And, if they should be so fortunate as to have any kind of roof over their heads at all, it is a sure bet that it is a lean-to shanty, instead of a quaint bungalow. Who could forget the report made to the public by former President Jimmy Carter and his lovely wife, Rosalyn, who visited the poorer quarters in the outskirts of Atlanta, Georgia and saw the impoverished people of the greatest nation in the world living in cardboard boxes and rotating drinking water that they had made by boiling effluent from the street sewers? We have got to stop assuming that everyone else's plight is somehow self-induced or only temporary, or that it is never as egregious as those who are really concerned about it tell us it is. Herein rests the secret to true world peace; sharing the spoils of Christ's Resurrection with every nation and race; making our faith and love so powerful and attractive that every soul on the Earth and beyond the moon wish to share it; and calling upon other people's consciences to such brilliance that every billionaire in Creation will crave spending themselves broke feeding the poor souls they may never know in this life, racing one another to the bank-teller lines to retrieve their cool cash and giving it to the shivering war veterans sleeping on the curb outside. This is the meaning of elevating the charity and dignity of human life; and absent of it, there is no question that raw evil will strike at our heels once again. It is only a matter of time before we become developed and changed into the people whom Jesus wants us to be; whether we allow Him to help us at the outset or not. No empire other than His can live forever on the Earth because time, itself, will wear it down. Customs change, generations mutate, ideals dissolve, blood-lines weaken, relatives become estranged, enemies disappear, new foes arise, and the world as we know it marches on. None of these things is inevitable; but they seem to be almost permanent because *we* are so slow in accepting the sublime overtures of God. Perhaps we should not say that everything we have ever known and accepted as being human ritual will pass-away in our age; but there is always a suffix at the end of every day which allows us to imagine the best of all possible worlds to broach the eastern horizon tomorrow. We are not as divided from our neighbors as most of us let on; for we are common in many cumulative ways; what we perceive as being our lineage from the past, our share of the present, and our destiny in the future. No one wants to let go of the memories that have shaped their character and strength, nor the wisdom which always keeps us hanging-on.

However, it is also as imperative that we arrive at the conclusion that we are more frail and helpless than we really care to admit. The 20th century seems to have been filled with more world warring than flashing moments of spectacular genius; and our accomplishments have always seemed to become overshadowed by the uncertainty of our reckless nature. The hundreds of years that humanity has put behind him are nothing when compared to the indelible Truth which is yet to be revealed inside the void of our own lacking. We cannot find the answers to the secret of human existence in our reactions to deadpan questions, trite cliches, or canned responses because our modes of mass-communication do not contain the spiritual integrity to keep us properly informed. The legends who have guided us through the perils of our youthful history were, in themselves, also sinners; but they became giants because of the fragile circumstances in which they were cast. We should learn from their mistakes, imitate their ingenuity, proclaim their sense of duty to our children at home, and commit their memories both to our hearts and to the ages. They have given us a foundation of freedom upon which to build a world of true liberty; one that has been driven completely to the bedrock of the human spirit; American, Europan, Asian, African, Oriental, and all the other origins by which the modern world has come of its own. I do not believe that the greatest record of our history has already been inscribed, signed, sealed, and delivered through the back door of Heaven to God. We are striving to be an immortal people whose vestige has yet to be measured; a good flock of Christ's children that has yet to follow Him back home; and an army of warriors fighting at the hottest flashpoint in the battle for justice whose best days are still to come. The clock cannot kill us, but it might easily dilute our tenacity. Although our labors of Love may be strenuous, our progress can never recede. Once we have conquered another bunker and taken another hill on our march toward divinity, it is then ours for the keeping; never to be surrendered to imperfection again. I suppose this is one of the mystical aspects of pure Love; once you have seen it, it shall always be within range of your clearer sight. Christians have learned that not only is the power of human Love all-seeing, it is also part *hypostatic*; meaning that we are called to focus upon alleviating the plight of our fellow humanity as a reflection of the creative magnum of God resting in our souls. When we "put on" Christ as a means of yearning for Salvation, we inherit the same holiness He has called upon us to achieve for the past twenty centuries. This is the magic of our faith; for we are the ones who must concede that everything the Almighty Father says is true.

Therefore, following the course of Christianity allows us to understand ourselves from the inside-out. We are likewise proud and afraid to walk the narrow passage for fear of falling astray; but we are also courageous enough to know that Jesus will be alongside to catch us if we somehow teeter and fall. These are the very visions which must have been flashing through the mind of President Bush when he was thrust into the role of American giant from the stately Well of the House that day. It is a product of the Truth; and it must surely be the same thread of valor which has connected all peoples of sanctified vision; from surgeons to mentors; scientists, ministers and popular charismatic leaders. They teach us that the fallout from our trials does not always have to be negative because we can sense the new bonds which are created when it comes time to reunite our peoples under a single labor of Love. We are able to envision our own losses through the pain of our neighbors; the shattered lives around us give us pause to reassess our own priorities for living; and the common anonymity of the human family sheds its disguise, and true heroes suddenly spring from beneath the texture of what might have otherwise been our future; now never to transpire quite like we thought it would. The material world is the "womb" in which legends are conceived; and we are created by God to live this like purpose; to search for a destiny, stake a claim, and to share the common dreams of every man. *Indeed, each and every one of these commissions is centered in Him; and this is precisely the reason why we are all prospering under one Cross.* It is the purpose behind our breathing and trying, the nature of our concentric "being" in the Sacred Heart of Jesus Christ, the momentum behind our expressiveness, and the real climax why we are never truly afraid of dying in His favor when all our days are through. There will never be a last *hurrah!* to the existence of humanity because Our Savior has raised us above and beyond the vast tumult of the ages. We are simultaneously perpetual past the element of time and everywhere in physical space because of the supernature of His Love; veritably slung-shot past Eternity because our Almighty God has refused to part with His people. Even with all our faults and omissions, He still loves us to His death and would never deny us again.

When we seem to be too befuddled about what we are doing or confused about the most subtle of things, we might imagine seeing or hearing Him through the eyes of our faith somewhere beyond the distant stars with His Holy Face turned toward the heights of the Firmament so we cannot see Him sheepishly laughing up His sleeve like a proud grandfather watching his son's little boy falling off a horse. America is in good hands these days because of our Maker; and this should be the reason why we stand humbly beneath the open skies and hail the King of the Cross as our final peaceful dominion; from Daytona to Seattle, and from Maine to the Mexican border. We are a land of revelers and mavericks, and statisticians and pilgrims; and as long as we hold fast to our Judaic Matzos and Eucharistic Hosts with the strength of our most gracious spirits, we will be safe inside the Holy Providence of the Omnipotent God who gives us life. If it is in miracles that we discover Him best, there is no short supply of them from which to choose. I would be wholly negligent in my imparted duties if I concluded this volume of my ongoing series of manuscripts without referencing one of the most profoundly supernatural events to have ever occurred in any century under the espousal of God. There is a Diary in print which was penned by a cloistered nun in her native Poland from 1934 until her untimely passing at the age of 33 on October 5, 1938. Her name was Sister M. Faustina Kowalska, who was born on August 25, 1905 in the village of Glogowiec, Turek County, the Lodz Providence of Poland. As early as the age of seven years in 1912, she began to miraculously hear the voice of the Holy Spirit deep within her soul, which portended her miraculous visions to come. She suffered a long-term respiratory illness for most of her life, and her sudden relapses often made it difficult for her to continue her work. She wrote most of her Diary in retrospect, sometimes penning her memories of years out of their proper succession; but she managed to complete the Opus that God had asked her to accomplish. The reason I have incorporated her biography into this chapter is because I have referenced heretofore on several occasions *The Divine Mercy of Christ*. It was through His humble servant Sister Faustina that this powerful Chaplet for spiritually lost sinners was revealed to humankind. Our Lord showed her a miraculous image of Himself standing in a pearly-white raiment with a pair of red and pallid rays emanating from the center of His breast; red flowing toward His right, and white to His left; and with one Hand raised in blessing, the other touching His garment near His Sacred Heart. He asked Sister Faustina to remember what she had seen and to paint the image with the signature JESUS, I TRUST IN THEE as best as she knew how. The first version of the Image of The Divine Mercy was completed by Eugene Kazimierowski in 1934, and the most recent in 1982 by Robert O. Skemp. This is a widely known devotion to the Sacred Heart of Jesus in the Catholic Church to this day, and coincides with the celebration of the Feast of The Divine Mercy on the first Sunday after Easter.

Sister Faustina's vision of the Lord Jesus occurred on February 22, 1931, which is also the Feast of the Chair of Saint Peter. She wrote everything down that she heard from Him, especially detailing her interior visions, the literal record of her interlocutions; how she endured her periods of doubt, distress, and moments of spiritual darkness; the acts of mortification and penance that Jesus sought her to perform, the gradual regression of her physical health, her intercessions with the Blessed Virgin Mary, the daily prayers she wrote in private, and many petitions and resolutions she offered in reparation for the errors of sinful humanity to enlist The Divine Mercy which Jesus had seen fit to reveal through her devotions and piety. I have chosen to recite her Retreat Resolutions from January 1937 which were reprinted in an English translation of her Diary which was commissioned by the Congregation of Marians in the Diocese of Springfield, Massachusetts. (Eden Hill, Stockbridge, Mass. 1987). She prefaced the litany with her Diary entry, *"...Particular examen: remains the same; namely, to unite myself with the Merciful Christ (that is; what would Christ do in such and such a case?) ...and, in spirit, to embrace the whole world, especially Russia and Spain."* If I may add one particular of a personal note; I too have been given a Diary from the Blessed Virgin Mary which I have previously mentioned as being my first book, *Morning Star Over America*; and I logistically arrived upon placing Sister Faustina's Retreat Resolutions from January 1, 1937 in *When Legends Rise Again* on the date of January 1, 2002, completely unplanned and not premeditated by me. This should not come as a total surprise because the messages I have received from Our Holy Mother began on February 22, 1991, precisely sixty years to the day from when Sister Faustina was shown her supernatural vision of The Divine Mercy of Jesus. The following is an unedited context of her pious Resolutions upon that solemn occasion in 1937.

General Resolutions

I. *Strict observant of silence—interior silence.*

II. *To see the image of God in every sister; all love of neighbor must flow from this motive.*

III. *To do the Will of God faithfully at every moment of my life, and to live by this.*

IV. *To give a faithful account of everything to the spiritual director, and not to undertake anything of importance without a clear understanding with him. I shall try to clearly lay bare to him the most secret depths of my soul, bearing in mind that I am dealing with God, Himself; and that His representative is just a human being, and so I must pray daily that he be given light.*

V.   *During the evening examination of conscience, I am to ask myself the question: what if He were to call me today?*

VI.   *Not to look for God far away, but within my own being to abide with Him alone.*

VII.   *In sufferings and torments, to take refuge in the Tabernacle and to be silent.*

VIII.   *To join all sufferings, prayers, works, and mortifications to the merits of Jesus in order to obtain Mercy for the world.*

IX.   *To use free moments, however short, for prayers for the dying.*

X.   *There must not be a day in my life when I do not recommend to the Lord the works of our Congregation. Never have regard for what others think of you (for human respect).*

XI.   *Have no familiar relationships with anyone. Gentle firmness toward the girls, boundless patience; punish them severely but with such punishments as these: prayer and self-sacrifice. The strength that is in the emptying of myself for their sake is for them a (source of) constant remorse and the softening of their obdurate hearts.*

XII.   *The presence of God is the basis of all my thoughts, words, and deeds.*

XIII.   *To take advantage of all spiritual help. To always put self-love in its proper place; namely, the last. To perform my spiritual exercises as though I were doing them for the last time in my life, and in like manner to carry-out all my duties.*

I am not really certain whether the pen *is* mightier than the sword, but it is obvious that our souls can be spared the fatal slash of God's overwhelming Justice if we will only heed the Commandments of His Word. Sister Faustina did this through a dutiful faith which was beyond reproach; and she was but a simple woman of little means. Can we not construe through her experiences, however, as a matter for the record of the intervening Spirit of God having spoken to mankind for thousands of years, that Jesus Christ *wants* something from those with greater affluence? He realizes that His Father did not ask Him to endure the agony of His Passion and the mortality of His Crucifixion for no good reason. In these six words: *Salvation is ours for the taking*, we understand that the choice for our future rests in our hands; not that we can save ourselves; but we have been accorded a venue to Redemption in the Blood of Jesus Christ. The Saints knew it; as well as all the writers, poets, publicans, tax-collectors, popes, paupers, and presidents about whom we have heretofore spoken. The question we must pose is whether we assume that the seventy-billion mortal souls, give or take a few, who have already lived and died are simply crammed into oblivion somewhere, or if they are instead; as Our Lord confirms, sitting before Him with their lives laid-bare, awaiting the final call from His Almighty Patriarch to lay Creation to rest one last time. I am not a wealthy man by any measure; and I have no clique of friends who ask me to accompany them on weekend outings or attend brown-bag lunches everyday. In many ways, it is rather lonely being a good Christian in America because most of our peers and acquaintances cannot grasp the thought of "selling everything we have, and giving it to the poor," as Jesus implores in the Bible. I have come to know Salvation through the Roman Catholic Church whence I was a little boy and my mother and father accompanied me to Holy Mass every week. I shall forever love and hold them dear to my heart for the seed of faith they allowed to be planted inside me from those many years ago. And, thankfully to God, I have entered a relationship with Jesus Christ which is shorn of all ambiguity because of the paranormal intercession of His Mother, Immaculate Mary, the Queen of Heaven and Earth. The prominence of every successful human experience is determined by how we interrelate our actions with God's Love; no matter what we might be thinking, saying, or doing; and if it is for the greater transference of His Holy Grace to the rest of the world, then we are living the finest of our hours. I shall never concede that humanity is too lost to be found again in the preordained circumference of the circle of Love. If there are apathetic people who have been offended by this book, or atheists who are outright up-in-arms, then my objectives have been happily achieved. We will soon be subjected to the Truth in our arraignment before the Lord; and when that time arrives, I shall stand beside those whose faith may have been a little weaker than they would have liked in order to tell Jesus that I will vouch for the worthiness of their souls. I Love humankind with the intensity of the Risen Christ-Child who wears the Crown of Glory under which we are peacefully composed. Let us join together again, like His Father has intended from the very beginning of time, and be obedient to this Messiah who will take us home someday. As God confirms about these final moments, "...*a Shoot shall sprout from the stump of Jesse; and from His roots, a bud shall blossom. The Spirit of the Lord shall rest upon Him: a Spirit of Wisdom and of understanding; a Spirit of counsel and of strength; a Spirit of knowledge and of fear of the Lord; and His delight shall be the fear of the Lord. Not by appearance shall He Judge, nor by hearsay shall He decide; but He shall Judge the poor with Justice, and decide aright for the lands afflicted. He shall strike the ruthless with the rod of His mouth; and with the breath of His lips He shall slay the wicked. Justice shall be the band around His waist; and faithfulness a belt upon His hips.*

Then, the wolf shall be a guest of the lamb; and the leopard shall lie down with the kid; the calf and the young lion shall browse together, with a little child to guide them. The cow and the bear shall be neighbors; together their young shall rest; the lion shall eat hay like the ox; the baby shall play by the cobra's den; and the child lay his hand on the adder's lair. There shall be no harm or ruin on all My Holy Mountain; for the Earth shall be filled with knowledge of the Lord, as water covers the sea. On that day, the Root of Jesse, set up as a signal for the nations, the Gentiles shall seek out; for His Dwelling shall be Glorious." (Isaiah 11:1-10)

Epilogue
Our Conversion Has Come Due

If human vanity were only skin deep, perhaps the excision of our outer-skin would suffice to render us beautiful again. Since it is not, God has been required to travel to the prodigal pit of our mortal constitution to cleanse us from within. And, as bad as this hurts, sometimes, He seems to be saying that there is a causal relationship between physical pain and spiritual purification. Toward such imminence, the cost for our moral cleansing has been paid by His Son on the Cross. So, what remains for us to be frightened about? Are there still people who rise from their beds at daybreak and say, "I'm at the top of the morning, but I am still deathly afraid of heights!" Such is the birth of our engagement with our fellow human beings to teach them that the worst of life is nearly over. For anyone who believes that the connection between how we treat one another and what our Creator thinks of us is in any way a false correlation, or that the mandates which are impressed upon our consciences through the Holy Scriptures constitute vitriolic malarkey, there is sufficient evidence to prove them quite wrong. It is probably inaccurate to assume that God wishes to speak profanely to those who reject His Love, and that this must be what our agony is all about; but even He knows that the use of such expletives would only serve to drive us farther away. So, there is a much more Divine reason for joining Our Lord's mortification than for the simple purpose that God wants to bring us to our knees in unmitigated torture. However we arrive at our deduction, there is no refuting the fact that people who attempt to engage Heaven for the goal of attaining Eternal Salvation without acknowledging Jesus as their Crucified Redeemer are living entirely on the wrong side of history and in complete opposition to God's priceless Domain. Followers of any false prophet who would lead their flock away from the Cross procure only the contraception of their own immortality by being deprived of the counsel of the Holy Spirit, the Bread of Life, and the Blood of Absolution. The lifting of our spirits before the presence of Heaven is not the same as the phenomenon of physical levitation because the latter implies defying the force of gravity; and there is none to be known in Paradise. Our souls are weightless right now, but are burdened onto the ground because of the constancy of our flesh. We conquer the elements of physics and the record of our own past when we die in Jesus Christ; and we are sanctified forever thereafter. Whenever we bury ourselves in a novel or become lost to the whistling winds, we somewhat achieve this same sensation, but on a singular plane. Once we are rescued from death by our dear Lord Jesus, we are capable of attending many locations at once; riding the waves of the ocean without a keel beneath our feet, sitting in grand perspective on the plateau of a mountaintop, and hovering above our relatives and friends beneath the dossals in a Church sanctuary.

Such is the simultaneous repose and resurrection of our spirits having flown past the globular horizon and onward to the endless enterprise of Divine space; a bastion of fulfillment beyond parameters and constraints; not foreign to everything we might encounter here on Earth, but synonymous with each protraction that is afforded by God through His own reserved command. This revival of mankind is the Divine expectation of our transfer into His mystical infinity and the cosmic berth of the afterlife; a real and true environment as it is prophesied in the Sacred Scriptures; hailed by the Holy Paraclete stationed at the capstone of the Earth, and by the Truth as it is revealed inside our hearts upon our auspicious acceptance of Jesus as the Savior of our souls. Therefore, any pious practices in which we choose to participate to evince the Cardinal Virtues of our religious faith is a signal to God and Creation, alike, that we wish to overcome our physical existence; and this opens our consciousness even wider for Him to divulge ever-greater dimensions of what is yet to come. Again, since we are all subject to the ticking of the clock; time is of the essence, and it is only our enemy if we expend it solely as a tool to augment our efforts toward perpetuating material gain. Our access to perfect Wisdom can become as vitreous as glass if we will just open our eyes and see past the immediacy of our tangible surroundings. And, the indispensable key to such revelations revolve around the same central thesis— *conversion.* We may try to rename it, subject it to the test, circumvent its purpose, censure its necessity, and ignore the consequences of our denial; but Eternal Life shall never be bestowed upon a lost sinner whose soul has not been converted to accepting Jesus Christ; even if it is their last opportunity when their spirit departs the flesh. If we are the trumpeters in the last age of the Earth, then our report has finally come due; for God is standing beyond the horizon with His hands cupped behind His ears, waiting in great anticipation for us to signal our response and echo the sound of the playing of *taps* for the world we leave behind.

We can learn from envisioning His presence that life in America should never hinge upon what our public laws allow, but how we define what we do within the strictures of morality, instead. He continues to ask us everyday whether we can see the Truth very well. Anything we learn through the vision of the heart is discernable only by enlarging our consciences like the pupils of our eyes in the dark through the divination of our desires to know the factual nature of our invincibility better. We must do this promptly because the Earth has become so blackened by hatred these days; which necessitates the broadness of our faith to become even more expanded to recognize what is truly worth seeking anymore. Inasmuch as we would rather take life with a grain of salt, it is never wholly shed of grief and sorrow. Its surfaces are oftentimes marred by unconscionable tragedies and cataclysmic unease. We can make them more glossy and "smooth to the touch" by offering them to Jesus as our gift of ullage toward the distillation of our brothers' hearts; and this will lift the burden of culpability from them while they are completely unawares. In essence, they become the little children whom He has always wanted them to be. We often wonder why the best times in our lives seem to passed-by more rapidly than the click of the shutters inside the cameras which produced the photographs we look at now to remember them by; seeing the images of all the faces who shined with such guile and innocence; the toddlers waving their hands into the lens; and even the background walls and tapestries of our homes that could render volumes about the Truth of Love if only they could speak. We seem to be frozen in time by such commemorations, both pictural and mental; because they reflect the record of our legacies. We see the tail-finned automobiles that stood behind us at the picnic grounds, in the back yard, and at the cemetery; and perhaps an unwary squirrel scampering up an oak tree and the leaves of grass beneath our feet which seem many lifetimes away from us now. We can have all these things back again if we recommend them as our hopes in Christ; indeed, His Holy Mother has told me so! We can retrieve all the feelings of affection and security that reside in the traces of our memories for as long as our hearts desire, once our souls have arrived in Paradise.

Conversion? Why not now? How much longer can we desist in growing the attraction of our fibrous "beings" into the manifestations of the immortal unknown? It seems as though we pay no mind to climbing the great sequoias in central California to procure a better perspective of nature; so why is it so difficult for our faith to sense an equal benefit of such a panoramic view while kneeling in prayer in our rooms; where we can ascend to the highest peaks of our benign spirituality without ever lifting a foot or bothering to try to hang on? We can do this through our religiosity, by our perfected belief in Christ Jesus, and through the strength of the Holy Spirit. If we wish to become wise in a world of ignorance, we will accomplish it by sending our spirits aloft in supplication like satellites to strike-up a conversation with Heaven; all while continuing to complete our mission of forthcomingness right here on the bevels of the ground. The Love of God is our central nourishment when hatred and despair strip our pantries clean of anything comforting that would keep our emotions from spiraling out of control like a dislodged feather having been shed by an eagle into the winds of a storm. When we become depressed and decide to, "pack it in and hang it up," our happiness can be rejuvenated by sounding-out the sweet melodies of the Mosaic Psalms to give us hope again. This regenerative exchange becomes the synthesis of our new beginning, the architecture of our refurbished temperament, and the germination of the seeds from within our souls that help us bloom alongside the foliage by the flowing Streams of Paradise. If the acclamation of President Bush is to ever come-to-pass; that we shall never tire, falter, or fail; then we have no other choice than to enlist the theatre of the advocacy of God; for only in Him can any righteous human endeavor ever succeed. There is nothing either foreign or frigid in the stratospheric resiliency of our mutual pardon; whether it be between worlds, nations, dominions, or races. This should become the thematic penchant for our viable cohesion through which the 21st century has already begun. Woe be unto us if we allow the peeved constellations in the distant beyond to rain holy retribution upon the globe in the absence of our trying. Humanity-whole is not a parliamentary House of Lords in which our indoctrination must flow by virtue of some "peer of the realm." We are seated into equality because we have been borne that way by the Will of the Father; and the framework of His Divine disposition is the source and candor of our immortal legitimacy. We own an inalienable right which was bequeathed to us by Jesus from the Cross to continue to *be*; long after we have bade farewell to the diminishing world. Should we decline to accept this new Birth, it would bear the resemblance of a capital inequity for which there is no defense.

Jesus Christ is the darling of our daylight dawn and our harvest moon, alike; and He needs no covert or secretly systematic stratagem to accomplish the conversion of the world. Neither is there any high-strung "divide and conquer" theory that faithful Christians live by where they run about the countryside jabbing bayonets into the abdomens of anybody who will not listen to their preaching. Everything about our beliefs is above board; revealed only in accordance with the kindness of the Truth, and sensitive to the personal dignity of everyone involved. It is true that Our Lord told us that He was brought into this world as the Prince of Peace; but He has also come to establish division; father against son, mother against daughter; two against three, and three against two. This was more of a prophecy than a wish on His behalf because He knew full well that there would be certain family members asking their relatives to stop cramming their religious sentiments down their throats. There will be no such division once everyone completely understands the irrevocable requirements of the New Testament. Every soul must accede to the fact that we must judge for ourselves how best to fall in Love with God, or take the risk of being lost inside the void of death forever. This is not always an easy matter because some people cannot muster the foresight to believe in Him, let alone make a judgement as to whether He is worthy of their allegiance and affections. Indeed, some of our peers do not parse their words in telling us about it, often blowing-off their steam of disapproval to rival the ejecta of those volcanoes I referred to earlier. All they seem to be interested in is hailing the false virtuosity of our historical Manifest Destiny or how one race is supposedly superior to the rest by result of some random flash of God's genius which never really occurred in the first place. Even if a majority of the Americans who lived in the 1800s believed in an imaginary doctrine that it was the inevitable destiny of the United States to expand across the entire continent of North America, who is to say that Jesus Christ will not appear within the next few hours and demand it to be rolled completely back to the east coast again? After all, stranger things have occurred! I am not proposing that Our Divine Lord looks disdainfully upon the progress we have made in this country; at least none which would have us believe that He has played any part in siccing the dogs from Hades to chomp at our heels; the ones which are still hounding us through the actions of the vile criminals residing half-way around the globe. This is not to say, however, that we have never been properly forewarned that our deviations from His statutes would cause great harm to our indigenous inhabitants and their carefully cordoned land. Furthermore, we are assured that we can extract full exemption from such misfortune by becoming part of the pristine excellence of Heaven. How do we know this to be true? Because the Bible proclaims that, *"...in His goodness and Wisdom, God chose to reveal Himself and to make known to us the hidden purpose of His Will by which, through Christ, the Word made Flesh, mankind might in the Holy Spirit have access to the Father and come to share in His Divine nature."* (Ephesians 1:9, 2:18, Peter 1:4)

All anyone would need to do is open the Bible upon which most of our presidents have placed their left hand to take the oath of office and it would be spelled-out quite frankly in black and white lettering on the pages. It continues, *"...God, who through the Word creates all things and keeps them in existence, gives humankind an enduring witness to Himself in created realities."* (Romans 1:19-20). A more objective observer could never draw any clearer connection between the unseen Kingdom of Paradise and the visible mortal world than this. The point we should remember is that everything revealed from God is meant to be bequeathed to the succeeding generations of living beings thereafter. By all means, credit must be given to our forefathers and their children; and even most of the parents of the 20th century. It was not until our post-modern age, however, when "the cookie really started to crumble." Many Americans are slowly relinquishing the sacred traditions of the Church in exchange for a more casual approach to celebrating the Rites and Liturgies. Even worse, they are deliberately skewing the meaning of certain Bible passages to suit their own lifestyles, altering its text altogether in an attempt to prove false propositions, and completely abandoning the etiquette which has made the Church stand-out as the most enduring institution on the Earth as the center of all spiritual persuasion. We must be reminded that, *"...sacred tradition and Holy Scripture form one sacred deposit of the Word of God, committed to the Church. Holding fast to this deposit, the entire holy people, united with their shepherds, remain always steadfast in the teaching of the Apostles, in the common life, in the breaking of bread; so that holding to, and practicing and professing the heritage of our faith, it becomes on the part of the bishops and the faithful a single common effort."* (From Pope Pius XII, Apostolic Constitution, *Munificentissimus Deus*, November 1, 1950.) Therefore, if we work to sustain the cohesion between what is inscribed in the Bible and the traditions which have been transferred through the centuries into our possession, we will see our living faith shine again like a city on a hill that will make the one about which Ronald Reagan spoke look like a dim streetlight in a suburban bowery somewhere.

In the proclamation of the Second Vatican Council (Vatican II), it is assured that, *"...there exists a close connection and communication between sacred tradition and Holy Scripture. For both of them, flowing from the same Divine wellspring, in a certain way merge into a unity and tend toward the same end. Sacred Scripture is the Word of God inasmuch as it is consigned to writing under the inspiration of the Divine Spirit. Sacred tradition takes the word of God entrusted by Christ the Lord and the Holy Spirit to the Apostles, and hands it to their successors in its full purity so that, led by the Light of the Spirit of Truth, they may in proclaiming it preserve the Word of God faithfully, explain it, and make it widely known."* (Dogmatic Constitution on Divine Revelation, Second Vatican Council, Number 9.) In other words, the Church is demanding of the ages that its integrity never be abridged by any nebulous amendments or pared through the workings of sinful humankind without the guidance of the Supreme power from whom she was founded. Saint John ends his Gospel by telling us that there are many other things Jesus did, but if these were to be described individually, the world could not contain the books that would be written.   Saint Paul also admonishes the Christians of Thessalonica, *"...brothers, stand firm and hold fast to the traditions that you were taught, either by oral statement, or a letter of ours."* (2 Thessalonians, 2:15). His purpose here is to provide for the passage and superintending of everything Christ has revealed through His Church by the Holy Spirit, all the way from His day to our point in linear time. The healing, protection, and purification of America will be manifested only after we have returned to our adherence to the ages-old traditions which have maintained the integrity of our faith, the innocence of our actions, and the trusting nature of our interior motivations. Therefore; and with respect to these revelations; our people must begin to rise-up against any force which serves to diminish the holiness for which the Apostolic Church is calling, in consortium with the sacred traditions that have been heretofore held for 2000 years. Exposed by virtue of this Light, it is absolutely obvious that we must cease and desist our participation in condoning the abortion of unborn children, ban the use of contraceptives, illegalize assisted suicide, rescind laws that allow for the infliction of capital punishment, censure homosexual and lesbian unions, eradicate social injustice, amend unfair labor laws, uphold the celibacy of our priests and nuns, deny permission for ordained priests to be married, address the afflictions of the impoverished and neglected, forgive the debts of foreign nations, reduce our military armaments, preserve our natural environment, liberate those who are living under dictatorial oppression, lift all international trade sanctions, lower excessive transfer tariffs, improve working conditions for manual laborers, end the practice of racial profiling, parole our rehabilitated prisoners, and ban the use of fetal cells for medical research and laboratory experimentation, explicitly to the prevention of human and animal cloning. Every single one of these issues is addressed in the communion of the Holy Scriptures and the sacred traditions of the Roman Catholic Church.

We have somehow misconstrued the meaning of "freedom" in America to imply that we are not required to otherwise obey the Divine Laws of God in whom we have placed so much trust. How does it look for the United States Congress to open for business by invoking the Wisdom of our Divine Creator, and seconds later, enact a new law that provides for additional funding for the extermination of an entire class of unborn citizens? In addition, if someone were to write a condensed narrative about common civility and public morality in America today, they might appropriately conclude it with, "...died circa 1962," and describe the cause of its mortality as succumbing to the intentional latent effects of removing prayer from our public schools. Its death certificate is a matter of public record in the *Journal of Decisions by the United States Supreme Court,* if there is such a thing. Banning the pursuit of spirituality in public education when it was ruled was especially destructive because it was enacted in the face of the reluctance of many levels of our government to allow the Civil Rights movement to move forward uninhibitedly. I believe that our country could benefit from a reminder about how pathologically autistic our approach to social change has been. It is generally recognized that Americans are quite proficient in making good speeches; and we do pretty well at delivering the goods most of the time. There is no doubt, however, that our verbal conscience seems to have fallen into a dead silence; and the dock of our moral warehouse is sitting rather empty right now. We can make the necessary changes to render us holy again if we implore God to help us. He knows His people and the nature of the world better than anyone else alive, save His Son, Jesus Christ. He reigns from within the center of our most elegant works of art and literary expressions. When someone spends months painting a replica of a wintery twilight scene depicting the silhouettes of the leafless trees against the western horizon, God knew that it would be done from the foundation of the Earth; so He made the crows black to prevent their color from clashing with the spiraling branches in which they often perch to watch the traces of the foregone sun disappear. Indeed, this painter would be able to employ only the simple colors of black and white for this masterpiece; not unlike those Scriptural passages upon which the president places his hand to take the oath of office. This is simply another visual revelation of His Divine sense of harmonic resonance with the images that are generated in our hearts. We are His people who are perfectly united with Love; and we should never be comfortable without our personal relationship with the Almighty Father who is its essence and origin.

If there is to be a convergence of capitalism and Christianity that will have any meaning toward the lasting effect of the purpose of our founding fathers, let it become the intersection of Truth and Wisdom, justice and peace, honesty and service, and patience and cohesion. We are one nation not only because our ancestors heartily strived for a new land upon which to forge the bedrock of their dreams, but because God has given us a mission unlike any other in the Western hemisphere. We cannot mandate any citizen of our great republic to take a stance for evangelizing Christianity any more than we might ask the Canadians to surrender their sovereignty and concede their natural landscapes to their Yankee neighbors to the south. Those who believe in God and know that Jesus Christ is the innate effectuation of every freedom that our earliest colonialists aspired to achieve also know that the vision of their hopes may not have been realized in their day. We seek a resolution to the problems of a community wherein human societies are joined together for the cause of making the entire of mortal existence a little easier to bear. There are no quick fixes to our ailments; and democracy is not some benign catholicon, universal remedy, or panacea for enhancing the rituals of social interaction between the sprawling plains and curvaceous valleys of any ideological government and its constituent countrymen. Bobby Kennedy reminded us a long time ago when speaking on the subject of violence in the wake of the assassination of Dr. Martin Luther King, Jr. that achieving social justice is not always as easy as it seems. *"...too often, we honor swagger and bluster, and the wielders of force,...we excuse those who are willing to build their own lives on the shattered dreams of other human beings. Some Americans who preach nonviolence abroad fail to practice it here at home. Some who accuse others of rioting and inciting riots have, by their own conduct, invited them. Some look for scapegoats; others look for conspiracies. But, this much is clear: violence breeds violence, repression breeds retaliation; and only a cleansing of our whole society can remove this sickness from our souls. For there is another kind of violence; slower, but just as deadly destructive as the shot or the bomb in the night. This is the violence of institutions, indifference, inaction, and decay...that afflicts the poor, that poisons relations between men because their skin is different colors. This is the slow destruction of a child by hunger, and schools without books, and homes without heat in the winter. This is the breaking of a man's spirit by denying him the chance to stand as a father, and as a man, amongst other men. And this, too, afflicts us all. For, when you teach a man to hate and to fear his brother,... that he is a lesser man because of his color, or his beliefs, or the policies he pursues;...that those who differ from you threaten your freedom or your job, or your home, or your family; then you also learn to confront others not as fellow citizens, but as enemies to be met not with cooperation, but with conquest; to be subjugated and to be mastered. We learn at the last to look at our brothers as aliens...with whom we share a city, but not a community; men bound to us in common dwelling, but not in a common effort. We learn to share only a common fear, only a common desire to retreat from each other, only a common impulse to meet disagreement with force. For all this, there are no final answers for those of us who are American citizens...The question is whether we can find in our own midst, and in our own hearts, that leadership of humane purpose that will recognize the terrible truths of our existence. We must admit the vanity of our false distinctions,...and learn to find our own advancement in search for the advancement of all."* (April 5, 1968, Cleveland, Ohio). I wish to thank Bobby Kennedy for reaching retroactively beyond his grave to shine the Light of God's hope upon the end of my book. Someday in Eternity, he will become President of the United States; and this legendary giant will make the preceding excerpt a part of his inaugural address. His legacy and the contribution of all the legends who shall rise again in Christ is the true remaking of the American dream for every soul on Earth beneath the Holy Cross.

Index

The Passionate Stations of the Way of the Cross

I. JESUS IS CONDEMNED TO DEATH BY PONTIUS PILATE
When Jesus came out wearing the crown of thorns and a purple cloak, Pilate said to them: "Behold the Man!"—John 19:5

II. JESUS CARRIES THE CROSS
He emptied Himself and took the form of a slave, being born in the likeness of men.—Philippians 2:7

III. JESUS FALLS THE FIRST TIME UNDER THE CROSS
Here is My servant, My chosen one, not crying out loud, not shouting, not making His voice heard in the street. —Isaiah 42:1-2

IV. JESUS MEETS HIS FAITHFUL MOTHER, MARY
Come, all you who pass by the way, look and see whether there is any suffering like My suffering.—Lamentations 1:12

V. SIMON OF CYRENE HELPS JESUS CARRY THE CROSS
A man named Simon of Cyrene was coming in from the fields, and they pressed him into service to carry the Cross.—Mark 15:21

VI. VERONICA WIPES THE FACE OF JESUS WITH HER SCARF
He was spurned and avoided by men, a Man of suffering, accustomed to infirmity, one of those from whom men hide their faces.—Isaiah 53:3-4

VII. JESUS FALLS A SECOND TIME UNDER THE CROSS
It was our infirmities that He bore, our suffering that He endured; upon Him was placed the chastisement that makes us whole; by His stripes, we are healed.—Isaiah 53:4-5

VIII. JESUS COMFORTS THE WOMEN OF JERUSALEM
A great crowd followed Him, including women who lamented over Him; beating their breasts. Jesus turned and said: "Do not weep for Me. Weep for yourselves, and for your children.—Luke 23:27-28

IX.   JESUS FALLS A THIRD TIME UNDER THE CROSS
The Lord laid upon Him the guilt of us all. Though He was harshly treated, He submitted and opened not His mouth.—Isaiah 53:6-7

X.   JESUS IS STRIPPED OF HIS GARMENTS
They took His garments and divided them four ways.—John 19:23
They divided My garments among them, and for My vesture they cast lots.—Psalm 22:19

XI.   JESUS IS NAILED TO THE CROSS BY THE SOLDIERS
Just as Moses lifted-up the serpent in the desert, so must the Son of Man be lifted-up that all who believe may have eternal life in Him.—John 3:14-15

XII.   JESUS DIES ON THE CROSS TO REDEEM HUMANITY
Jesus cried-out in a loud voice, and then gave up His spirit.—Matthew 27:50

XIII. JESUS IS TAKEN DOWN FROM THE CROSS (The Deposition)
They shall look on Him whom they have pierced, and they shall mourn for Him as one mourns for an only son.—Zechariah 12:10

XIV. THE BODY OF JESUS IS LAID IN THE PASCHAL SEPULCHER
Then, having brought a linen shroud, Joseph of Arimathea took Him down, wrapped Him in the linen, and laid Him in a tomb which had been hewn out of rock.—Mark 15:42

The Anima Christi

Soul of Christ, sanctify me; Body of Christ, save me. Blood of Christ, inebriate me; water from the side of Christ; cleanse me. Passion of Christ, strengthen me. *Love of Christ, heal me*; O good Jesus, hear me. Within Your Wounds, hide me; let me never be separated from You. From the evil one, protect me; at the hour of my death, call me. And, close to You bid me; that with Your Saints, I shall be praising You for all Eternity. *O Lord, grant me repose and sanctuary in Your loving Heart, as I give you rest in mine.* Amen.
(Italicized phrases - Requested additions by the Most Blessed Virgin Mary.)

The Hail Mary

Hail Mary! Full of Grace; the Lord is with Thee! Blessed art Thou amongst women, and Blessed is the Fruit of Thy Womb: Jesus. Holy Mary, Mother of God; pray for us sinners now, and at the hour of our death. Amen.

The Our Father

Our Father, who art in Heaven, hollowed be Thy Name; Thy Kingdom come; Thy Will be done on Earth, as it is in Heaven. Give us this day our daily bread; and forgive us our trespasses, as we forgive those who trespass against us. And, lead us not into temptation, but deliver us from evil. For Thine is the Kingdom, the power, and the Glory forever to come. Amen.

The Glory Be

Glory Be to the Father, the Son, and the Holy Spirit. As it was in the beginning; is now and ever shall be; world without end. Amen.

The Apostles' Profession of Faith

We believe in one God, the Father Almighty, maker of Heaven and Earth; of all that is seen and unseen. We believe in one Lord, Jesus Christ: the only Son of God; eternally begotten of the Father, God from God, Light from Light, true God from true God; begotten, not made; one in Being with the Father. Through Him, all things were made. For us men and for our Salvation, He came down from Heaven: by the power of the Holy Spirit, He was born of the Virgin Mary and became Man. For our sake, He was Crucified under Pontius Pilate; He suffered, Died, and was buried. On the Third Day, He rose again in fulfillment of the Scriptures. He ascended into Heaven and is seated at the right hand of the Father. He shall come again in Glory to Judge the living and the dead, and His Kingdom will have no end. We believe in the Holy Spirit, the Lord, the giver of life, who proceeds from the Father and the Son. With the Father and the Son, He is worshiped and glorified. He has spoken through the prophets. We believe in one Holy Catholic and Apostolic Church. We acknowledge one Baptism for the forgiveness of sins. We look for the resurrection of the dead, and the life of the world to come. Amen.

Notations

www.ingramcontent.com/pod-product-compliance
Lightning Source LLC
Chambersburg PA
CBHW060253100426
42742CB00011B/1731